OVER THE EDGE

OVER THE EDGE

THE TRUE STORY OF FOUR

—

AMERICAN CLIMBERS' KIDNAP

—

AND ESCAPE IN THE

—

MOUNTAINS OF CENTRAL ASIA

GREG CHILD

Ⓥ

VILLARD NEW YORK

To

Sergeant Turat Osmanov

Captain Ruslan Samsakov

Captain Beishen Raimbekov

and all the soldiers killed in action

during the conflict around the

Karavshin Valley in August 2000

ACKNOWLEDGMENTS

Thanks are owed to many people for helping make this book possible, but a deep debt of gratitude is owed to several in particular. First of all, I wish to thank Tommy Caldwell, John Dickey, Beth Rodden, and Jason "Singer" Smith for trusting me to tell their story, and for being so open with me about a difficult experience. Likewise I am grateful to Beth and Tommy's parents Robb and Linda Rodden, and Mike and Terry Caldwell, for their cooperation. Special thanks are due to my agent, Susan Golomb, of the Susan Golomb Literary Agency, for her representation, her advice, and her confidence in me, as well as in the four climbers who are central to this story. Special thanks also go to Bruce Tracy, my editor at Villard. This story had its genesis as a feature article in *Outside* magazine, and I want to thank editor in chief Hal Espen for the wisdom, counsel, and understanding he extended to me during the writing of that story and this book. I am also grateful to Elizabeth Hightower, my editor on the story for *Outside*. The other climbers who were swept up in the drama in the Ak Su and Kara Su valleys in August 2000 who shared their experiences with me deserve thanks too, namely, Kate Dooley, Natasha Kolysnik, Stefan Hiermaier, Radan Svec, and Roland Laemmermann. I also wish to thank the mother of Turat Osmanov, who welcomed John Dickey, Jason Smith, and me into her house and who shared her son's life with us. Thanks to Elena Domatov, Erika Monahan, and Larissa Collum for translating Russian tapes and text, and to Salley Oberlin, who transcribed countless hours of taped interviews. To my interpreter in Kyrgyzstan, Erkin Atabekov, I say thanks for your invaluable work and your friendship. Others who helped me on the road to this story include Ivan Samoilenko in Russia, and, in Kyrgyzstan, Turat Akimov, Alexander Kim, Igor Shestakov, Garth Willis, and General Bolot Januzakov, secretary of the

Kyrgyz Security Council, who allowed me access to Kyrgyz military facilities and personnel. Among the soldiers who helped me piece together the military actions of August 2000, I am especially grateful to Lieutenant Colonel Akyl Dononbaev. Finally, to my friends who stood by me during the writing of this book, I say a very big thanks. And thanks to Dewey, who stood with me during the writing of this book, and whose memory will be with me forever.

CONTENTS

INTRODUCTION

The world changes fast. In 1995 I visited Kyrgyzstan with a team of American climbers, where I spent a month exploring one of the most beautiful and spectacular alpine rock-climbing areas on earth. The canyons, peaks, and glaciers that we had traveled to were in a remote corner of the Pamir-Alai range known to climbers as the Ak Su and Kara Su valleys. My memories of that time are of idyllic days camped on verdant meadows alongside rushing rivers, of encounters with friendly Kyrgyz shepherds, and of climbs on towering granite pinnacles up to four thousand feet in height. This vertical playground rightly deserved its reputation as the Yosemite Valley of Central Asia, and for twenty years Russian, European, and American climbers had flocked there.

Fast forward five years to August 2000 and that idyll would change in one brutal instant when fanatical militants of the Islamic Movement of Uzbekistan (IMU), which operates out of secret bases in Tajikistan and Afghanistan and which is linked to Osama bin Laden's Al Qaeda network, would creep over mountain passes toward the Ak Su and Kara Su valleys to ambush and murder Kyrgyz soldiers, terrorize local shepherds, and kidnap ten climbers from expeditions from America, Germany, Ukraine, and Uzbekistan. The hostages would be used as human shields, and for ransom. The ultimate objective of the Taliban-inspired invaders was to continue across Kyrgyzstan to attack the regime of the Uzbek leader Islam Karimov, and, it is suspected by Kyrgyz officials, to pave a trail for smuggling tons of opium. The week-long running battle that ensued between the heavily armed militants marching their hostages through the mountains and the Kyrgyz commandos who ultimately turned back the attack would be a terrifying experience for shepherds, soldiers, and hostages alike, all of whom were taken by surprise by the IMU invasion.

This is the hour-by-hour story of those violent days, from their innocent beginnings as a climbing holiday to the invasion that would slaughter nineteen Kyrgyz soldiers, to the remarkable escape of the two groups of hostages.

Over the Edge began as an article in *Outside* magazine in November 2000, titled "Fear of Falling." I wrote that article immediately after the four Americans who'd been taken hostage returned to America. Tommy Caldwell, John Dickey, Beth Rodden, and Jason "Singer" Smith had been forced off a mountain wall by gunfire, had survived a firefight in which a Kyrgyz army hostage was murdered practically in front of them, and had been marched for six nights through the mountains guarded by murderous Uzbek militants, and they'd escaped by pushing one of their captors from a cliff. They were still shell-shocked when I interviewed them, and the story in *Outside* related the experience of what the Americans saw and felt as hostages.

In this book, Caldwell, Dickey, Rodden, and Smith remain the principal characters through whose eyes events are drawn, but the story is greatly expanded, through additional interviews with those four, as well as with other hostages, soldiers, and the terrorists who survived the attack on Kyrgyzstan, whom I visited in a Kyrgyz prison in March 2001.

This is also the story of a story that refused to stop unfolding even during the months it was being written. Among the bizarre twists and turns that arose after the hostage drama was over were the discovery that the terrorist the Americans believed they had killed by pushing from a cliff was alive; allegations that the climbers made up their story; and the return to Kyrgyzstan by Dickey and Smith, with me, to meet in a prison cell the rebel who'd held them at gunpoint, and whom they pushed from a cliff in order to escape.

When I embarked on this story about Americans in trouble in a faraway country, the IMU was barely known outside State Department offices. Yet I sensed as I researched this secret army that the world would soon know more about Central Asia's explosive mix of terrorist armies and warlords, repressive anti-Islamic dictators, Taliban fanatics, and endless jihad.

Little did I suspect that I would write the closing chapters of this book in the shadow of September 11, and that in his address to the nation after the attacks on New York and the Pentagon, President Bush would name the IMU as one of the principal targets alongside bin Laden in the war in Afghanistan. Indeed, there appears to be a sense of closure to this story with the news in November 2001 of the death of Juma Namangani, the leader of the IMU and a lieutenant of bin Laden, in an American bombing raid. Namangani had orchestrated the raid on Kyrgyzstan, and it would have been in his strongholds in Tajikistan and Kyrgyzstan that the foreign climbers would have languished, had the hostage-taking gone as planned.

This story has its share of villains, and it has some brave Kyrgyz soldiers, but it is not a story about heroes. The climbers swept up in the events of August 2000 are people little different from the rest of us. Though their climbing skills taught them a thing or two about survival, their individual characters and their compassion for one another were what kept them alive. Like anyone who has witnessed warfare and death, they feel pain over the memories that they recount in this story. It is their hope that others may learn from their experience.

Castle Valley, Utah, December 2001

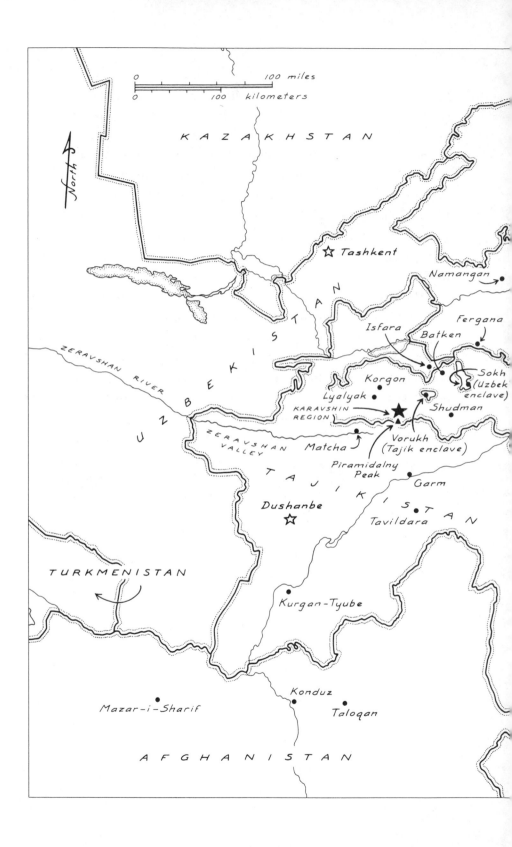

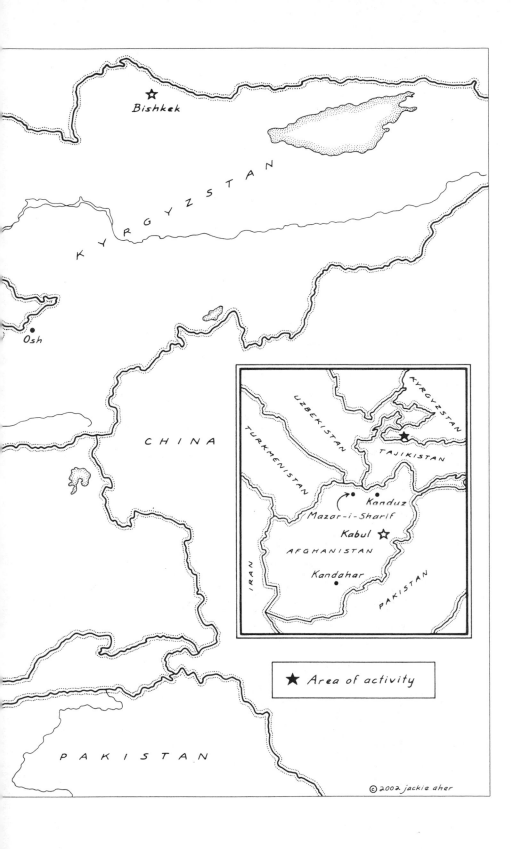

Osh

CHINA

PAKISTAN

© 2002 jackie aher

KYRGYZSTAN

Bishkek

UZBEKISTAN

TURKMENISTAN

TAJIKISTAN

KYRGYZSTAN

Kunduz

Mazar-i-Sharif

Kabul

AFGHANISTAN

Kandahar

IRAN

PAKISTAN

★ Area of activity

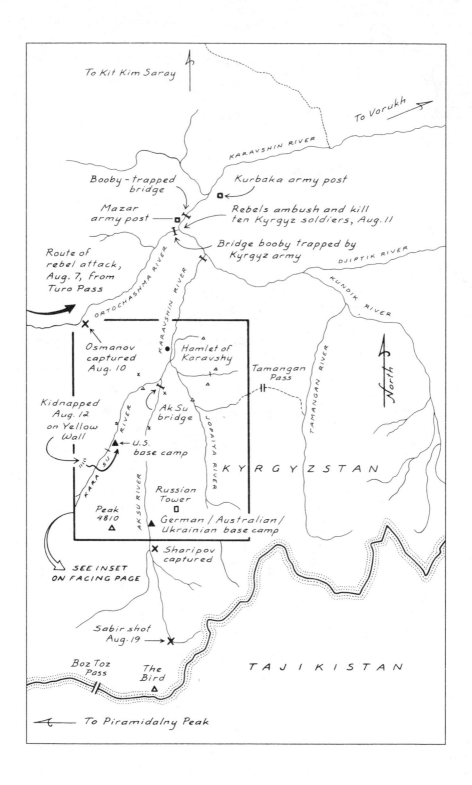

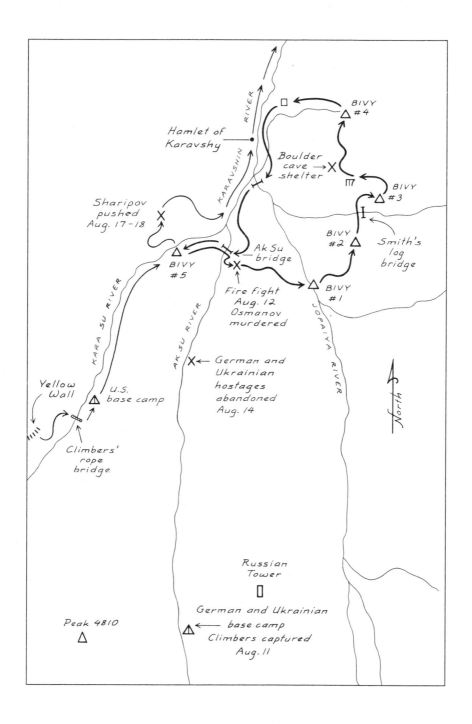

North

Hamlet of Karavshy

Boulder cave shelter

BIVY #4

BIVY #3

Smith's log bridge

BIVY #2

Sharipov pushed Aug. 17-18

Ak Su bridge

BIVY #5

Fire fight Aug. 12 Osmanov murdered

BIVY #1

German and Ukrainian hostages abandoned Aug. 14

KARAVSHIN RIVER

KARA SU RIVER

AK SU RIVER

JOPAIYA RIVER

Yellow Wall

U.S. base camp

Climbers' rope bridge

Russian Tower

Peak 4810

German and Ukrainian base camp Climbers captured Aug. 11

⟶ "Loop" of hostages' journey

OVER THE EDGE

1.

FIRST CONTACT

―――

KARA SU VALLEY, KYRGYZSTAN

AUGUST 12, 2000

The first shot hits the wall at 6:15 A.M.

Its echo fills the air as sunlight pours through the gaps in a jagged ridgeline of the Pamir-Alai Mountains of Kyrgyzstan and brightens the deep canyon of the Kara Su River.

Deep in sleep, bunked one thousand feet off the ground on the side of a cliff in two portable cliff tents, called portaledges, the four climbers wake instantly at the ping of lead hitting granite somewhere on the wall beside them. Instinct tells them that it's the sound of a stone falling down the cliff, or the clunk of a boulder being pushed along in the roaring, glacier-fed river below, but when the second bullet strikes thirty feet below them, and the rifle report that follows it echoes through the gorge, they all sit bolt upright.

"What the hell was that?" Jason "Singer" Smith shouts the question as he dons his climbing helmet to protect his head from rockfall.

"We're being shot at," Beth Rodden calls from the portaledge adjacent to Smith. Beside her is her boyfriend, Tommy Caldwell.

"That's irrational," Smith replies. "It's probably local hunters."

The explanation sounds reasonable enough. The valleys below—the Kara Su, where the climbers' tent camp is located, and the adjacent Ak Su—are the herding and hunting grounds of seminomadic Kyrgyz shepherds. Ibex, the large and woolly breed of mountain goat, and even the rare snow leopard are sometimes their quarry in these hills.

Then the third bullet hits the cliff twenty feet above the two portaledges. Rock dust flies out of the crater, spattering the platforms on which the climbers are camped.

"Shit! That was definitely for us!" John Dickey shouts, reflexively curling into a fetal position. He's lying in his sleeping bag, next to Smith.

They are bunked on the Yellow Wall, a vertical facet of the twelve-thousand-foot Mount Zhioltaya Stena. It is day two of their climb, and week two of their monthlong rock-climbing expedition in this former Soviet republic. Like many destinations on the international climbing circuit, the region they are in—located near Kyrgyzstan's mountainous border with Tajikistan, and known to climbers as the Karavshin, after the area's main river—is remote. Being eighty miles from war-torn Afghanistan, it's also in a volatile part of the world. Yet to these climbers it doesn't seem so far off the beaten track. For two decades the fortresslike granite towers of the Karavshin have lured an international scene of Russian, European, and American climbers.

Up on the wall, the four Americans ease their heads over the sides of the portaledges and peer down into the gathering light.

"There—on the rubble straight below us," Smith says. "I see three men."

"What the hell could they want?" Caldwell asks. He and Rodden have been dating for five months, ever since they fell for each other in Yosemite Valley in California that spring. Based on Caldwell's native Rocky Mountain time, today, August 12, is his twenty-second birthday. Among the gear and food they have hauled up to their cliffside camp, Rodden had secretly packed a candle and an instant chocolate pudding to celebrate.

"Maybe they want to rob us," she suggests, recalling a trio of comically light-fingered local shepherds who over the past few days have been blatantly pilfering from the base camps of the expeditions camped in the valleys below. "But if they wanted to do that, they'd just go to base camp and steal all our stuff, right?"

"Maybe it's a surprise birthday party for Tommy," Smith quips in his signature sardonic tone.

"No, dude, it's gotta be the airline trying to tell us that they've found our lost bag," Dickey says. He and Smith have a habit of trying to outdo each other with wisecracks. Dickey is referring to the hike he and Smith made several days ago, to search for a village with a phone so they could contact their Kyrgyz travel agent about a lost duffel bag. The bag had gone astray somewhere between San Francisco and Bishkek, the Kyrgyz capital, and it was loaded with climbing gear.

"That's really funny," Caldwell says, nervous and deadpan. "I just hope they're really good shots and they're only trying to scare us, rather than really bad shots who are trying to hit us."

"They may not even know we're camped up here," Smith says. "They might be shooting at our portaledges for target practice. Hell, maybe this is just how the locals get your attention around here." Since arriving at their base camp they had been visited by many shepherds and soldiers, most of them armed with shotguns or rifles.

"Well, they've got my attention," Caldwell says.

Smith waves his arm and calls down, "Hey, don't shoot! We're up here!"

The men on the ground shout back. Drowned out by the white noise of the river, their reply is unrecognizable. Smith grabs Dickey's camera. A two-hundred-millimeter lens is mounted to it. Smith's bunk site gives him a better view of the ground, and he aims the camera at the men below.

"One of them is waving at us. It looks like he's telling us to come down."

A hush falls over the bivouac as the climbers digest the observation. Sitting side by side in their sleeping bags and their nylon fleece jackets, they exchange worried looks; Rodden and Caldwell clasp each other's hands. That they are being sucked into a vortex of danger is apparent.

"Someone has to go down, to see what they want," Caldwell says.

"Go down?" Rodden says, alarmed by the suggestion. "Are you sure?"

"Okay. Tommy, John, we'll throw for it. Even draws. Odd man out goes down." Smith leaves Rodden's name off the list of contenders.

"I'll go," Dickey says, settling the issue.

Smith looks at his bunk mate and nods. At twenty-five, Dickey is the oldest among them. He's the most traveled; he sports a beard, which gives him an appearance of maturity; and his way with people is relaxed and confident. He's also the scruffiest-looking one of them all, and he figures that might earn points with whoever is doing the shooting. They uncoil the tangle of their five ropes that are clipped to the wall around their portaledge camp and tie them end-to-end to make a single, thousand-foot strand. They lower one end of the rope to the ground, and Dickey connects his aluminum rappel device to it. Then he clips the device to his waist harness and eases over the edge of the portaledge, like a diver rolling off of a raft. Locking off the rope with a firm grip of his right hand, he hangs beside the portaledge, and Smith hands him one of their Motorola two-way radios. Dickey slips it into his pocket.

"Pass my tobacco," Dickey adds as a parting request.

"What?"

"It might come in handy down there. Maybe these guys need a smoke. It'll show them we're friendly." He shrugs, at a loss for anything further to add to the surreal situation they have woken to. Elsewhere in his travels the laconic Texan has found the offer of a cigarette to be a useful gambit for defusing tense situations with rough customers. Smith passes the pouch of Drum, then shakes his friend's free hand.

"Good luck, dude," Smith says.

Dickey swings into the void. It is 6:35 A.M., twenty minutes since the first shot hit the wall. His descent will take another half hour. He spins slowly as he glides down the nylon strands, pausing to hang on an ascender clamp every two hundred feet so he can disengage his rappel device from above each knot, then reattach it below the knot. He performs the rope maneuvers carefully yet efficiently. In the back of his mind he's thinking, "We are being shot at, the shooters are ordering us down, I'm descending into a holdup. But what else can I do?" Five hundred feet above the ground the angle of the cliff becomes less steep and Dickey's toes touch the wall. He comes to a steel bolt, drilled into the rock by Caldwell a few days earlier. The bolt marks the point where the old Diagonal Route, first climbed by Russians years earlier, crosses the new climb that the Americans are bivouacked on. Dickey hitches his rope to the bolt with a carabiner and continues sliding down. When he is fifty feet above the ground he sees the gunmen clearly for the first time. "My heart nearly leaped out of my throat," he would say of that first encounter. One man clasps a Kalashnikov assault rifle bearing a long banana clip; the other has a larger weapon with a two-pronged support mounted to its long barrel. A third armed man is positioned farther down the hillside in a stand of tall brush. The men wear a hodgepodge of camouflage army fatigues, the ragged sportswear of mountain villagers, and some stylish western mountaineering garments. They are not soldiers, and they are not shepherds. While Dickey hangs on the cliff, looking eye to eye with the gunmen, his radio squawks.

"Hey, John, how's it going?" Smith asks through the Motorola. "Whaddya see? Over."

"Shut the fuck up," Dickey replies in a sharp hiss. Intuition tells him it's better not to give the gunmen any idea of how many people are up there in the portaledges.

A man with a bushy black beard gestures insistently for Dickey to continue his descent. Dickey sucks in a deep breath and ropes down to the talus slope. On the ground, he detaches his rappel device from the rope. His heart is beating fast while he studies the gunmen. They now number two, the man in the brush having departed minutes earlier. They beckon him to come closer. Dickey strides through sliding gravel, trying hard to appear calm.

"Good morning," Dickey says slowly, clearly. "My name is John." He directs his thumb toward his chest to make it understood that he's introducing himself.

The heavily bearded man steps forward. He's stocky yet wasp-waisted, and he cradles his rifle close to his chest. A wild outburst of black hair is pressed underneath his camouflage cap. His pants are also camouflage, and the many pockets of his battle vest bulge with cartridge cases, a radio transceiver, and binoculars. On his hip he wears a pistol and a hand grenade. A sheath knife is mounted diagonally across his chest.

"Abdul," the man says, introducing himself. Months will pass before the group learns his real name; Abdul is his nom de guerre. He clenches Dickey's hand and shakes it with a bone-crushing grip, then steps back. His features are hawkish, his skin burnished by the sun. His pale-eyed gaze cuts into Dickey's psyche. The other man steps forward and offers his hand.

"Obid," this fellow says, pointing at himself and giving away a hint of a smile. Obid is bearded too, and like Dickey he's solidly built, nearly six feet tall. His black shoulder-length hair tumbles out from beneath a dark, greasy beanie. Dickey notes the leathery, calloused feel of his soot-blackened hand, then he points to the massive weapon Obid holds and mimes the act of shooting up at the wall. The man nods and points at himself. He's the shooter, and he appears proud of his marksmanship.

"Cigarette?" Dickey asks, holding out the tobacco pouch.

Abdul sweeps aside the offer with an abrupt wave of his hand and shakes his head disapprovingly. Then Dickey notices that Obid is holding a trekking-style ski pole owned by the climbers, which they left hidden at the bottom of the cliff. He also sees that under Obid's camo vest is a black Gore-Tex jacket bearing the fashionable Patagonia label. On his face are designer sunglasses, and on his back is a high-tech rucksack made by Salewa, a German manufacturer. These items don't belong to Dickey's team members, but clearly these men have not mail-ordered the gear either. At the very least, he figures, he and his friends are in the clutches of bandits who've been raiding the camps in the surrounding valleys.

Abdul holds up four fingers and points toward the portaledges. Dickey nods; yes, there are four in the party. Then Abdul's hands trace the outlines of a woman: curved hips, long hair, cupped hands to illustrate breasts. Dickey hesitates. He doesn't like the direction this conversation is heading. Abdul repeats the question, and Dickey nods; yes, a woman is among them also. Abdul points to the portaledges again and makes it clear that he wants everyone up there to descend. The order sends a "someone just walked over my grave" chill rippling up Dickey's back. He replies to Abdul with a show of hand signs: "No, it's too difficult and dangerous for those above to come down." But Abdul butts in and repeats his order. He points to Dickey's Motorola and says the word *radio*, in English, clearly suggesting that Dickey relay a message up to the portaledges immediately.

"Why?" Dickey asks with palms outstretched.

Abdul points toward their base camp and mimes the act of eating. Dickey stares quizzically at the man. Sure enough, he and his companion are lean as wolves. Could it be that all they want is a good square meal?

One thousand feet above them, Smith scopes Dickey's encounter through the two-hundred-millimeter lens. He snaps off frames of Dickey extending his hand to the gunmen, and of Abdul rejecting the proffered tobacco. When Dickey radios Smith he tells him that everyone must come down.

"What do they want?" Smith asks. "Over."

"I'm not sure," Dickey says. "Over."

"Do they speak English? Over."

"No. They just, er, well, you better come down. They want to go back to our base camp. For, er, breakfast. Over."

The logic underlying Dickey's statement is absurd, but Smith doesn't question it. He knows Dickey well enough to glean from his quavering, nervous tone that something is wrong. After he signs off he reports nothing of this feeling to his companions in the other portaledge.

"Okay, I'll go next," Smith says. "Tommy, you follow me. Hopefully we'll clear this up, and Beth won't even have to come down."

Smith clips himself into the rope and slides out of the portaledge, leaving Rodden and Caldwell buckling up their climbing harnesses and slipping on their shoes. Smith leaves Caldwell with the radio. When Smith reaches the ground he radios up and tells them to come down. Despite their wishful thinking, Rodden is not spared the forced descent.

Weighing a petite ninety-five pounds, Rodden has difficulty pushing the ropes through her rappel device. All together the five ropes weigh over forty pounds. The friction of rope sliding through her rappel device heats the metal enough to make spit sizzle, and a flap of skin on her hand gets dragged into the device. When she reaches the ground at about eight o'clock, she is breathing hard and bleeding from her palm. She fumbles with the hot rappel device and drops it on the ground, then she holds back on the slope, taking in the scene of her companions sitting on the rocky ground, guarded by two heavily armed men.

"Good morning," Abdul says to her in heavily accented English. He seems to have learned the phrase from Dickey a few minutes earlier. Abdul gently shakes Rodden's hand. The gunman and the young woman exchange names. He is polite, almost deferential to her.

Obid steps forward and mimics the greeting: "Good morning." He and Abdul chuckle, as if amused by the foreign sounds coming out of Obid's mouth.

"What do these guys want?" she asks, trembling.

Half out of optimism, half out of concern for Rodden, who is small and almost childlike in appearance, Dickey coolly, ridiculously, reiterates that all that these men want from them is a little breakfast. Though the experience unfolding before her is beyond her comprehension, the twenty-year-old Californian isn't fooled. They are in trouble, and she knows it. Abdul's and Obid's eyes track her as she crosses the rocky slope to stand beside Caldwell. Her climbing companions, she notes, take short, nervous breaths, and their eyes dart about quickly. Fear is in the air, as thick and pungent as smoke.

Abdul signals to them that it is time to move. His tone is nonchalant, without alarm or urgency, yet it is clear that he is in control. He is, undoubtedly, the commander. They stand and depart, leaving their gear hanging on the wall. It's the last they'll see of their portaledges, their racks of climbing hardware, or Dickey's seven-thousand-dollar collection of cameras and lenses.

Abdul and Obid flank their rear and aim them downhill and along the riverbank. They hike in single file, toward a rope spanning the Kara Su River, which the climbers rigged a week earlier to aid their access to the Yellow Wall. But several hundred yards before the rope bridge, Abdul motions to the climbers to roll up their pants and wade across a fast-moving, thigh-deep stretch of the river. Abdul hands Rodden a trekking pole so she can fight the current, and they cross. It is 11 A.M. when they arrive at their base camp, a cluster of bright yellow North Face tents pitched on a flat, grassy meadow. There the four climbers are shocked by what they see.

Their tents, which a day earlier they sealed shut from pilfering fingers by taping the zipper tabs of the doors together, are slit wide open at the walls. Clothes, equipment, food wrappers, and empty cans litter the meadow. A puddle of vomit in the center of camp attests to the gunmen's feeding frenzy; evidently, the American food was too rich for someone's stomach.

"This is not a good scene," Smith mutters, breaking a silence they have kept since leaving the bottom of the cliff.

The third gunman—the one who had been standing in the brush at the base of the Yellow Wall—is now posted a few yards away on the meadow, his assault rifle slung at his hip. A fourth man sits at the edge of the camp, with his back against a boulder. Abdul grunts curtly to the gunman in the meadow. He approaches the Americans, and Abdul introduces him; his name sounds like "Su." In contrast to his full-bearded cohorts, Su manages only a few soft, downy hairs on his upper lip and chin, most of them around a pea-sized black mole near the corner of his mouth. He has the look of a callow farm boy, but the way he stares back at the Americans unsettles Smith. He does not extend his hand. He offers no greeting. The only expression that Smith can read in Su's dark almond eyes is anger. He is wearing Caldwell's running shoes, gloves, and wool hat. On the small rucksack on his back he has clipped a lightweight solar panel, also booty belonging to the Americans.

"This guy is scary," Smith mutters to Dickey.

Su returns to his outpost, while Abdul and Obid loot the tents. The four climbers have been herded beside the fourth man, who sits with his arm resting on a sleeping bag stuffed into a green sack. He wears a beige T-shirt and khaki army fatigues with a tobacco pouch protruding from the cargo pocket. He is smooth-faced, like most of the Kyrgyz they have met.

"Who is this guy?" Dickey whispers.

"I don't know," Smith whispers back. "He's one of these bandits, isn't he?"

"Beth, isn't he the soldier we met a few days ago?" Caldwell asks.

"Oh, yeah, he is! He came here, to our base camp! He was with some other soldiers, and they checked our passports," Rodden says, recalling the meeting that occurred while Smith and Dickey were searching the mountain villages for a phone.

The man nods at Caldwell and Rodden and quietly tells them his name. Sergeant Turatbek Osmanov of the Kyrgyz army—Turat for short—is a prisoner too. He speaks no English other than a few common words, but when Su isn't looking, he makes hand gestures and scratches numbers and symbols in the dirt at their feet, like he's playing a game of charades. He counts out the number of soldiers he'd been with when he visited this base camp nine days earlier—there'd been two others besides him—and his hands conjure the shape of the small dog that had been with them. Then he communicates the following: there was a battle; he was captured; more shooting, his signing suggests, is imminent. Then he repeatedly scratches the number 17 into the dirt. The climbers cannot understand his meaning. Does it refer to gunmen or soldiers, men alive or dead? Finally, he holds up three fingers and sweeps his hand across his throat.

"Oh God," Caldwell mutters when he understands that Osmanov has made the universal symbol for death—the slit throat. The implied message is that their captors will kill the men, keep the girl, steal what they want from their camp, and head on with their crime spree.

"Nyet, Nyet!" Osmanov says when he sees the Americans' stricken faces. But the story he gets across with a series of rapid theatrical gestures is hardly more encouraging: Osmanov was captured with some fellow soldiers; the gunmen killed his comrades—maybe by knifing them, judging by Osmanov's jabbing motions. He has been kept alive only to guide his captors through the mountains. The soldier points to dark spatters on the leg of his pants—the blood of his friends. He makes the gesture for a cigarette, then points to the bandits: "Nyet," he whispers, waving his finger to indicate they do not smoke, a fact that Dickey already knows.

"Vodka: nyet," Osmanov adds.

So, the gunmen neither smoke nor drink. Dickey, for one, understands Osmanov's meaning: their captors are staunch Muslims. Militants. Perhaps not mere thieves, but guerrillas, rebels or revolutionaries. Su looks across at the prisoners. Osmanov shuts up and sits back, putting on a face as hard as stone.

Abdul emerges from the large yellow tent that the climbers use as their main dining area and summons Dickey and Smith inside. Leaving Caldwell and Rodden sitting with Osmanov, they approach the tent fearfully. Anything seems possible at this juncture. Even having their throats slit.

"What do they want?" Rodden asks insistently while Dickey and Smith disappear into the tent. "What are they going to do with us?" She's near to tears, quaking whenever the gunmen glance at her, tense with the thought that at any moment she could be dragged away and raped.

"Don't worry," Caldwell says, drawing her closer. "I'm not going to let you out of my sight."

Rodden thinks for a moment, then calms down and looks him in the eyes. "Tommy, whatever happens, don't risk your life for me."

When Su's attention returns to the broad, green valley, Osmanov turns to the couple and resumes chattering and making hand signs. Seeing that he has terrified the girl with his talk of blood and death, the soldier makes clear the message that no, they will not be killed. He rubs his thumb and forefingers together, making another universal symbol—the sign for money—and he points to each of the Americans. The pieces of the puzzle are fitting together in all their minds. Before they left America they'd heard reports about Islamic militants in Kyrgyzstan kidnapping foreigners and holding them for ransom. They had not imagined that this hazard applied to the well-traveled Karavshin region, so the information had settled into their minds like background material.

Inside the big yellow tent Dickey and Smith find Abdul and Obid digging through the duffel bags containing the Americans' food. They've been ripping open packets and candy bars, nibbling at the contents, tossing aside what they deem unpalatable and shoving foods they like into rucksacks. Now they want to know the contents of each can and packet. A strange game of charades begins. When Abdul holds up a can of chicken meat the climbers cluck, *"Bok bok bok."* When Obid points to a strip of beef jerky they intone, *"Moo."* Smith and Dickey understand that these Muslims don't want anything that smacks of *oink*.

Smith picks up a packet of dried fruit sticks that the climbers had been unable to stomach and says, handing one to Obid, "Hey, try one of these. The sour-apple flavor is really awful, at least we think so." The gunman bites into it, winces at the tart taste, and throws the fruit stick aside. Dickey laughs uneasily at his friend's ability to squeeze a joke out of their predicament, then their terror returns.

Abdul tosses another rucksack at Smith and hands him random items to pack: batteries, candles, matches, canned meat, packets of cookies, candy bars. Pointing to the other rucksacks in the tent, Abdul communicates that the Americans must pack their jackets, hats, and gloves, and they must wear long pants too. He tosses a sleeping bag at Dickey, who packs it. Soon four rucksacks brim with forty to fifty pounds of supplies. While packing, Dickey turns to Smith. A crooked, nervous smile contorts his lips.

"We're hostages," he says flatly.

2.

TRAVELER ADVISORIES

The four Americans came to Kyrgyzstan looking for adventure, but they did not hope to find it at the point of a gun.

They are young, but they comprise a remarkable pool of rock-climbing talent. A self-assured, boyish-looking, and opinionated twenty-two-year-old Utah native, Jason Smith lives in California in a Ford van that is frequently found parked in Yosemite Valley, where he spends most of his time climbing. He has made a slew of notable ascents, including, at the age of twenty, a solo climb of a four-thousand-foot plug of rock called Mount Thor, near the Arctic Circle on Canada's Baffin Island. To make the climb, he lived alone on the cliff for fourteen days. His nickname, Singer, is derived from his penchant for stitching up kitschy clothing on an old sewing machine.

Beth Rodden, twenty, is from Davis, California. Though her angelic face and diminutive stature make her look five years younger than her age, her appearance belies her athleticism. She is one of the few women—and the youngest—to have climbed at the top 5.14 rating of rock-climbing difficulty.

Her soft-spoken, sunny-faced, and crew-cut boyfriend, Tommy Caldwell, lives in the Rocky Mountains of Colorado. Built like a cross between a pit bull and a greyhound, he has laid claim to the first ascent of what is possibly America's hardest sport climb, a route he'd named Kryptonite. The one-hundred-foot climb, on a wall of limestone shaped like a crashing wave, near the town of Rifle, Colorado, is regarded as difficult enough to qualify for the breakthrough rating of 5.15. While practicing, Caldwell took hundreds of falls onto his climbing rope before he succeeded in reaching the top. Though tenacious and immensely strong on rock, and something of a new star of the climbing scene, Caldwell is known more for modesty than for bravado.

Texas-raised John Dickey, twenty-five, is a budding photographer who moved to California from San Antonio, Texas, six years earlier. The son of a Church of Christ deacon turned Methodist, his favorite stomping ground for climbing is the High Sierra.

It is Smith who organized their "mini-expedition" to the Karavshin, planning it from his back-of-the-warehouse office at The North Face in San Leandro, California, where at the time he headed up A5 Equipment, a small division within that larger mountaineering-and-ski-wear manufacturing company. A5 designs products for hard-core climbers, like the portaledges they'd been bivouacking on when the gunmen opened fire. Smith, like Rodden, was also one of the up-and-coming climbers in The North Face's clan of semiprofessional outdoor athletes, and when the two of them suggested their expedition to the company's marketing department, The North Face agreed to fund it, hoping to acquire photos that they could use to advertise their products. The Karavshin region reigns as one of the best spots on the planet for big-wall climbing. Its geologic twin, Yosemite, with its sweeps of glacier-carved granite soaring to twenty-seven hundred feet, is the established world mecca of big-walling. It is also the virtual second home of the four climbers, and it is where they all got to know one another. On the biggest cliff in Yosemite, El Capitan, they collectively climbed a score of routes. Some of those routes took as long as a week to ascend, others as little as a day, on dawn-till-dusk speed ascents.

Since Smith had already shivered through a season in Baffin Island's big-wall country while climbing the frigid Mount Thor, he was keen to experience a sunnier climate, where the rock does not chill your fingers to the bone whenever you touch it. Smith and Rodden settled on the Karavshin region, for its temperate latitude and for its legendary status among Russian climbers. Smith invited Dickey along as photographer, and Rodden invited Caldwell, her main climbing partner ever since they had formed an inseparable bond in Yosemite during the spring of 2000. Ironically, Caldwell was to go to the Karavshin earlier that year with other climbers who were planning to make an adventure documentary, but the expedition had been canceled because some members had caught wind of warnings on the State Department's Web site about Islamic insurgents kidnapping foreigners and fighting with government troops in southern Kyrgyzstan in 1999.

I had climbed in the Karavshin in 1995, on an expedition that was also sponsored by The North Face. Our team of eight included climbing luminaries like Lynn Hill, Conrad Anker, and the late Alex Lowe, and we had found a pastoral scene with a scattered population of Kyrgyz farmers tending yaks, cows, sheep, and goats. We also found a slew of virgin routes on the walls of Peak 4810, Peak 3850 (so named for their heights in meters), and the Russian Tower, which Russian climbers call Slesov Peak. Soviet climbers learned about the Karavshin region in 1936, when geologists prospecting for tin in the Turkestan Range (the subrange of the Pamir-Alai Mountains that contain the valleys of the Karavshin) stumbled across the spectacular gorges of the Ak Su and Kara Su. Climbers helped the prospectors in their explorations, and among them was the famous pioneer of Russian alpinism, Vitaly Abalakov. Back in 1936, the gear and techniques needed to climb vertical four-thousand-foot rock cliffs didn't exist, so Abalakov's team focused on the higher-altitude ice peaks that lie deeper in the mountains, beyond the Ak Su and Kara Su valleys. They made an unsuccessful attempt on the area's tallest mountain, Piramidalny Peak (18,073 feet). A few years later came World War II and then the Cold War, and the Karavshin remained untouched by climbers for fifty years. When another generation of Russian climbers rediscovered the area in 1986, big-wall climbing had come of age, and a golden era for Soviet climbing began when climbing camps, funded by the Russian Ministry of Sport, allowed Russians to pick off dozens of routes on the towers lining the valleys.

There are mountains all over the world, but the number of spots where Ice-Age glaciers carved out big walls from the granite bedrock is an exclusive shortlist: Yosemite; Baffin Island; Greenland; the Trango Towers of Pakistan; Chamonix, in the French Alps; and by the late 1980s, the Karavshin. The two ten-mile-long valleys—the Kara Su and the Ak Su— became the testing ground for Russia's best climbers, and later for foreigners who visited the area on climbing exchanges. Those exchanges were among the earliest acts of glasnost, or "openness," during the years when Russian president Mikhail Gorbachev sought to free up the Soviet Union from its social and economic isolation. By the mid-1990s the Karavshin had also created a small but healthy hard-currency-earning adventure-tourism business for Russian, Uzbek, and Kyrgyz climbers who took care of the logistics for westerners wanting to climb there.

When I visited the Karavshin in 1995, Tajikistan was still fighting its 1992–1997 civil war, yet Kyrgyzstan—dubbed "the island of democracy" among Central Asian countries—was at peace. None of us on that trip encountered any hint of hostility, and we never saw a soldier or an army outpost. Quite the contrary, my memories from that expedition are of an idyllic alpine paradise, where friendly local shepherds would beckon us into their simple houses and feed us yogurt, bread, and hot tea, and where climbers visited one another's base camps to exchange climbing stories and equipment and knock back shots of vodka. Two Russian teams and another American group were camped near us, having either helicoptered in from Tashkent in Uzbekistan (as we did) or traveled across borders by vehicle and packhorse.

In the mid-nineties it was still unusual to meet Russian climbers, and I recall a brisk trade in equipment between us. Russians bartered pitons and ice screws made of strong, lightweight titanium, which they manufactured (when supervisors weren't looking) in the plants where the famously silent Soviet submarines were built; westerners brought rock shoes with sticky rubber that gripped the cliffs securely. One pair of western rock shoes would fetch a fat bundle of titanium gear. The Russians especially appreciated the trade, as their rock shoes were flimsy rubber-soled bedroom slippers or clumsy rainproof overshoes called *galoshkies.* When I asked one Russian climber how he'd managed to make so many titanium pitons in a state-owned factory, he replied, "The government pretends to pay us, and we pretend to work."

Of the climbing there I remember sinking my hands into cracks that led like highways up towering sheets of blond granite, azure skies, and views from the heights of the Ak Su and Kara Su Rivers, which appeared as foaming white threads merging into one river—the Karavshin—at a perfect Y intersection. Those of us on that 1995 trip spoke glowingly of our experience, possibly contributing to the Karavshin's growing reputation over the next four years as a world-class mountain playground. During the 1990s, climbing magazines and journals from every country regularly reported on the new routes climbers were adding to the Karavshin, and as recently as August 1999, companies like Mountain Travel-Sobek took paying clients trekking through the region, even camping at the base camp near the Yellow Wall where the American climbers would be kidnapped. That same year the Russian Mountaineering Federation held a big-wall climbing contest in the Ak Su valley, attended by two dozen Russian, French, British, Spanish, and American climbers. During that competition a violent standoff between Islamic guerrillas and the Kyrgyz army erupted sixty miles away, yet all remained peaceful in the Ak Su and Kara Su and the competition went on without a hitch.

But by the end of the twentieth century the frontiers of adventure were also the frontiers of political instability and civil conflict, and the quest to experience the world's last unspoiled places increasingly led climbers and explorers into unexpected peril. Ethnic unrest, militant Islam, poverty, drug trafficking, and social rot became the automatic legacy of Central Asia's independence from the Soviet Union, which collapsed in 1992. Fearing trouble in Kyrgyzstan, Mountain Travel-Sobek canceled its Karavshin trip for 2000. Lonely Planet Online was succinct in its warning to travelers heading for the boondocks of Kyrgyzstan: "There's a great temptation to hop off the bus in the middle of nowhere and hike into the hills, but this is not recommended if you value your life." While intimations of peril led some trekkers and climbers to cancel their plans in the Karavshin for summer 2000, the dangers of the rapidly changing political situation in southern Kyrgyzstan eluded others, as no less than five teams of climbers and trekkers from France, Germany, Ukraine, Australia, and the United States converged on the Karavshin.

OBTAINING VISAS to visit Kyrgyzstan was a simple matter for the Americans. They simply downloaded application forms from the Web site of the Kyrgyz embassy in Washington, D.C., and mailed them with their passports and a fee of fifty dollars. By e-mail Smith contacted a Bishkek-based tour operator called Ak Sai Travel to cater to their in-country travel needs. Svetlana Fedina, Ak Sai's deputy director, quoted him a fee of $9,400 to set up a helicopter flight from Bishkek to the wilds of the Karavshin. He wired the money into Ak Sai Travel's bank account about two weeks prior to departing. "I received absolutely no information from Ak Sai Travel on danger, and I received no warning from the Kyrgyz embassy," Smith would say later.

Prior to leaving for Kyrgyzstan, some of the climbers did scan the Internet for information about the country they would be visiting. The U.S. State Department's Web site at www.travel.state.gov had several lengthy entries about Kyrgyzstan, among them a Consular Information Sheet dated November 17, 1999. Such sheets provide basic information about safety and travel conditions for every country in the world. Under the subheading "Safety and Security" was the following caution: "Due to military and insurgent activity throughout most of southern Kyrgyz Republic and the Kyrgyz-Tajik border areas, the Department of State cautions U.S. citizens to avoid all travel west and south of the southern provincial capital of Osh." This notice also informed readers that U.S. government personnel were prohibited from traveling to this area, and it explained that in August 1999 Islamic militants had launched an armed offensive from Tajikistan into southern Kyrgyzstan. The information continued: "The militants have kidnapped foreigners and Kyrgyz citizens in an effort to win recognition of their demands, including the formation of an Islamic State. The Kyrgyz government has launched counter-attacks against the insurgents and fighting in southwestern Kyrgyz Republic continues. Close contacts with local population do not provide a guarantee of safety."

Some of the climbers recall seeing State Department postings for Kyrgyzstan that mentioned Islamic militants and kidnappings, but they incorrectly interpreted the information as being out-of-date, describing events that had happened a year earlier and that pertained to other parts of Kyrgyzstan. "The advisory for Kyrgyzstan seemed low-key," Tommy Caldwell would say, recalling his personal assessment of the warning. "We decided it was not very alarming." Smith would also contact an acquaintance who had worked in Kyrgyzstan and ask if the country was safe. His friend felt all would be well and encouraged Smith's team to visit Kyrgyzstan.

To the best of their recollections, the Americans also missed seeing an update a couple of mouse clicks away on the same Web site that gave a more recent and more worrisome overview of the situation in southern Kyrgyzstan. This was a supplement to the Consular Information Sheet, called a Public Announcement. Public Announcements are not intended as a scale or a level of warning. The State Department issues them to "disseminate information quickly about terrorist threats and other relatively short term conditions that pose significant risks or disruptions to Americans."

The Public Announcement for Kyrgyzstan dated June 15, 2000, reiterated that travel south and west of Osh was inadvisable and described conditions in the region as being "fluid and potentially dangerous." The announcement told of the kidnapping of four Japanese during the armed offensive of August 1999, and their release after a counterattack by the Kyrgyz military and the imminent onset of winter. "The possibility exists that militants could again launch an armed incursion into the southern Kyrgyz Republic and seize foreign hostages," the report warned. The Karavshin region, lying 160 miles southwest of Osh and abutting the Tajik border, lay well within the hot zone described in the State Department's Public Announcement.

Yet for all the explicitness of the danger in southern Kyrgyzstan, the alert stopped short of being a full-fledged Travel Warning, a sort of red light that advises Americans to avoid a country completely. Neither Kyrgyzstan nor Uzbekistan to the north was on this keep-out list. Tajikistan, war-torn Afghanistan, and pariah nations like Libya and Iraq were on the Travel

Warning list, yet so was Pakistan, a country that thousands of trekkers and mountaineers visit every year despite its being a hotbed of narcotics trafficking, a training ground for terrorists, and a recruiting center for Taliban fighters in its religious schools, or *madrassas*. I had been climbing there myself, on seven expeditions between 1983 and 1996. I'd never felt threatened in Pakistan, though the atmosphere between locals and westerners was sometimes tense; "Death to USA" and "Death to Israel" are, in some towns, the graffiti of choice.

Adding more confusion to the climbers' attempts to interpret the various types of warnings on the State Department's Web site was the inclusion of peaceful Australia on the Public Announcement list. As host of the 2000 Olympic Games, it was, the State Department felt, a potential terrorist target.

The State Department Web site made clear the dangers in southern Kyrgyzstan, yet the climbers "surfed" through these sites, rather than studying them. Knowing that dozens of climbers had visited the Karavshin in recent times, they went ahead and planned their trip. In June 2000 I happened to be in Yosemite with Mark Synnott, climbing the Nose of El Capitan, when Jason Smith, paired up with Lynn Hill, sprinted up the climb from below and joined me on a ledge for a few minutes. He told me he was off to the Karavshin region later that summer; I replied that the climbing there was fantastic and that he'd have a great time. Neither of us knew much about the political situation in Kyrgyzstan. I, for one, have to confess that in sixteen expeditions to the mountains of Asia, Africa, and South America, I have never checked a State Department Web site to see if the country was safe—though I will in the future.

If the climbers had searched through the Internet beyond the State Department's site they would have found a labyrinth of filings about the trouble around Batken in southern Kyrgyzstan, and they would have seen the name of the Islamic Movement of Uzbekistan, or IMU. If they had keyed the name of that organization into a search engine, they may have found, among a bewildering array of stories, a rambling document titled "In the Name of Allah the Most Compassionate the Most Merciful."

Dated August 25, 1999, and signed by a man named Az Zubair Ibn Abdur Raheem, who called himself the Head of the Religious Leadership of the IMU, the document announced that the IMU's military commander, Mohammed Takhir Farooq (Yuldashev), had declared "the start of the Jihad against the tyrannical government of Uzbekistan and the puppet Islam Karimov and his henchmen." *Jihad* means "holy war," or "holy struggle," and the document stated the aims of the IMU's struggle: to free five thousand Muslims held in Uzbek jails, to overthrow the government of Uzbekistan's President Karimov, and to establish an Islamic state in southern Uzbekistan in which the eye-for-an-eye form of Islamic law known as Shari'a would rule. It also declared holy war against Kyrgyzstan, for allegedly arresting and handing over to "Karimov's henchmen" thousands of Muslim Uzbeks who had migrated as refugees into Kyrgyzstan.

Warning that the IMU's mujaheddin—its soldiers of God—are ready for battle, the declaration offered chilling advice to tourists considering a visit to Uzbekistan or Kyrgyzstan: "They should keep away, lest they be struck down by the mujaheddin."

Few foreigners realized it, but the fighting men of the Islamic Movement of Uzbekistan had declared open season on tourists in Kyrgyzstan.

3.

YOU HAVE NEVER BEEN

TO TBLISI!

FROM SAN FRANCISCO TO KYRGYZSTAN

JULY 25-27

At 3 P.M. on July 27 the last pieces of luggage from the British Midlands flight roll off the baggage carousel at Manas International Airport in Bishkek. The odyssey of the four American climbers started in San Francisco two calendar days earlier with a British Air flight to London. There they transferred to British Midlands Airlines for the continuation of their journey to Bishkek, but during the flight the pilot had fallen ill so the plane had made an unscheduled stop in Tblisi, the capital of ex-Soviet Georgia and the birthstate of Joseph Stalin. The passengers had been put up in a good hotel in Tblisi, but by the time their flight reached Kyrgyzstan it was fourteen hours behind schedule.

As they drag their heavy duffels full of camping and climbing gear off the carousel in Bishkek and dump them onto trolleys, the climbers again count out nineteen instead of twenty bags. They learned they were missing a large black duffel in Tblisi, where they'd had to recheck all their bags. The airline representative there had told them to report the missing bag in Bishkek, so at dawn, red-eyed, jet-lagged, and with Russian phrase book in hand, Caldwell marches up to the desk of an airline agent in the gray-tiled lobby of Manas Airport.

"I speak English," the uniformed ethnic Russian woman wearily informs him as he muddles through a greeting in Russian.

"Great. Thanks. The airline has lost one of our bags."

"Where have you come from?" the clerk asks, studying the baggage receipt that Caldwell hands her.

"Tblisi."

"No. You have not come from Tblisi. This is London flight. Never went to Tblisi."

"The plane was sent to Tblisi because the pilot got sick," Caldwell explains.

"*Nyet.* Tblisi, *nyet,*" the clerk repeats an octave higher. She points a long red-painted fingernail at the abbreviations on the baggage-claim tag: "LON-FRU." "Frunze"—"FRU" in airline baggage-speak—is the Soviet-era name for Bishkek.

"That's right," Smith says, arriving at the counter to help Caldwell. "The plane came from London, but it stopped in Tblisi."

"Tblisi no!"

"Tblisi yes!"

"Forget Tblisi!" the woman shouts.

As Smith grows impatient, Caldwell steps back in. He leans on the counter and slowly explains the problem. His friendly smile and cowboyish drawl put the woman at ease. She lets him get as far as the pilot falling ill, but the second his story lands in the Georgian capital she waves the baggage receipt in the air and shakes her head.

"No!" she thunders. "You have never been to Tblisi. Forget Tblisi!"

Morning has broken by the time they are done filling out the lost-bag claim, which makes no mention of Tblisi. Wheeling a fleet of trolleys through Kyrgyz Customs, they exit the airport and meet Svetlana Fedina, deputy director of Ak Sai Travel.

"Your flight was very late," she tells them. "The helicopter is now waiting. We must go to our office quickly, then you will fly."

Fedina elbows a path through a throng of taxi drivers offering over-priced rides into the city and ushers the Americans to a minivan. They fill the van with bags and people and add a taxi to carry the overflow, then the convoy makes the half-hour drive into suburban Bishkek to the offices of Ak Sai Travel. Distinguished only by a large yellow sign mounted on a gray stucco wall on Sovetskaya Street, Ak Sai's offices overlook a busy intersection where Russian-designed Ladas blow smoke beside shiny Mercedes-Benzes. Ak Sai is in the business of making travel within Kyrgyzstan easy for foreigners. Its many years in the travel business have brought the firm contacts with everyone from military-helicopter pilots and permit-stamping bureaucrats to mountain guides and mule drivers. A streamlined travel process in a foreign country is like gold to an expedition, and Ak Sai Travel had come recommended to Smith as an outfit able to get things done, by one of Smith's friends who had used it a year earlier.

In the office the climbers meet the ironically named Elena Kalashnikova, owner and director of the company. Built stout as a fireplug, she's an ethnic Russian, with a warm smile and an efficient manner. Fedina translates for her. They hand Smith a frontier permit, required by the Kyrgyz government for travel to the border areas.

"If you wish, we can arrange an interpreter. He can look after your base camp too. Ten dollars per day."

Smith and his friends decline her offer. "Who would he interpret for?" Smith says. "We'll be up on the walls, climbing. I don't think an interpreter will be necessary."

Business concluded, she escorts the group back to the waiting vehicles. Before Smith leaves the office, he raises the matter of the lost bag.

"It has climbing gear in it. It's important. Can you try to find it for us?"

"We'll try," Kalashnikova says, via Fedina, ushering the group down the stairs. "Now we must hurry to the airport because the helicopter is waiting. You will be in base camp tonight." She climbs into the van with the Americans, and the vehicles leave the parking lot.

As they drive to the helipad, back out near the city's old airport, the climbers are unaware that they have failed to register their presence in Kyrgyzstan with the American embassy. It's a voluntary formality advised by the U.S. State Department as a safety measure for its citizens. Nor do the Americans realize that because of their hasty departure from Bishkek, their passports won't be stamped by the Kyrgyz-government department for foreign registration known as OVIR—although OVIR registration is one of the items they have paid Ak Sai Travel to prepare for them. Although their passports have been stamped by the Kyrgyz immigration officer at the airport and their names have been entered in a ledger of travelers applying for frontier permits, no other agency in Kyrgyzstan will know the Americans are in the country. Neither Fedina nor Kalashnikova mentions anything about trouble in the region their clients are headed to.

MYSTERIOUSLY, however, three weeks earlier in Bishkek a young Australian climber named Kate Dooley and her two climbing partners, Nikki Sunderland and Claire Helme, were "warned by every local travel agency we spoke to not to go to this area due to what happened there last year." According to Dooley, when her group had "proved determined" to visit the Ak Su valley, despite initial warnings from the directors of Ak Sai Travel, the company "offered to help with logistics" by arranging overland transport and a frontier permit. Before they left for Kyrgyzstan the Australians had heard about the 1999 IMU incursion in the mountains near the town of Batken, and they knew about the kidnapping of the Japanese. But the women figured that the Karavshin was safe because it lay sixty miles west of the areas the rebels had invaded. They also calculated that because they planned to leave the mountains by early August they would be spared trouble, if indeed trouble arose, as the fighting in 1999 had occurred in late August, after summer heat had melted the snow on the mountain passes, allowing the rebels to enter Kyrgyzstan. "Turned out to be the right hunch," Dooley would later write.

Nevertheless, while she and her friends waited in Bishkek for three days preparing their trip, the repeated warnings left them feeling "really undecided" about travel in southern Kyrgyzstan. Yet travel there they did, and on a shoestring budget. Lacking the money to pay for a helicopter ride, they took a thirty-hour bus trip over potholed roads to Osh, then got onto another bus to travel to the village of Ak Sai. From there they hiked with packhorses for two days up the Karavshin River, arriving at a base camp below the peaks of the Ak Su valley on the afternoon of July 10.

THE VAN WITH THE AMERICANS ENTERS THE AIRPORT and drives up to a hulking Mi8 helicopter, property of the Kyrgyz military. There they meet Pavel, an English-speaking ethnic Russian who works for Ak Sai Travel. He'll fly to base camp with them, then return the same day to Bishkek. The Mi8, which Ak Sai Travel has chartered from the army, is piloted by an army colonel named Sydykov. The flight path will take the Americans southwest, over the cities of Osh and Batken, to Lyalyak, 350 miles away. The helicopter will then make a final short hop into the mountains of the Karavshin region and deliver the climbers to the Kara Su valley.

To keep such a huge machine airworthy is expensive: an hour of flight time retails for eight hundred dollars or more, with a third of that cost being fuel for the machine's 1,870-liter tank. In a country where the average annual income is $240 (a U.S. dollar buys 50 Kyrgyz som), the comparative cost of operating a twenty-four-seat helicopter is astronomical. So, the military subsidizes its helicopter corps by occasionally moonlighting for tourists. At the military air base near Manas Airport, European parachuting clubs have been known to charter army Mi8's and fill them with parachutists; coming to Kyrgyzstan and making multiple jumps from the Mi8 choppers is a bargain for foreigners. Flying tourists into the Karavshin or other mountain areas is not uncommon for the Kyrgyz military either.

The pilots welcome the Americans aboard through a door in the side of the helicopter and direct them to a row of cramped seats lining the fuselage wall. Their bags are loaded through the big clamshell doors in the rear. The fuselage is cavernous, the size of a garage; indeed, an Mi8 can transport a vehicle. Even with all of the Americans' duffel bags, there is room for more passengers. With that in mind, the pilots bring on board three civilians and sit them on the gear. A woman among them passes a baby forward through the cabin toward the more comfortably seated Americans. The child ends up in Rodden's arms.

Kalashnikova wishes them luck and waves good-bye, then the doors close. The pilots flick an array of switches in the cockpit, and the rotors of the Mi8 stir. Within a half minute the two 1,500-horsepower turbo-shaft engines are roaring, and the sweet smell of kerosene vapor becomes mildly nauseating.

The machine vibrates as it taxis down the runway on its big balloon tires, then it lurches forward and takes to the air. The grid of Bishkek's streets falls away, and soon they are flying over factories, then farms, then a lacework of pastures and rivers.

The helicopter flies for two hours, then touches down at the nonde-script town of Lyalyak, an arid outpost in the foothills of the Turkestan Range. The other passengers leave, then the helicopter lifts off again. Back in the air, the climbers look down on a landscape of desert badlands. Soon, though, the earth's crust ripples in a succession of sharp ridges, mountains appear, and the land begins to green. The helicopter gains altitude, flies over a ridge, and enters a steep-sided canyon—the Kara Su valley. The climbers press their faces against the round Plexiglas windows, watching raindrops spatter the windows as they fly through a squall. Poking through the clouds they see white summits ahead of them. Piramidalny Peak, the highest mountain of the region, marks the Kyrgyz-Tajik border. But it is the clean, glacier-carved granite walls lining the lower valleys that catch their eyes. They see that the rock is steep and solid. The canyon looks like everything that the young climbers had hoped for.

The pilot brings the helicopter down through low clouds to land on a flat, pebbly clearing beside the river. The rotors are still spinning as the rear doors swing open and the climbers and flight crew throw out the baggage. One of the crew siphons enough kerosene from the Mi8's fuel tank to fill the climbers' five-gallon jerry can. They'll use the fuel to run their camping stoves. Pavel steps out of the helicopter just long enough to point out the main rock towers around them.

"There is Usen, the big mountain. Next to it is Asan, the little moun-tain. And across the river is the Yellow Wall, a good one for the first climb here. Now I must leave, but it will make the pilots happy if you tip them."

"How much?" Rodden asks.

"Twenty dollars each."

Rodden counts out the cash and hands it over. Pavel and Smith set a date for the helicopter to return—the end of August—then Pavel climbs back on board. The climbers crouch against the windblast of the rotors as the Mi8 guns its engines, then rises and disappears down the valley.

Their base camp resembles a Zen garden. Lush grass and wildflowers surround lichen-mottled boulders and twisted old fir trees, called *archas* by the locals. Previous expeditions have built tables and seats from stacked stones, as well as a short wall to shelter campers from cold gusts blowing down from the Asan-Usen glacier to the south. A clear spring bubbles out of a choke of rocks—just as well, because the river is dark and silty. The words *Kara Su* mean "black water"; in the other valley, the Ak Su, the water is clear and sweet. The words have roots in old Tibetan, though Tibet is far away. Language, however, is well traveled in Central Asia. The passes that connect Kyrgyzstan, Tajikistan, Uzbekistan, and Afghanistan are centuries-old trade routes, all branches of the economic highway known as the Silk Road. Everything tradable—food, livestock, pots, pans, weapons, opium—has traversed Central Asia's borders in caravans of camels, yaks, mules, and, where roads have been bulldozed, in trucks. Language, ideas, religions, wars, revolutions, and the business of smugglers have traveled across these passes too.

The climbers laugh and joke as they set up their base camp. Carefree, living for the moment, devoted to their sport, and at the prime of their athletic lives, they are excited to be in Central Asia's own Yosemite Valley.

But unbeknownst to them, thirty-five miles to the south in the Zaravshan Valley of Tajikistan, trouble is brewing as twenty-three heavily armed men march in their direction. The men are a ragtag group in their late teens or early twenties, and they come from many places: Tajikistan, Uzbekistan, Afghanistan, even as far away as Russia's Ural Mountains near Siberia. They bend under the weight of heavy rucksacks, bandoliers of bullets, Kalashnikov assault rifles, machine guns, and grenade launchers, and they move inexorably uphill into the alpine highlands of the Tajik-Kyrgyz border. They are the mujaheddin of the Islamic Movement of Uzbekistan, and they have been traveling undetected for days, out of secret bases in Tajikistan. Their mission is to slip over the border and link up with five more rebels in the highlands of the Karavshin region, then fight their way north into Uzbekistan.

At dusk that night the rebels camp within a few miles of the Kyrgyz border, on summer pastures where yaks graze, just below the line of perpetual snow where glaciers and snowfields remain frozen year-round. Piramidalny Peak and the mountains radiating out from its ridges stand in front of them like an impenetrable barrier, but fifteen-thousand-foot passes with names like Turo and Boz Toz will let them slip through the mountains onto the glaciers that flow like frozen rivers toward the lower valleys. Kyrgyz shepherds will show them the way. Some of the shepherds assisting the IMU will say they were pressed into service under threat of death; others will help them from a common bond in Islam, or for money. Yet the rebels have much work to do before they crest the mountains and invade Kyrgyzstan. They'll have to blaze trails through deep snow, find paths around crevasses, and use shovels to hack steps into slippery slopes of winter-packed snow. Then they'll ferry their supplies, establish a forward line, reconnoiter the route into Kyrgyzstan, and spy on the Kyrgyz-army outposts along the way.

While the Americans pitch their high-tech dome tents beside the Kara Su, on the Tajik side of the border the rebels build their own ramshackle camp in the frigid shadows of the mountains. They rig tarps over boulders, dump spadefuls of snow into blackened cooking pots that they set over kerosene stoves, and lay out their bedding. Some of the mujaheddin are sluggish from the altitude. Their leaders know that these men need time to adjust to the heights if they are to be strong enough to fight, but altitude-ill or not, at the call for *maghrib*, or evening prayer, all the mujaheddin dutifully form a line facing the setting sun and chant prayers memorized from the Koran. They kneel and rise, kneel and rise, paying homage to Allah. When their prayers are done, they crawl under their quilts and shiver side by side through the night, listening to the news from Tajikistan and Afghanistan on a small AM/FM radio, fondling strings of black prayer beads, and smiling and laughing into the video camera that one of the rebels points at them to record their mission. Tucked into their beds they look nothing like terrorists and murderers. They look like teenagers on a camping trip.

4.

A WALK DOWN THE KARAVSHIN

KARA SU BASE CAMP AND KURBAKA ARMY CAMP

JULY 27–AUGUST 1

For the shepherds of the Karavshin, life is a simple ritual of farm chores interspersed with periods of prayer. Men range the valleys on horseback or on foot, herding yaks and cattle or hunting; children tend goats and sheep; women bake bread in clay ovens, milk cows, churn butter, prepare yogurt in sacks made from the tanned bellies of sheep, and look after toddlers. They are among Kyrgyzstan's poorest folk, living in their mountain homes without electricity or running water, far from any roads. They are also semi-nomadic, leaving the valleys at the onset of each winter and heading to the lowlands until spring, when the snow covering the high country melts and they pack their belongings onto horses and donkeys and return to the high alps with their animals. So, when four Americans land by helicopter and set up base camp, everyone for miles around wants to meet them.

Among the first locals to visit the American newcomers is a twenty-year-old shepherd named Ulan, who arrives soon after the helicopter departs, on the evening of July 27. Ulan lives with his aging parents in a *khosh*—a local word for farmhouse—a half mile down the valley. The same families have inhabited the region for generations, and Ulan is happy for the chance to meet some new people. Dickey takes up the Russian phrase book, and he and Ulan embark on a conversation: "Where is your home? How old are you? What is your job?" Ulan explains that he will soon leave the valley to study English, and tells them he is a soldier, a reservist they assume.

The next morning, July 28, Ulan returns to the camp, bringing a jug of fresh milk for the climbers. He also brings his son, Rulan, and Rodden gives the youngster a gift of a small soccer ball. By midmorning a dozen more locals have strolled into the camp. Rodden snaps Polaroids of them, handing them out as gifts. Most of the visitors are children, and they arrive while the Americans are sorting through their duffel bags, organizing the camp they plan to live in for the next month. Clothes, sleeping bags, and shiny piles of climbing gear are everywhere. The children are fascinated by the equipment, and they inspect everything, pulling at ropes, opening and closing the snapping gates of carabiners, jangling the "cams" and "nuts" that the climbers will soon be using to climb the surrounding cliffs. Some of the children know a few words of English: "Give me?" they ask whenever they see something they really like. The Americans have so many things, surely they won't miss a carabiner or a pen, the children are thinking.

"Ah, compact disketta!" exclaims one of the men, admiring Smith's CD player. His name is Murat Kalnarazov. Coincidentally, five years earlier I stayed in this hospitable shepherd's home, down near the junction of the Kara Su and the Ak Su Rivers at a sprawl of farms called Karavshy. He and his family served me and my two companions yogurt, bread, and tea from a long-spouted brass pot. We spent the night on the packed-earth floor of his porch on our way to a pass that led to the Ortachashma River and the trail to the Turo Pass—the very path the terrorists were now headed toward. Kalnarazov's uncle tried to sell us a snow-leopard pelt that night for eighty dollars, and we struggled to explain to him that killing the rare spotted cat was regarded as a crime in our home countries. When we departed, Kalnarazov was astonished, even offended, that we insisted he accept a five-dollar bill as payment for putting us up.

Smith places the headphones of his music machine on the shepherd's head. Kalnarazov's eyes widen and his round, ruddy face breaks into a smile when Smith's favorite Black Sabbath CD starts pounding his eardrums. Smith nicknames the shepherd Homer, after the father in the TV cartoon show *The Simpsons*.

"Singer, I figured out what we lost in that missing duffel bag," Dickey breaks in while Smith and Homer rock out.

"What?"

"Two of our climbing harnesses, a rope, my rock shoes, one of the fuel bottles for the stoves, a water filter, three of our four bivy sacks, a sleeping bag, and my Gore-Tex rain jacket."

"Damn," Smith says. "That's a shitload of stuff."

Not having these items will hinder their ability to climb. In particular, the loss of one of their two kerosene bottles renders their second stove useless, making it difficult for the climbers to break into teams of two. The stoves are necessary for boiling and sterilizing water and cooking the dehydrated meals they have brought from America. Over the next couple of days, as they learn of even more items lost in the missing duffel, Dickey and Smith decide that they must find a way to get a message to Ak Sai Travel, to tell them it is imperative that they locate the missing bag from the airline and get it to base camp, perhaps by bus to the town of Batken, then by horse to base camp.

"Hey, Ulan," Dickey asks, thumbing through his Russian phrase book. "Where is the nearest telephone?"

"Telephone? Ah, Vorukh."

"Vorukh? A village?"

"*Da.* Village."

"How far?"

Ulan ponders a moment, mentally converting Russian numbers into English.

"Thirty kilometers," he answers, pointing down the river.

"Then it looks like you and I are going for a walk, dude," Smith tells Dickey.

―――――

ON THE AFTERNOON of July 31 Smith and Dickey set off to search for a telephone. They take one five-mile-range Motorola radio, leaving Rodden and Caldwell with a pair of two-mile-range Motorolas. They carry light rucksacks, with little clothing because the weather has turned fair and hot; for food they take a couple of packets of instant noodles and some energy bars, as they plan to be gone for only two days. In the meantime, Rodden and Caldwell have decided that they will begin climbing on the Yellow Wall. It is the closest cliff to base camp, and at a little under two thousand feet it is the smallest wall in the valley. Caldwell and Rodden have viewed the wall through a spotting scope and have decided to try to do a new route up a series of cracks splitting the center of the cliff. The four climbers agree that while Dickey and Smith are away, Rodden and Caldwell will carry supplies up to the base of the Yellow Wall and climb the first few hundred feet of the route, "fixing," or installing, their climbing ropes over the rock as they go, and returning to base camp each evening. Dickey's role as cameraman means he'll want to get up on the wall with Caldwell and Rodden and catch the action of the climb, so everyone agrees that they'll wait to camp on the wall until Dickey and Smith return.

Before Dickey and Smith leave base camp they schedule daily radio contacts with Caldwell and Rodden for 9 A.M., 12 noon, 3 P.M., 6 P.M., and 9 P.M. But almost as soon as they depart the canyon walls block out radio reception. The two are not on the trail long when a woman on the other side of the river steps out of her hut and waves to them.

"*Chai, chai!*" she calls, inviting them to her house for tea.

"No, we have a long walk," they yell back, pointing downstream.

But Kyrgyz hospitality inevitably wins, and they cross the river on a wooden footbridge to the hut, which is a square, flat-roofed cabin chinked with sod and clay. Inside, they sit on a well-worn rug while the woman sets porcelain cups in front of them. She wears a wildly bright floral-print skirt and scarf, and her waist-length raven hair hangs in two long, glossy braids. She serves soup stiffened with balls of dough, then yogurt and tea. The man of the house arrives and joins them. The climbers use their phrase book and again ask about a phone. It takes a few moments for their host to grasp their meaning, but when they mime the action of dialing a rotary phone and placing the receiver to their ears, he gets their drift.

"*Carta!*" he says. That's the Russian word for "map," and on a piece of paper he sketches the network of rivers and the farmhouses around them. At a point near a three-way intersection of rivers—the Karavshin, the Kundik, and the Ortochashma, the man draws a hut surrounded by long-horned skulls.

"What is this?" Smith asks.

The man puts his fingers to his forehead, miming some sort of horned beast while repeating a word they cannot find in the phrase book.

"*Tatonka! Tatonka!* Buffalo! I bet he's seen the director's cut of *Dances With Wolves*," Smith jokes.

The climbers puzzle over the meaning of the horned skulls, while the shepherd completes the map. After a few miles, he indicates, they'll find a soldier camp and, maybe, a phone.

"That's even closer than Vorukh," Smith says. "If he's right about a phone there, we'll make the call and be back in camp by nightfall." Thanking the man for lunch and the hand-drawn map, they continue along the trail. Farther downstream, near the confluence of the Kara Su and Ak Su Rivers, they pass another *khosh* and meet an old man and his grandson. The dwelling is the home of Murat Kalnarazov; the old man is Homer's father, the boy is Homer's son. They dub the pair Grandpa Simpson and Bart, and they show them their map. Grandpa and the boy accompany them across a footbridge and down the valley for some way. Bart speaks patchy English.

"Hello! *Soldat* camp?" the youngster says. "I take you. One hundred dollar!"

"Oh, only one hundred dollars?" Smith says, laughing. "You must think our pockets are just full of Ben Franklins."

"Shoes," Bart says, pointing to Smith's trainers. "Give me."

"What will I wear then?" Smith replies. "Well, maybe later, at the end of the trip," he says, suddenly pitying the boy, whose toes protrude from ragged rubber gumboots no doubt inherited from an older brother or two.

Grandpa Simpson and Bart bid them good-bye, then the Americans pass more huts and cross another river. At 4 P.M. they encounter Homer himself along the trail. They show their map to the shepherd and make it understood they are headed to the soldier camp. The man sucks in his breath and makes a wounded sound, then shakes his head. His gestures indicate that the soldiers will steal their money and the camera hanging around Dickey's neck. The man holds out his arms and mimes the gesture of having his wrists shackled.

"Man, these soldiers must be frightening!" Dickey says to Smith. "Are we gonna end up in jail? You sure we should head down there?"

Smith is uncertain, but their path is set. They leave Karavshy, walking down the Karavshin, past broad beds of river-worn stones, past apricot orchards and more shepherd huts. About seven miles from base camp they cross a footbridge where the Kundik River joins the Karavshin. A mile beyond that they reach the junction of the Ortochashma River and cross another bridge. There they find a hut surrounded by bleached ibex skulls perched on sticks.

"Tatonka!" Dickey exclaims.

"More like *Blair Witch Project*," Smith says. The pair dub the site "the Head Chopper's Place."

The long curved horns staked out around the little hut with its stone-walled courtyard suggest the supernatural. The two climbers do not know it, but the place is a Sunni shrine and a graveyard, known to local people and soldiers as Mazar. The clay-walled building is empty, though. Heeding the warning of the shepherd that the soldiers are thieves, they hide Dickey's camera and both of their trekking poles in a cavity under a nearby boulder. They continue along the Karavshin, through a narrow canyon with water-polished walls, then cross the river on another footbridge. It is nearly dark when they arrive at the army camp. Called Kurbaka, the camp lies among a cluster of stone walls and ruins on a goat-dung-covered field. In bygone times Kurbaka was a fort. As soon as they are within sight of the camp, two soldiers armed with automatic weapons shout at them to halt.

"This is gripping!" Smith says while the soldiers stride toward them.

The soldiers make the Americans empty the contents of their rucksacks onto the ground. They inspect everything, then examine their passports and their frontier permit.

"Americanski? Alpinista?"

"Da." Yes is one of the few words of Russian they know.

The soldiers have already encountered the Australian women climbers, or *alpinistas* as climbers are called hereabouts, on July 9 when they had hiked through on their way to the Ak Su valley. More recently, in fact a day earlier, German climbers also en route to the Ak Su passed through Kurbaka as well. Earlier in the season, French trekkers had visited the valley. The soldiers relax and help the climbers repack their rucksacks, then they escort them into the camp. The officer in charge appears and shakes their hands. He wears a T-shirt with a safety pin attached to his chest—the equivalent of a Purple Heart in his army, a soldier will explain to Dickey. The man introduces himself in English as Captain Ruslan Samsakov.

Samsakov's friendly face puts them at ease. When he smiles, he reveals two gold-capped front teeth. He is a doctor in this army unit, and acting commander of the day. After he makes the Americans sign a logbook—in which Samsakov points out the names of the Australian and German climbers who had passed through—he asks them where they are going.

"We need a telephone." Smith explains about the lost bag and the importance of the things it contains for climbing in the mountains.

"No phone is here. In Vorukh is phone."

"Can we go there?"

"No. Vorukh is Tajikistan. With your permit, no."

"Is there another place with a phone?"

"Yes, but it is far. In Batken."

Suddenly the distance they must travel has tripled. "We must go there," Smith says.

"Can you speak Russian?"

"*Nyet.*"

Samsakov turns to his men and tells them that the two Americans want to travel all the way to Batken to make a phone call but they speak no Russian. The men have a good laugh at that.

"Do you know the roo-wit?"

"Roo-wit?" Dickey and Smith exchange puzzled looks, and then they realize Samsakov is struggling with his English, speaking phonetically. "Ah, the route! *Nyet.* We don't know how to get to Batken."

The soldiers laugh again. When Samsakov asks if they have a map and compass—the Americans have neither—the laughter rises to a guffaw.

What can these foreigners be thinking, the soldiers are wondering, wandering the hills in search of a telephone yet with no notion of where they are going? Dickey and Smith join in the laughter, aware of the absurdity of the situation. Yet detailed maps of Central Asia's mountains are extremely difficult and expensive to come by. The Kyrgyz government restricts access to maps for security reasons, and even units of the Kyrgyz army often do not have the Russian-made topo maps of the areas in which they are stationed. Five years earlier, on my trip to Kyrgyzstan, my friends and I wandered the mountains here just as free, with nothing more than a rough and inaccurate sketch photocopied from a French climbing magazine.

"Okay," Samsakov says after he has quit laughing. "Tonight you will sleep here. Tomorrow morning I will draw you a map."

Samsakov speaks with his soldiers, and the men escort the climbers to a doorless adobe hut. They enter it. A soldier stands guard outside and hitches a German shepherd on a leash to the outside of the building.

"Dude, this is aggro," Dickey says, realizing that they are now, essentially, prisoners of the Kyrgyz army.

"I suppose they figure this is for our own safety. Maybe if we get up in the middle of the night to pee, the guards'll shoot us. In which case this place is probably the safest pad around."

ROOSTERS ARE CROWING on the morning of August 1 when Samsakov wakes his guests. He has a sketch map on a scrap of paper. Speaking carefully, he runs his fingers along the lines of his map. He tells them to follow the river downstream, cross a bridge, then walk along a road to "a sanyon."

"Sanyon?" the Americans wonder aloud.

"Very close. Rocks," Samsakov explains, shaping a narrow, vertical-sided chasm with his hands.

"Oh, a canyon."

Samsakov apologizes for his poor English. In his Cyrillic alphabet, the letter *c*, which is usually a hard sound in English, is pronounced as *s*. He then sketches a horse trail winding up the north side of the Karavshin Valley, leaving the canyon about nine miles before the Tajik settlement of Vorukh.

"Here is up," Samsakov stresses, pointing to the horse trail. "Always up. Very up."

The trail climbs the flank of the valley, crests a pass, then descends to two villages, Kit Kim Saray and Tash Bulak. The distance from where they sit at Kurbaka to the villages is roughly twelve miles, he tells them. The trail continues past the villages to a road that heads west to Lyalyak—the town where their helicopter briefly landed—and then east to Batken. From the point at which the trail meets the road, it's a twenty-five-mile bus ride to Batken. Samsakov pens a note on the map in Russian, asking anyone the Americans meet on the trail to help them find their way to Batken and a telephone. Samsakov wishes them luck on their journey. Dickey and Smith leave Kurbaka feeling they have made friends.

THOUGH THE SOLDIERS at Kurbaka appear relaxed and cheerful to the climbers, the Kyrgyz army are stationed there because of the possibility of an invasion by the Islamic Movement of Uzbekistan, although Samsakov said nothing about this to the Americans. A year earlier, the IMU had taken Kyrgyzstan's army by surprise when their mujaheddin swarmed out of Tajikistan over mountain passes to the east. They occupied villages and killed soldiers and police; they held farmers, officers, civil officials, and four Japanese geologists hostage for weeks. The prisoners were used as human shields against Kyrgyz retaliation, and the rebels ransomed them in piecemeal fashion. The Japanese proved especially valuable, reportedly netting the IMU several million dollars.

No one in Kyrgyzstan could say for certain what the IMU wanted. Their strength—estimated from three hundred to a couple of thousand—was a wild guess. Their avowed motive—the overthrow of the Karimov regime and the installation of Taliban-style rule over a large part of Uzbekistan and Kyrgyzstan—seemed murky and idealistic. Experts would determine that the IMU's forays into Kyrgyzstan were an exploratory expedition to determine the strength of the Kyrgyz army and to tie up Kyrgyz forces during bigger raids on their real target, Uzbekistan. A raid on Kyrgyzstan would also determine if local Muslim people would support the IMU. The IMU's movements also coincided with the harvest of the Afghan opium crop. One study by the United States Department of State estimated that in 1999 a total of 4,581 metric tons of opium, from which 460 metric tons of heroin could be refined, were smuggled out of Afghanistan. One metric ton contains one thousand kilograms. The UN under-secretary-general for Drug Control and Crime Prevention that year blamed Afghanistan for 75 percent of the heroin and opium smuggled to Europe, and Kyrgyz officials say the IMU commanded 70 percent of that traffic. A lot of it passed through Tajikistan, Uzbekistan, and Kyrgyzstan as well as Pakistan, where much of the opium is processed into heroin. The value of that much opium and heroin was enough to finance an army.

Kyrgyz military strategists were unsure if or where the IMU would strike in the summer of 2000, but a glance at a map would show the well-traveled passes leading from Tajikistan to the valleys of the Karavshin to be a likely spot. The discovery early in the year 2000 of several tons of weapons and ammunition hidden in the village of Khodzha-Achkan had led the army to suspect a raid in the region, though this news, it seems, was unknown to tourists and their tour operators. Samsakov had probably prevented Smith and Dickey from making the short walk along the river to Vorukh because Vorukh was an enclave—literally, a separate state within a state—belonging to Tajikistan. Aside from the fact that their permit did not allow them to step onto Tajik soil, he may not have felt that the Americans would be safe there. Vorukh, a small triangle of land just fifty-five square miles in size, was believed to be a safe house for the IMU.

With the IMU's stated aim being to topple the Uzbek government, southern Kyrgyzstan found itself wedged between two belligerents. The 1999 IMU invasion had shown the rebels' willingness to march across Kyrgyzstan to get to Uzbekistan, killing soldiers, raiding villages, and taking hostages as they went. The Kyrgyz military, though untrained in mountain warfare and numbering just twelve thousand men, most of them conscripted, was not about to let terrorists use their country again as a staging post for their fight with Uzbekistan. The appearance of soldiers in outposts like Kurbaka was an effort to beef up security along Kyrgyzstan's porous borders.

The crazy quilt of Central Asia's interlocking borders was the brainchild of Joseph Stalin, who in the 1920s crudely lumped ethnic groups together and drew lines around them as a solution to administering the different peoples of his Central Asian empire. On a map, the borders of Tajikistan, Uzbekistan, and Kyrgyzstan appear to swirl around one another, with narrow peninsulas and inlets of one country penetrating or being indented by another. Adding to the complexity are enclaves like Vorukh and Sokh, which stand in Kyrgyzstan as ethnic islands of Tajikistan and Uzbekistan, respectively. Stalin created these enclaves as administrative stepping-stones between the countries. Today they are regarded as nuisances, creating border posts that block major roads, and offering havens for guerrillas and smugglers.

For modern-day invaders wishing to get from Tajikistan to Uzbekistan, whether to bring war, drugs, or both, the old trade routes through Kyrgyzstan via the valleys of the Karavshin provided the most direct route. The IMU had only to swarm over the mountains and fight their way down the Karavshin Valley into Vorukh, where they'd find caches of supplies hidden in the winter by sympathizers and agents. From the northern border of Vorukh the invaders would only have to cross six miles of Kyrgyz soil, then they'd be back in Tajikistan. Another fifteen miles across Tajikistan—which is poorly policed and famously corrupt—lay the Uzbek border and the spoken enemy of the IMU. The journey down the Karavshin, from the Turo Pass on the Kyrgyz-Tajik border to Uzbekistan, would cross five borders in just forty-five miles and would travel through some of Kyrgyzstan's poorest and most rugged country.

Did the IMU know that the Karavshin was a regular destination for foreign climbers? General Bolot Januzakov, secretary of the Kyrgyz Security Council, would tell me no, and he'd add that the IMU did not have the specific intention to kidnap foreigners. But their kidnapping of the Japanese in 1999 was a financial boon. Foreigners were as lucrative a cash crop as opium, and made handy human shields to ward off Kyrgyz or Uzbek guns. Hostage-taking has been part of guerrilla warfare throughout history. The Comanche Indians of the American West used hostages of other tribes as shields, slaves, and bargaining chips, and Chinese warlords held entire towns to ransom. If there were hostages to be taken in the base camps of the Karavshin, the IMU were not going to overlook them.

5.

LOST LUGGAGE

KARA SU VALLEY AND BEYOND

JULY 31–AUGUST 3

By the time Dickey and Smith reach the top of the pass indicated on Samsakov's sketch map, nearly seven hours have passed, and they have run out of water. Since leaving the Karavshin River at an altitude of about fifty-two hundred feet, they have plodded "up, always up," on a steep thigh-burning horse trail. At around ten thousand feet of elevation, the switchbacks level out at an expanse of rolling alpine meadows.

"This is trauma!" Smith exclaims wearily, dumping his rucksack and flopping into the long grass under the scorching sun, while Dickey curls up in the slim shade of a thorny bush. On the horizon they see the rock peaks of the Ak Su and Kara Su valleys. Russian Tower, Peak 4810, Usen, and a dozen others spike the cloudless sky, standing as symmetrical as the pyramids of the pharaohs. Behind them rise even taller mountains of snow and ice, like Piramidalny Peak. Smith and Dickey pick out the faces of the peaks they hope to climb in the days ahead, then the hot sun lulls them to sleep. It is midafternoon when the clopping of horses' hooves wakes them. They open their eyes to the sight of three armed Kyrgyz soldiers standing over them.

The soldiers, who speak no English, are alarmed to find two strangers in this remote spot. They hold the two Americans at gunpoint and make them stand and raise their hands in the air while they frisk them. Their attitude is stiff, but when they see American passports their moods lighten up. They record Dickey and Smith's passing in their logbook, then Smith shows them their map. The soldiers point the way to Kit Kim Saray.

Strangely, when the Australian women passed through Kurbaka back on July 9, Samsakov told Kate Dooley that her frontier permit was incorrect for the Karavshin. Samsakov, who struck Dooley as "an exceptional person," seemed willing to override the bureaucratic formality rather than turn them away from the mountains. He insisted, however, that their Kyrgyz interpreter, who was planning to head back to Osh after escorting them to base camp, should organize a frontier permit stamped by all the right agencies and send it to the Ak Su valley by mail, and then by horseman. Dooley never understood what was wrong with her original permit, and she became more confused when her new permit also caused her trouble. She feels sure it was identical to the American one, as she had seen their permit on the desk of the manager of Mundaz Tours in Osh; he'd organized frontier permits for both teams, on behalf of Ak Sai Travel. Yet the army would never question the permits of the Americans or the Germans when they walked through Kurbaka three weeks after the Aussies.

Dickey and Smith quicken their pace as they head down the other side of the huge hill they had climbed. It is getting late, and they begin to look for suitable spots to roll out their sleeping bags and sleep for the night, under the stars. Friendly Kyrgyz shepherds greet them as they stride downhill. One fellow walking along the trail pulls a point-and-shoot camera from a plastic shopping bag he's carrying and asks another passerby to snap a picture of him posing with the foreigners. Others pause to strike up halting multilingual conversations, or they proudly show the Americans their own identification papers. At every second house there's the offer of chai. The two climbers drop in elevation down the hillside, and for the first time on the trek they notice electricity cables running up through the valley. Then they enter a village where the people wear snug-fitting, embroidered pillbox caps, rather than the comical-looking pointy felt hats of the Kyrgyz. The pillbox-capped folk neither smile nor wave at them. They just stare.

"I don't think these people like the look of us," Dickey says.

"I hear you," Smith replies. "I'm feeling a bit uncomfortable. I think these people are Tajiks, or maybe Uzbeks. I hope we're in the right country."

In southern Kyrgyzstan, Uzbeks, Tajiks, and Kyrgyz often live in villages side by side. Some 700,000 Uzbeks live in Kyrgyzstan, mostly in the south, and some 300,000 Kyrgyz live in adjacent parts of Uzbekistan. Tajiks living in southern Kyrgyzstan are estimated at around 63,000, and a similar number of Kyrgyz are estimated to live in Tajikistan. Most of the several thousand residents of Vorukh are Tajik. Nearly all are Sunni Muslims.

They march on, till at dusk an old man steps out of the doorway of his farmhouse. He waves and calls to the Americans to stop.

"What do you suppose he wants?" Smith asks.

"Maybe he's got our duffel bag," Dickey replies.

The old man has a long wisp of a gray beard, like a sheaf of cobwebs. He is the fire watcher of Kit Kim Saray, the Americans will learn. He speaks not a word of English, but when he realizes that Dickey and Smith do, he points excitedly to a house across the hill, and bellows until the resident there opens his door. This man crosses a field toward them.

"With a voice loud as that, they don't need a phone around here," Smith says.

"My name is Beidel Dar," the man from across the field says in English. The Americans explain their mission to him, then Beidel Dar insists that they stay in his home for the night.

Sitting cross-legged on a threadbare red carpet under the amber glow of a kerosene lantern, they watch Beidel Dar's wife pour a pail of milk not ten minutes out of the cow into a pot and stir it over the fireplace till it is near boiling. She pours it into teacups and the Americans drink it down thirstily. It is delicious. She rounds out the meal with the customary bread and yogurt. When they have eaten their fill Beidel Dar begins to speak. He tells them that he had been a teacher in Batken when Kyrgyzstan had been run by Russia, and his life had been good. But after the Soviet Union collapsed and the Central Asian states became independent, subsidies for many goods vanished and the cost of living skyrocketed, though the wages of a teacher remained unchanged. He soon became so poor that he quit his job and returned to the village of his birth, Kit Kim Saray, to grow potatoes and herd goats.

"You are the first foreigners ever to come to this place," Beidel Dar tells Dickey and Smith.

"When did you last speak to someone in English?" Smith asks him.

Beidel Dar laughs. He hasn't been able to practice for years. He tells them that when he was a young man in the army he was stationed in Vladivostok in Russia. On the street he met two Italians who he thought might also speak English. On a whim, he decided to begin a conversation with a simple phrase: "What time is it?" They understood him, but he had been standing under a large clock on the face of a building and the Italians simply pointed to the clock and walked on. Beidel Dar was very embarrassed. Other than that, he has only met one other foreigner who spoke English, a Czech, in Batken, ten years ago. The Czech asked him directions to a department store, then had rushed off when Beidel Dar told him the way.

They stay up late while Beidel Dar gets his fill of speaking English with his guests. When they wake before sunrise on the morning of August 2, Beidel Dar surprises the Americans by announcing that he'll escort them to Batken. They hike for a couple of miles to a road flanked by power lines, running through the center of a broad, dry valley. The road, raised above the ground on a pile of gravel, is the remnant of a Soviet-era railway. At a roadside stop called Chai Dabar, they wait for the morning bus. Beidel Dar tells them the bus will cost thirty-five som, or seventy cents; he'll loan the Americans the money until Batken, where they can change some dollars for local money. But the 7 A.M. bus does not arrive, nor does the 8 A.M. bus. The few passing cars are jammed with people heading to the markets of Batken, and they have no room for more passengers. After ten o'clock all traffic stops and they sit in the ninety-degree heat. By noon they realize that they will never get to Batken.

"Maybe autobus is broken. We'll try tomorrow," Beidel Dar suggests.

"No, I think we have to go back," Dickey explains. "We told our friends in the mountains that we would be back in two days. Already we have been gone three days."

They turn around and hike back to Beidel Dar's house, where his wife prepares macaroni, onions, and goat-meat broth for their lunch. Beidel Dar is misty-eyed when the Americans leave on the early afternoon of August 2. He tries to refuse Smith's gift of a new pair of socks and four dollar bills, but Smith forces the socks into his hands and hides the money under a cushion, so that he'll find it when they are well along the trail. By nightfall the Americans have descended the pass and are camped beside the Karavshin. During the hike a soldier on a motor scooter passes them. Again their names are recorded in a logbook.

The next morning at Kurbaka they meet Samsakov and his soldiers.

"Did you make it to Batken?" Samsakov asks.

"No. Bus broken."

"Maybe you go second attempt on the house," Samsakov says.

"On the house?" Dickey and Smith puzzle over the meaning of this, then they figure it out: "Oh, on the horse. Thanks, that's really kind, but we have to go back and do some climbing."

"Okay," Samsakov says. "Maybe we see you in two weeks, in your camp."

As they hike back up the V-shaped river valley they encounter a strange creature crossing the trail. It is white, furry, multilegged like a scorpion, half the size of a human fist, and it has a menacing stinger on its tail that it waves about like an antenna. They've never seen a creature like it. "Could be a mammal, could be an insect," Smith says, baffled as to its phylum or genus. They add the sighting to the list of strange encounters these past few days, then they round a bend in the valley near the confluence of the Ak Su and Kara Su Rivers and switch on their Motorola.

Smith's radio call catches Caldwell and Rodden as they are clipping their waist harnesses onto their single-strand rope bridge, to slide across the churning Kara Su and return to base camp. The voice crackling over the Motorola is Smith's. He's singing a few bars of "Bohemian Rhapsody" by the rock band Queen.

"Hey, you!" Rodden responds on her radio. "We've been really worried about you! Did you find a phone? Over."

"We walked miles, but no phone. Tried to go to Batken. Spent the night with the soldiers. They shut us in a hut with a guard and a German shepherd at the door! Guns everywhere down there! We'll be in base camp tonight. Over." Smith talks enthusiastically, as if they've just had the most excitement they'd see on the trip.

WHILE SMITH AND DICKEY are hiking to Kit Kim Saray, Caldwell and Rodden are pushing their way up the center of the Yellow Wall, climbing toward a golden prow of rock jutting over the valley like a castle keep. They move up the wall in "pitches," or stages, determined by the boundary of their two-hundred-foot rope. The lower pitches ascend a slab polished so smooth by an ancient glacier that in places sunlight bounces off it with a mirrorlike glare. They climb this glassy surface by feeling out small edges with their fingertips and balancing the high-friction soles of their climbing shoes against bumps and crystals. Higher, above the slanting ramp of a 1980s-era Russian climb called the Diagonal Route, the cliff steepens, and cracks and fissures mark the way.

One climber "leads," the other "belays." The leader is the one in front, moving up the cliff; the belayer hangs at an "anchor" they have constructed from an array of devices that they have wedged into cracks. The belayer's job is to lock off the leader's rope using a friction device, if he or she falls. At the end of the pitch the leader constructs another anchor. Now it's time for the belayer to climb. The leader reduces the severity of any potential fall by inserting nuts and cams into the cracks and clipping the rope into these gadgets with aluminum snap links, called carabiners. Rigging such "protection" every few feet lessens the distance of a fall.

Caldwell and Rodden's aim is to make a free ascent from the bottom to the top, meaning that they'll climb the wall in a gymnastic style, utilizing the natural features of the rock for their fingers and toes, never hanging on the protection they place along the way. Getting that protection in the rock is their safety net, and sometimes they sweat and tremble to place it. Where the rock is glacier-polished and blank, Caldwell drills holes and taps bolts into them. To speed up the drilling he has brought along a battery-powered hammer drill. Its bit can penetrate the rock like a hot knife slicing through butter. Into the hole he inserts a strong steel bolt. With the electric drill the process takes a few minutes. But early in the climb, while he is balanced on the tips of his toes drilling out a hole, smoke pours out of the machine and the motor sputters out. It has short-circuited. He lowers it to Rodden and hauls up a masonry hand drill. Muscle, patience, and hundreds of hammer blows carve out the remainder of the hole. With the hand-driven tool it now takes a half hour to drill each hole. It's laborious work. But if they are not stopped by blank rock or a move they cannot master, the payoff will be two thousand feet of vertical, dancelike movement.

When not up on the wall, Caldwell and Rodden explore the Kara Su. The meadows are rampant with wildflowers and strong-scented herbs. Marmots inhabit the mazes of boulders. Enormous woolly yaks lumber about the grasslands. They find that the absence of Dickey and Smith brings a reprieve from the incessant rock music that their friends play through portable speakers connected to their CD players.

Rodden has known Caldwell since she was fifteen years old and he was seventeen, when they were teen competitors in the Junior Climbing Competition Association (JCCA) scene. Both of them consistently led their fields in the contests, which were held in indoor climbing gyms, on artificial walls made of plywood, on which climbs were created with modular plastic holds. Rodden's tiny build—as a teen she stood just five feet tall and weighed ninety pounds—gave her a formidable strength-to-weight ratio, and her innate sense of balance and her grace on rock gave her a winning advantage. When she graduated from high school with a 4.0 average in 1998, she began a semester in sports-nutrition studies at the University of California at Davis, but her passion for climbing led her to put college on hold.

Rather than steer Rodden toward academia, her parents, Robb and Linda, encouraged her to find herself through climbing. Robb Rodden, a fifty-three-year-old elementary-school principal, had climbed in the California Sierra when he was younger. Responding to his daughter's gift for climbing, he helped to start the JCCA, which still organizes youth competitions across America. Robb and his wife, Linda, an analyst with the University of California at Davis, have always been supportive, and protective, of their daughter, the younger of their two children.

At seventeen Rodden qualified to participate in the adult division of the World Cup sport-climbing competition circuit in Europe. World Cup competitions are elite events in which the top sport climbers compete on an artificial wall, in front of an audience and judges; the climber who climbs highest up the route wins. In Imst, Austria, in 1998, Rodden placed third in the women's contest, but her interests soon shifted away from the organized contests on artificial walls to climbing on real rock, which, to all climbers, is where the heart and soul of climbing is to be found. At an outcrop of volcanic rock called Smith Rocks, near Bend, Oregon, Rodden gained the attention of the climbing world when she completed one of America's hardest sport climbs at the age of eighteen. The route was named To Bolt or Not to Be, and it was given a rating of 5.14. Climbers rate difficulty using a scale that begins with 5.1, which is as easy as climbing a ladder, and tops out at 5.15, which indicates a piece of cliff that only immensely talented and strong humans, or geckos, can cling to. With no hold larger than the width of a pencil in its 120-foot length, To Bolt or Not to Be is a gruelling vertical marathon for the fingertips, and an exercise in balance and endurance. Only a handful of women had accomplished such a difficult grade, and the recognition that this climb brought Rodden launched her career as a professional climber, though unlike pro golf or basketball, the income derived from a climber's sponsorship contract is seldom enough to live on.

In 1999 an invitation for Rodden to join an expedition came from America's best-known woman rock climber, Lynn Hill, who was planning an all-women's expedition to free-climb a granite wall in Madagascar, a remote island off the East African coast. The climb was filmed for a television documentary. Rodden was offered sponsorship from The North Face soon after that climb. Pretty, childlike in appearance, and sweetly demure, her image offered a refreshing contrast in a climbing scene where muscle-bound males and heroics on Everest were standard fare. Rodden's innocent image took a glossy leap a few months after Madagascar in a photo spread in *Outside* magazine in which she appeared dripping wet, modeling skimpy sport shorts and a top, and entwined around a male climber's torso. The photographs were all about Rodden, as the male model's head was cropped out of the photo. The lusty images left her friends pleasantly surprised and suggested that there was more to the petite woman than her quiet demeanor implied. It was around this time—spring 1999—that Rodden began spending time in Yosemite. Climbing outdoors on Yosemite's tall cliffs, and soaking up the relaxed, bohemian atmosphere of Camp Four provided a contrast to the seriousness of the competition scene. The streetwise duo of John Dickey and Jason "Singer" Smith were among the climbers she befriended in Yosemite.

In June 2000 Rodden ran into Tommy Caldwell in Yosemite Valley. Her friend from the JCCA days was glum, having tried unsuccessfully to be the first to free-climb a big-wall route on El Capitan called the Muir Wall. "Why don't we try to free-climb Lurking Fear?" Rodden suggested, trying to cheer him up. This was another route on El Capitan that climbers had tried to free-climb, but a few sections of seemingly blank rock had stopped all contenders. While most young couples get acquainted at dances or in bars, Rodden and Caldwell began their courtship on the side of the two-thousand-foot west face of El Capitan. Given that they were both newcomers to dating, camping together on El Capitan presented them with a slew of embarrassing personal moments.

"Our relationship was progressing but still in its infancy," said Caldwell. "Obstacles such as using the poop tube in front of each other were something neither of us could bear." He was referring to the plastic container with a screw-top lid that a climber uses as a latrine and as a storage bin for feces while on a big wall. Poop tubes prevent the fouling of the cliff, and their use is mandatory, by National Park orders, on El Capitan. Use of the poop tube requires tolerance on the part of one's climbing partner, as two climbers may be suspended side by side on a wall, with nowhere to hide. This was almost too much for the young couple. "When nature's call became a shout," Caldwell said of their poop-tube antics, "one of us would quickly climb a pitch while the other answered the call."

By the end of June, after many days spent rehearsing the most difficult sections of the route, the pair went up on the wall one last time and put all the moves together. They rated Lurking Fear a solid 5.13, making it among the hardest routes on El Capitan. From that point on, they were seldom apart.

Tommy's father, Mike Caldwell, had been a bodybuilder during his twenties, and he held the Mr. Colorado title in 1972. In photos from that period he is as chiseled as Arnold Schwarzenegger. His devotion to sport and physical fitness defined his relationship with his son. Tommy couldn't hit a baseball due to a vision problem, but he was a powerful wrestler and swimmer in high school, though his lack of competitive juices held him back from being a real champion. Climbing, being a competition within oneself rather than against others, suited Tommy's nature much better. His father noticed his son's affinity for climbing and threw himself into it as much for Tommy's benefit as for his own love of the sport. Today, framed newspaper clippings of the father-son team's climbing achievements line the hallway of the Caldwell home in Estes Park, and Mike Caldwell—now an avid fly fisherman—will rattle off the list of the climbs they've done together to all who'll listen: Tommy's first climb, with his sister Sandy, at age three when the whole family climbed a bulbous granite peak above Estes Park called the Twin Owls, to fly kites; Devils Tower in Wyoming, at age six; Long's Peak at eight; Lost Arrow Spire in Yosemite at ten; the precipitous Diamond face on Long's Peak, via a 5.10 route, at twelve. While Mike was a middle-school teacher and working as a guide for the Colorado Mountain School, he roped up with fourteen-year-old Tommy and went to the top of twenty-one-thousand-foot peaks in the Bolivian Andes, like Illimani and Huayna Potosi, and Europe's Matterhorn and Mont Blanc. More than anything Tommy excelled at sport climbing. He was climbing 5.12, then 5.13, then 5.14, all in his teens. For most devotees of climbing, that's a lifetime of achievement right there, but for Tommy Caldwell it was all done before he was old enough to legally buy a beer.

Prior to turning fifty, Mike Caldwell himself had climbed hard sport routes, and he delighted in belaying his son on the intensely strenuous climbs that became Tommy's hallmark. By age twenty-one, Tommy had climbed rock in South Africa, Europe, and China. In Korea, where his sponsor, the rock-shoe manufacturer Five Ten, produced their climbing shoes, he had served as a sort of corporate climbing envoy, taking the company staff up routes on their local cliffs.

As a couple, Rodden and Caldwell began to see their exploits written about in climbing magazines and their faces appearing in the advertisements of companies they endorsed in the outdoor industry. By the time the expedition to Kyrgyzstan came around, Caldwell and Rodden—a wholesome, athletic, fun-loving couple devoted to climbing—had become celebrities and role models.

SMITH AND DICKEY GREW UP under very different circumstances.

The day Jason "Singer" Smith turned eighteen, in 1996, he left his hometown of South Jordan, near Salt Lake City, Utah, and headed to Yosemite Valley to feed his compulsion to climb. Like many young climbers living the dream there, he hired on at the Yosemite Lodge as a housekeeper for minimum wage, making beds and cleaning cabins after guests had left; on days off, he climbed. When a solo ascent of El Capitan took him longer than he'd expected and he missed work for three days, he quit before his boss could say "You're fired" and moved into Camp Four, the cheapest campground in Yosemite. For six decades this dusty patch has been the valley's principal "hang" for climbers and has served as a cultural focal point for climbing.

As a budding teenage climber, Smith learned from the school of hard knocks. In the Wasatch Mountains above Salt Lake, while climbing on the cliffs of Little Cottonwood Canyon with a friend named Aaron Martin, Smith stood poised on a slab of granite 120 feet off the ground, reaching up for a tombstone-sized flake of rock that looked stable enough to pull up on. The force of his fingertips wrapping around the flake was all that was needed to dislodge it. The flake and Smith went to the ground. When Martin got down to Smith he found him swaying on his feet, deep in shock, and bleeding from a slew of gashes around his face and head. Smith had blown ligaments in his ankles and a knee, twisted his hip, and sprained his arm. The only reason he survived was because he'd landed in a patch of spring snow.

At the hospital Smith's divorced parents showed up at the same time. Since they'd split up when Smith was four years old, his parents had often gotten together around his hospital bed following their son's not infrequent misadventures. "Hey, I really like it when I get hurt because you guys laugh and tell jokes and are civil to each other," he recalls saying to them through a haze of painkillers.

Smith has never understood why his parents divorced, but he recalls trying to be helpful by carrying his dad's suitcase out of the house the day he left. Smith and his father, Dave, a Salt Lake City cop of twenty-five years, still spent plenty of time with each other, and Smith credits Dave for introducing him to the mountains on childhood hiking, camping, pheasant-hunting, and fishing trips in the Wasatch and Uinta Ranges of Utah. Though the family lived in the predominantly Mormon town of South Jordan, religion never figured in Smith's family. As a youngster he occasionally went on patrol with his father, and he vividly recalls his first encounter with death when his father's squad car was called to a high-speed collision: two cars driving at eighty miles per hour had hit head-on; one driver had walked away, the other had been "pasted all over his windscreen." Smith drifted away from his father during his late teens, even felt angry at him when he chided Smith for climbing too much and doing little in the way of career building, but by his early twenties the two of them felt the need to build bridges back to each other. One day, out of the blue, Smith called the by-then-retired policeman and asked, "Have you ever shot anyone?"

"No, but I wish I had," Dave Smith replied. He then related two tales of the beat, the sum of which totaled an answer to his son's question. His first story began with a shoot-out in a parking lot and ended with his partner lying on the ground with a bullet in his chest and Smith trying to stem the bleeding with his hands.

In the second story Smith is on patrol, solo, in the foothills above Salt Lake City when he surprises a burglary in progress at a closed gas station. One assailant is on foot committing the robbery; the second is behind the wheel of a pickup truck. Smith calls, "Freeze!" and draws his pistol. The man on foot gets in the car, which starts slowly rolling away. Running to the moving vehicle, Smith reaches into the window and grabs the passenger by the shoulder. Pointing his pistol at the man's head, he orders the driver to stop. When the passenger reaches toward the floor of the car Smith knows what's coming next: a weapon will be aimed back at him in a split second. He considers shooting but hesitates; a shot at point-blank range will surely kill the man. The next second the driver punches the accelerator and the truck takes off. Smith tries to detach himself, but his belt catches on a hook on the side of the pickup. While being dragged along the street Smith shoots out the front and rear tires. The car swerves into a ditch and the men run off into the night. Smith was unharmed, and the robbers were apprehended the next day, but Smith regretted not seizing the moment and taking action right then and there.

Jason Smith credits his stepfather, a "natural healer" whom he called Dr. Larry while he was young, for helping him develop his creative side. Dr. Larry was given to pranks like cracking eggs over his stepson's head during breakfast cook-ups, or making Smith dig a deep hole in the yard, then to immediately fill it in again. The seemingly pointless labor would be rewarded when Larry would poke the garden hose into the freshly dug earth and mix up a sloppy mud pit for Smith and his friends to play in.

By the time he was twenty Smith was a regular in the Yosemite climbing scene and had developed a penchant for solo climbing. Solo climbing is, by definition, climbing of any kind without a partner. But within the arena of the lone ascent there are solo climbs done with a rope using self-belay techniques, and solo climbs done without a rope or any other equipment. Ropeless solos of free climbs are regarded by some climbers as the most pure, yet most risky, expression of the sport. Pure, because the climber, untethered to a rope, is deeply committed to the act of climbing. Risky, because any mistake can result in a fatal or crippling fall. Because of the danger, few climbers practice soloing. When Smith made a ropeless ascent of a thousand-foot 5.11 crack climb called the Rostrum, it was something of a milestone for him. He had climbed the Rostrum previously with a rope and a partner, so he knew he could do it without falling. But to actually commit to the solo and not let the fear of falling interfere with his ability to climb—that was the challenge.

In 1998, not long after he began working part time for The North Face, he decided to venture into an altogether different realm of soloing, on the thirty-six-hundred-foot wall of Mount Thor on Baffin Island. The route he planned to climb was an "aid route" named Midgard Serpent that had been ascended only once before, by two top-notch big-wall climbers who had spent fifteen days on the wall. The climb would take Smith just as long, but he'd have to do all the work alone, first climbing up each pitch using a complex self-belay technique with ropes, then rappelling back down, and then reascending the rope to hammer out all the gear. He'd also have to haul approximately four times his body weight in supplies and water.

The big-wall solo experience is marked by hard work and determination, but the appeal is solitude. A Camp Four eccentric known as Chongo summed up the allure of big-wall soloing like this: "When there's only one in the crew, everybody gets to be captain."

Smith's big climb took place near the Inuit native town of Pangnirtung on the Arctic Circle, where, in midsummer, the sun never sets. To get his four hundred pounds of food and gear up the Weasel valley to the bottom of Mount Thor, Smith carried it in stages for twenty miles, over tundra that he described as "a most disagreeable surface for hiking, best likened to walking on a wet down-feather bed." On the wall he lived in a portaledge and spoke to no one for three weeks. The route spat him off three times, sending him tumbling through the air for forty feet each time when pieces of gear popped out while he hung suspended from them.

Halfway up he came to a wide ledge that cut across the face, and at the far end he could see the haul bags of a Japanese solo climber named Go Abe. He'd been soloing a route hundreds of feet to the right of Smith's route in 1999 but had died in a fall. The higher Smith climbed, the more the isolation and the arduous nature of his pilgrimage affected him. Recording his thoughts in a journal, he questioned the sanity of his lone mission and considered abandoning his climb and rappelling down. But at other times he reveled in his self-imposed drama, watching snowstorms blow in and out and being the sole witness to geologic events like the collapse of a massive chunk of the mountain, which avalanched from hundreds of feet up, creating a cloud of dust as tall as the cliff and leaving the ground littered with blocks of rock the size of houses.

A book he had lugged up the wall, called *Frogs into Princes* by Richard Bandler and John Grinder, ended with a quote that spoke to Smith's growing access to the mystical on the wall. Smith's account in the *American Alpine Journal* contained a passage from it: "At any moment that you find yourself hesitating or if at any moment you find yourself putting off until tomorrow something you could do today, then all you need to do is glance over your left shoulder and there will be a fleeting shadow. That shadow represents death, and at any moment it might step forward, place its hand on your shoulder and take you. So that the act that you are presently engaged in might be your very last act and therefore fully representative of your last act on this planet. When you hesitate, you are acting as if you are immortal."

On the flat summit he walked for the first time in thirteen days, then he clipped a small parachute to his haul bags and threw the beasts off, to float back to the tundra. Just before he headed down the less steep back side of the mountain, Smith wrote, "In many ways I was ecstatic that such an experience was close to being over; in others, I felt that I wanted it to go on. I wanted something more. In some warped sense, I wanted an epic; I wanted to get really worked."

Epic is a term used in climbing to describe a situation that has gotten wildly out of control. Two years after his soul-searching ascent on Baffin Island, Smith would find his epic in Kyrgyzstan, but it would not be the epic of his choice.

JOHN DICKEY HAD been climbing around Yosemite for a year before going to Kyrgyzstan. Though he took his climbing seriously, he was neither as competitive nor as athletically minded as Caldwell or Rodden, nor was he inclined to push the envelope by soloing. He enjoyed the lifestyle, the landscape, and the camaraderie of the sport; he felt content to be a participant rather than a trendsetter. He and Smith became friends in Yosemite sometime in 1997, when Dickey would drive out from San Francisco to climb and pursue his other passion, photography. Their self-deprecating brands of humor complemented each other, and when the Karavshin expedition was coming together Smith invited him along as the team photographer.

Dickey was born in Indianapolis, but when he was two months old his father, an accountant in the civil service, moved the family to northern Italy so he could work for the military. They lived in Florence, and his mother worked as a nurse for the Red Cross and for church outreach services. Dickey's grandfather had been a minister of the Methodist church, and Dickey's own parents became devoted followers of the Church of Christ. Eventually, his father became a deacon in that church.

When the family left Italy and moved to San Antonio, Texas, they entered Dickey in preaching contests. By age nine he was immersed in Bible-study classes and religious competitions. Bible Bowl was a contest of Bible trivia that required one to memorize and recite verse and Scripture. These were large events, held in Houston, Dallas, and Lubbock, in which contestants expounded for ten minutes on Scripture themes in front of an audience and judges. He knew the life of Christ backward. But his church was strict, and by the time he was a teenager he was bristling against its rules, like one that forbade boys from sitting in a chair within ten minutes of a girl having sat there. Even his parents began to find their church somewhat askew from their own views, and by the time he was seventeen they shifted to a Methodist church.

By age fourteen, though, Dickey had decided that he did not need a church to direct him to a sense of God; God is resident in all humans, he believed at that time. By seventeen he stopped attending church except on special occasions. He grew his hair long and adopted the dress of a "metalhead stoner." He told his parents he smoked pot and that he was moving to California just as soon as he saved enough money from his after-school jobs to buy a cheap Volkswagen van. His father worried over his lost son and imposed drug tests and lectures on the evils of California. When Dickey finally had enough to buy his van, his father surprised him by giving him a brand-new Toyota pickup truck. Though very pleased with the gift, Dickey was not happy with the obligation of having to stay in Texas for the truck to be paid off. After he got through being angry with his father for doing this he settled down to bussing tables in a restaurant by night and doing seventeen units at school by day. More than anything, Dickey wanted his family to accept him. "I didn't want to be at odds with my family. Our whole childhood, my sister and I had a very religious upbringing. We always had to appear good and hide the bad from our parents. I wanted that to stop."

When summer 1993 came around, Dickey quit school, hitched a U-Haul trailer to the truck, and said his good-byes. Family ties were temporarily severed. Dickey turned his back and left for California with his girlfriend (whom he moved in with, to the disappointment of his father). Dickey did not speak to his family for several months, though now they see and talk with one another often. In 1996 he totaled the Toyota. In 1998 he graduated from San Francisco State University in recreation and leisure studies with an emphasis on outdoor adventure, business management, and leadership. His parents "immediately chilled out" when he graduated. "They were so proud of me. They just wanted to see that I wasn't going to be a burden on society or some criminal punk."

A HALF HOUR after the radio call with Smith, and late on the afternoon of August 3, Rodden and Caldwell walk into their base camp on the Kara Su. There waiting for them they find three armed Kyrgyz soldiers and a dog that runs around camp, wagging its tail and sniffing at the new American smells. One of the soldiers is a sergeant. He does not introduce himself by name, and he speaks no English. He's friendly but businesslike as he checks their passports and a copy of their frontier permit. The sergeant—whom they'll later know as Turat Osmanov—records their passport details in his logbook, then bids them good-bye. He and his men walk toward the trail leading to the Ak Su valley.

6.

SIGNS OF TROUBLE

KARA SU AND AK SU VALLEYS

AUGUST 4–12

Dickey and Smith wake the next morning, August 4, to aching knees. Their four-day trek to and from Kit Kim Saray—a round trip of nearly sixty miles—was longer and more strenuous than they had bargained for. That morning at breakfast they eat ravenously, noting that their already thin waistlines are slimmer by a belt notch. Their mission to find a phone failed, but the experience of crossing into a world where no westerner had set foot before excited the explorer's gene resident in each of them, while their interactions with Ruslan Samsakov, Beidel Dar, and the other people along the path struck a deep chord. Roaming from one mountain village to another seemed more adventurous than climbing a mountain.

Smith is tired, so he spends the day lounging around in his tent, reading Hemingway. While he rests, Rodden, Caldwell, and Dickey hike upriver, and Dickey shoots photos of Rodden and Caldwell climbing on the massive cubes of rock that litter the valley. By evening raindrops are pattering the nylon shells of their tents in base camp, but the clouds pass quickly and stars fill the dark sky.

The climbers wake the next morning, August 5, to the rasping sound of cow tongues licking the outsides of their tents. A herd of half a dozen piebald milkers stand lapping dew off the nylon and chewing their cud. When Smith sees one of the cows grinding up their dishwashing sponge in its mouth he runs the cows out of camp and down the trail. Marauding donkeys earlier raided the cooler they had fashioned out of stones in a shady spot beside the Kara Su, eating the cheese and tortillas the climbers had brought from the States.

After breakfast Rodden and Caldwell return to the Yellow Wall. By now they are five pitches up, and they have rigged several hundred feet of rope between the ground and their high point. The Yellow Wall can be climbed in a day by several established routes, but Rodden and Caldwell's climb is far more difficult than the existing routes. In any case, the young couple are enjoying each other's company and are content to keep plugging away at their route. Over breakfast Dickey and Smith make plans to climb the rock face of Asan, which stands upriver near the head of the Kara Su and the point where the river spurts from glacial ice. Asan and its taller brother, Usen, are named after twin warriors in an old Kyrgyz legend. The mountains bristle with routes, most of them established by Russian climbers in the late 1980s. Dickey and Smith are swinging their rucksacks onto their backs, about to leave for their climb, when a woman marches into camp.

"G'day, I'm Kate," she says, extending her hand. Her accent immediately identifies the fit-looking redhead as an Australian.

Dooley and her two companions, who have remained at their base camp in the Ak Su, have crammed in an impressive number of climbs between the snowstorms that fouled much of July's weather. She sits down with the two Americans and they hear about her ascents. They summited a steep rock buttress on Peak 4520 first, then they tried to climb the Central Pyramid, but were driven off by a blizzard. They were luckier on Pamir Pyramid, climbing to the top via a rock feature resembling a huge open book. Finally, they climbed the fabled Perestroika Crack on Russian Tower. When they descended, they found that the German expedition had arrived and set up a base camp a ten-minute walk from their own. Dooley goes on to tell Smith and Dickey that she and her friends hope to fit in one more climb before their planned departure from the mountains on August 7. Coincidentally, the women are planning to climb Asan too, and the purpose of Dooley's jaunt around the hill separating the two valleys is to reconnoiter the peak.

"We were just about to leave for Asan when you showed up," Dickey says, so the three of them head up the valley for a look.

As they hike, the Americans tell Dooley of their lost duffel bag, and of their journey to Kit Kim Saray to find a phone. When she hears about their lost fuel bottle, she offers to sell them an extra one that they've brought with them. They agree that one of the Americans will hike over to the Ak Su to pick up the fuel bottle on the sixth or seventh of August.

After they hike upstream and get a view of the cliffs of Asan in the early afternoon, Dooley heads back around the hill to her base camp. When she reaches her camp and her companions, she is surprised to find Ruslan Samsakov and several other soldiers there, along with five donkeys. A captain, Baktiar Shergeliev, and a major, Djizelbek Subanbekov, are with Samsakov. They have been waiting several hours for Dooley's return.

"Hi, Ruslan!" she says cheerily to the soldier.

But the news Samsakov brings is hardly what she wants to hear. He has orders to escort them out of the Ak Su and down to his camp at Kurbaka, because, he says, they do not have the right type of permit.

Dooley was under the impression that they had sorted all that out with the new permit. Two days earlier a horseman had delivered the updated frontier permit to the Australian camp. And in any case, they are due to leave in a couple more days. Why the rush? she wonders.

"I'm sorry, Kate," he explains. "My orders come from the big chief."

Dooley has returned to base camp too late for the group to head down to Kurbaka that evening, so the soldiers make camp beside the Ak Su, planning that the whole group will leave the next day. The soldiers join the women under the tarpaulin they have draped over a rock, as a kitchen, and they spend the night singing songs from each others' countries.

On the morning of August 6 Dooley and her team pack up under the watchful eyes of the soldiers. They don't understand why they have to leave, while the Germans who arrived less than a week ago can stay. When she raises the question, Samsakov just tells them that the German permit is in order. The soldiers load the women's gear onto the donkeys, and by noon they are hiking down the canyon toward Kurbaka. Dooley keeps the fuel bottle out of the loads, strapped to her rucksack in case one of the Americans arrives in camp to buy it. She waits again for them at the bridge at the junction of the two rivers, near Murat Kalnarazov's house. But no one comes. Caldwell and Rodden will cross over to the Ak Su to buy the fuel bottle a day too late.

"It was very strange," a young German climber named Stefan Hiermaier will tell Caldwell and Rodden when they walk into his camp looking for the Australians. "The soldiers took them away."

OVER THE NEXT TWENTY-FOUR HOURS the Australians become increasingly confused by the situation unfolding around them. At Kurbaka, Samsakov tells them they must wait until he has spoken to his superiors. He enters the radio shack, and when he comes out he tells them, "You are under arrest." His manner suggests he regards the matter as a joke.

Dooley demands to know why. Samsakov becomes apologetic. He explains that the Ministry of Internal Affairs wants to interview the women because they are in a restricted zone and that they may have to go to Ravat to talk with them. Tonight Samsakov says the women will camp at Kurbaka.

"What is the Ministry of Internal Affairs? Where is Ravat? What is wrong with our new permit?" Dooley and her friends demand to know.

"Ministry of Internal Affairs used to be KGB," Samsakov tells them.

The mention of the KGB gives Dooley and her friends pause. Clearly, things are heating up around these parts, though they do not understand what's going on. Samsakov tells Dooley that they should never have been allowed into the area in the first place. He talks about their permit being imprinted with an Uzbek seal, rather than a Kyrgyz seal, making it invalid. Dooley gets the impression that her team had only been allowed into the mountains because Samsakov had "stalled the chiefs as long as he could" so the women could get some climbing done. She also suspects that the travel companies had taken shortcuts and given her a less-than-legitimate permit. Whatever the case, Dooley's team has fallen under the scrutiny of the Kyrgyz equivalent of the KGB, and Samsakov tells them they'll have to come up with a reason to explain why they have been in the mountains so long without the right permit. He and Dooley begin "scheming" up excuses to help them avoid trouble. They decide that in his next radio call Samsakov will tell the Ministry of Internal Affairs that the women had some injuries among their team and were forced to dally at base camp.

The Australians camp the night of August 6 in a dusty field. Early on the morning of August 7 Samsakov walks over to Dooley at her tent and says with a smile, "You are free." He has radioed his superiors, and they will now permit the women to head down the valley to Vorukh, then on to Osh and Bishkek. Samsakov suggests that they again use the five donkeys the soldiers used to carry the Australians' gear down to Kurbaka. He points out four scruffy-looking men sitting around the edge of the army camp, brooding and looking nervous, and he explains that they are the owners of the donkeys. They are four Tajiks from Vorukh, and they'd been arrested a few days earlier for not having the right kind of permits for being in the area. The Tajiks were taken for questioning to Ravat, which lay twenty miles to the northwest, on the road to Batken. But now the muleteers are free, and they have just that morning returned to reclaim their animals.

While they are discussing using the donkeys, a Kyrgyz horseman rides into Kurbaka. He has been sent by Ak Sai Travel to pack out the gear of the Australians. His appearance is on schedule—August 7—and the women load their packs and duffels onto his horses. Dooley cannot stop wondering what is really behind their early eviction. Throwing them out of the valley two days ahead of schedule strikes her as an exercise in futility. As the caravan gets ready to head down the valley, Samsakov bids Dooley and her friends good-bye.

"Now I have to go to the Americans in the Kara Su and make them leave, because they have the same permit as you," he tells her.

"You'll need a lot of donkeys!" she says, thinking of the wealth of equipment and the many duffel bags she'd seen in the American camp. "They have a lot of gear!"

But neither Samsakov nor any soldiers will ever make it to the American camp.

AROUND THE SAME TIME that the Australians are being evicted, at a checkpoint near Vorukh, four Ukrainian climbers from the cities of Rostov-on-Don and Kiev are arguing heatedly with the Kyrgyz soldiers who are turning them away from the entrance to the Karavshin Valley. The Ukrainians have traveled overland from Tashkent in Uzbekistan. They've been to the Karavshin before, and they've already bribed their way through Tajik border guards, just like on every other trip.

"You don't pay anything, you don't get anywhere," said one of the Ukrainians, Natasha Kolysnik, explaining the way things work in Russia and Central Asia.

But the Kyrgyz soldiers at Vorukh can't be bribed, and they won't let them pass. The atmosphere at the checkpoint is tense. A mass of Tajiks on either side of the border are trying to cross. There is shouting, jostling, and scuffling between soldiers and civilians. In recent days Kyrgyz and Uzbek troops have been rounding up Tajiks in border towns whom they suspect of having ties to Islamic extremists. A helicopter arrives, and a dozen heavily armed Kyrgyz border guards get off and take positions around the checkpoint. It looks like a riot is about to occur. An officer among the Kyrgyz detachment tells the Ukrainians that the border is sealed, that fighting with bandits is certain, and that a local policeman has been killed already. The officer makes the Ukrainians load their gear into the Mi8, and despite their protests, he has them flown to the army base at Batken. Police and soldiers search their bags there. They even have to turn out the contents of their pockets. The Ukrainians assume they are being checked for narcotics. The discovery of climbing gear changes the mood of the officers in charge.

"They were going to arrest us, but when they saw we were sportsmen just going climbing, they treated us like normal people," said Natasha Kolysnik.

As the morning passes, the Ukrainians get friendly with the helicopter pilots. A deal is struck: for five hundred dollars the pilots will fly them to the

Ak Su valley. The flight is unofficial, off the logbook. The money goes straight into the pilots' pockets.

On the morning of August 7 the Mi8 departs with the Ukrainians. Dooley sees the helicopter flying over Kurbaka while she is packing to leave, and Caldwell and Rodden hear it while they're hiking over the hill toward the Ak Su, where they hope to find Dooley and buy her fuel bottle.

The pilots are nervous as they bring the chopper down to river level beside the German base camp. They keep the rotors spinning fast, disgorge their passengers and payload, and take off at speed. The Ukrainians' arrival brings the number of climbers in the Ak Su and Kara Su to fourteen.

Days later, the officer who turned the Ukrainians back at the border would ask them all why they had sneaked around him, despite his warning of war. "We were crazy," one of the climbers would answer. Vasilii Kolysnik, Natasha's husband, had never had trouble in the Karavshin before. He felt certain that the army was just overreacting to some local ethnic situation.

"BAD MEN," the Kyrgyz horseman warns the Australians, pointing to the Tajik muleteers hiking with them down the trail to Vorukh. Though the Tajiks' donkeys carry nothing belonging to the Australians, they shadow the women for two hours, leering at them, walking beside them too close for comfort, and making lewd comments behind the veil of language. When Dooley feels the hand of one of the Tajiks reaching from behind and groping her she loses her temper and shoves the man. He stumbles down a short embankment in a cloud of dust, then picks himself up and laughs. Minutes later he is back alongside her, dogging her down the trail.

"Fuck off!" she screams at the man in Russian.

Her anger shocks the muleteers, and the men march ahead. The women do not catch sight of them again.

About a mile before Vorukh the climbers stop and spend the night in a farmhouse. The next morning, August 8, they reach the border. Here they find a checkpoint guarded by two young soldiers. The checkpoint did not exist a month earlier when the women had traveled up the Karavshin River on the way to base camp. The soldiers are friendly but adamant that the women cannot cross into Vorukh because they have no permits to enter Tajikistan. For the women, the situation is maddening—the army wants them out of the Karavshin Valley, but the soldiers at the entrance to the enclave are preventing them from leaving even though they had crossed Vorukh a month earlier unchallenged. Border hassles in the Third World are only resolved by patience, so the women sit in the shade of a tree and wait for something to change. The soldiers are friendly; they are simply following orders. The women let them listen to tunes on their Walkman, they snap photos of the soldiers, and they pose holding their rifles, while the soldiers share some of their food with them. Six hours pass. Then three cars appear speeding along the dusty road.

The vehicles stop at the checkpoint. A crowd of men wearing suits and ties, as well as a few well-armed soldiers, get out of the cars. They order the women to their feet and examine their passports. "They were very official and pompous, and we were a bit too laid-back for them," Dooley would later note. The men are from the Ministry of Internal Affairs—the erstwhile KGB.

"Have you seen any unusual men in the mountains?" an interpreter asks them. "Men with beards? Men wearing sneakers?" The men ask a lot of questions and record their answers in folders.

Other than the Tajik muleteers, who struck Dooley as wandering around without purpose, the women have seen nothing out of place. When the interview is over, the officials tell the women they cannot travel through Vorukh.

"But we have to get through Vorukh," Dooley tells the officials. "Our travel agent has arranged a car to be waiting for us in the village of Ak Sai, on the other side of Vorukh. If we don't get to that car, we won't be able to get to Osh."

Eventually, a deal is struck. They can cross Vorukh by car. Their horseman, it transpires, has a brother who lives near Ak Sai, and he owns a Lada automobile. The horseman rushes ahead to fetch it. The Lada arrives by nightfall and takes the women the few miles across Vorukh, back into Kyrgyzstan. They spend the night in the house of the car's owner. Joining them there is an interpreter named Aibek, who arrived in Ak Sai in the car arranged by Dooley's tour operator; this car awaited them on the Kyrgyz side of the border, and Aibek had crossed Vorukh by other means. Aibek has been sent to help the women cross the myriad of new checkpoints that have sprung up in the past few days. Late that night a Kyrgyz policeman arrives, and he too quizzes the women about unusual men in the mountains. Beards and sports shoes seem to be the distinguishing characteristics of these mysterious men, judging by the questions.

FOURTEEN NEW CHECKPOINTS manned by heavily armed soldiers slow the 125-mile drive between Ak Sai and Osh to a crawl. The Aussies reach Osh on August 9, and Bishkek at midnight on August 11. On the morning of August 12 Dooley marches into the office of Ak Sai Travel. Svetlana Fedina is visibly relieved to see her. She tells Dooley that newspapers are reporting that "Taliban" men have crossed into the Fergana Valley and an attack around Batken is feared. She has been worrying about the Americans, who, she says, would be targets for the terrorists.

For the first time Dooley begins to comprehend the reasons for the military buildup. She assumes now that her eviction by Samsakov was because of the rebel incursion Fedina is describing. It might also have something to do with her team's gender.

Tajik newspapers did, in fact, break the news on August 6 that insurgents had crossed the Tajik border into the Surkhandarya region of southern Uzbekistan, 180 miles southwest of the Karavshin, and clashed with Uzbek border guards and Tajik government troops. On August 7 Uzbek news reports said that fighting had killed ten Uzbek soldiers and several rebels. The report named the IMU as the invaders and Juma Namangani as the leader, and it claimed that the rebels were the same ones who had invaded Kyrgyzstan in 1999 and kidnapped the Japanese geologists. The same day BBC Radio monitored Az Zubair Ibn Abdur Raheem of the IMU claiming responsibility for the incursion into Uzbekistan. On August 8 Kabar, the official Kyrgyz-government news agency, reported an attack on southern Uzbekistan by one hundred rebels. "The aim of invasion of these groups was to create ammunition, arm, and food storehouses in bordering regions of Uzbekistan to prepare and conduct terrorist actions in the territory of Uzbekistan. The bandit groups are well equipped with modern armaments, sniper arms, and grenade cup dischargers," said the report.

Kyrgyz military sources later confirmed that by August 8 IMU rebels had been seen by shepherds in the mountains above the Karavshin. But Dooley was unaware of these details. She tells Fedina that although security was tightening up around the mountains, they had seen nothing unusual and the Americans were fine. Fedina calms down but is not entirely mollified.

"We may send a helicopter to bring them out early," she says. "It might become dangerous there."

"Don't worry," Dooley tells her, "Ruslan will look after them."

7.

JUMA NAMANGANI AND

THE ISLAMIC MOVEMENT

OF UZBEKISTAN

Russia's invasion of Afghanistan and the collapse of the USSR; the Afghan and Tajik civil wars; Central Asian dictators; Islamic jihad; Osama bin Laden; warlords, guerrilla armies, and the Taliban; opium and heroin smuggling; kidnapping and ransom—they all play a role in the evolution of the Islamic Movement of Uzbekistan.

Few people in Central Asia, other than those in government or security positions, had heard of the IMU before February 16, 1999, when six car bombs exploded across downtown Tashkent, the capital of Uzbekistan. The car bombs blew up during a period of one and a half hours in the middle of the day, killing 16 people and injuring more than 120. One of the bombs, planted in a rattling thirty-nine-year-old Uzbek-built GAZ-21 car, somehow passed through security guards to park near shiny government sedans delivering officials to the front steps of the Cabinet of Ministers Building in Independence Square. The politicians were gathering to hear a speech by Uzbek president Islam Karimov, who was due to arrive in a matter of minutes.

According to official Uzbek-government accounts, the two young drivers of the GAZ-21 got out of the car, opened the trunk, and began to walk away quickly. Guards posted at the government building thought their actions looked suspicious, so they started following them. The drivers produced two submachine guns, and a shoot-out began. Meanwhile, another car bomb exploded in front of a nearby theater while its drivers were also firing at police. The GAZ-21 exploded a few minutes later, but its target was spared, as Karimov's car was late for the meeting. None of the bombers were caught. In the words of Karimov himself, the terrorists "left virtually no tracks and escaped."

Two hours after the bombings, President Karimov and the leaders of his security and police forces announced that Islamic militants, or Wahhabis, as Islamic extremists are sometimes dubbed in Central Asia, were the culprits. They blamed a little-known outlawed organization called the Islamic Movement of Uzbekistan, and its leaders, Takhir Yuldashev and Juma Namangani, as the would-be assassins. The men, both Uzbeks, had lived in exile in armed camps in Tajikistan since 1992. In the coming months Uzbek courts would sentence them to death, in absentia. Other suspects included outlawed Islamic organizations, like Hizb-ut-Tahrir (the Party of Liberation), which, though anti-Karimov, claims to shun violence as a means of enacting political change. The only political candidate to ever legally challenge Karimov in an election, Muhammad Solih, leader of the Erk (Freedom) party, was also accused. Solih had lived in exile in Europe since fleeing arrest in 1994, after the Karimov government banned his party.

In the months following the bombings, human-rights observers estimate that between four thousand and five thousand people were arrested for antigovernment activities. Nearly all the suspects were Muslims. Reports of a "concentration camp for religious extremists" in Karakalpakstan in the remote west of the country began to surface. According to a Russian journalist, Vitali Ponomarev, writing for the Human Rights Information Center in Central Asia, "The repression of believers assumed dimensions comparable to those of Stalin's purges during the 1930s. . . . After the explosions on 16 February, the police conducted a kind of mini-census of the population, including on the list of potential Islamic terrorists all men between the ages of 18 and 35 absent from their place of permanent residence." President Karimov appeared on state TV after the bombings and announced: "Fathers would answer for the crimes of their sons." Among the many suspects arrested under this ruling was Zikir Khasanov, the father of one of the men who would later be arrested and stand trial for the bombings. After two months in detention in the basement of the Uzbek Ministry of Internal Affairs Building, Zikir was hospitalized and died. Human-rights observers say that he had not had contact with his son for eighteen months and knew nothing of his political beliefs.

In summer 1999 a closed Uzbek Supreme Court trial from which family members and media were largely excluded found several men guilty of the bombings and sentenced them to death. In their confessions the men admitted that they were members of the IMU, and they named its leaders as being the masterminds of the bombings. They stated that their aim was to overthrow the Karimov government and to forcibly establish Islamic rule in Uzbekistan. In January 2000, on the eve of the holy Muslim holiday of Ramadan, the Uzbek government announced that the executions of the IMU conspirators had been carried out. Acacia Shields, a representative for Human Rights Watch in Uzbekistan, attended parts of the trial.

"In all the bombing trials that we were permitted to attend, there was no material evidence linking the defendants to the bombings, much less the IMU to the bombings," she said. "We're left without any evidence whatsoever that the government caught the right people."

SOME OBSERVERS SAY that the climate of intrigue and corruption in Uzbekistan is so deep that the Karimov regime may have staged the Tashkent bombings itself, to create a pretext for a harsher crackdown on Islamic movements, though few doubt that the IMU and its mysterious creator, Juma Namangani, were to blame.

The terrorist leader was born in the Uzbek town of Namangan in 1969 as Jumaboi Ahmanjonovich Khojaev. He abandoned the family name, Khojaev, and adopted the name of his hometown around 1992, after he took up arms against the government of Islam Karimov. Namangani's road to radicalization began in 1987, when he was drafted into the Soviet army fighting in Afghanistan, where he served as a sergeant in the paratroop corps for three years. The savagery of that conflict—commonly regarded as the moral and spiritual equivalent of the Vietnam War for the former Soviet Union—and the stubborn resistance of the Afghan mujaheddin deeply affected Namangani; and he converted to Islam. When he was discharged around 1989 he returned to his home in southern Uzbekistan and undertook the serious study of Islamic scriptures under a *Qori*, or spiritual leader able to recite the Koran from memory.

While Namangani studied the Koran, the last Soviet divisions were leaving Afghanistan in defeat. The ten-year war had killed fifteen thousand Soviet troops and more than a million Afghans. More than four million Afghan refugees fled the country, most into Pakistan. Cities were in rubble, and there was no plan for rebuilding the country. When the Soviets withdrew, worn down by the guerrilla tactics of the mujaheddin, seven different Afghan factions began fighting among themselves for control of the country. These paramilitary clans had received arms and training from Inter-Services Intelligence, the Pakistani equivalent of the CIA. The American CIA also helped them, delivering Stinger missiles that knocked out deadly Soviet helicopter gunships. The fight against the Soviets had become a holy war that attracted legions of non-Afghan Muslims. Osama bin Laden, a Saudi, was one of the men who joined the struggle. He used his personal fortune from his family engineering firm to create a guerrilla force that he personally led against the Soviets, and he was himself wounded in battle.

In the post-Soviet/Afghan conflict, the warring factions fought over an already pulverized country. Two predominant groups emerged: the Taliban and the Northern Alliance. The Taliban were the antiwestern religious extremists who drew a constant supply of fresh troops from the *madrassas*, or religious schools, that sprang up in refugee camps in Pakistan during the 1980s and '90s. Wrote former prime minister of Pakistan Benazir Bhutto of the insidious *madrassas*: "The boys that were sent there by their parents to be nourished and educated were taught extremism, intolerance, subjugation of women, and violence. All of these elements are antithetical to the Holy Book and the teachings of the Prophet. When the children were not being brainwashed, they were trained in hand-to-hand combat, the use of weapons and terrorist strategy. The schools became the recruitment centers for the fanatic administration that ultimately took control of Afghanistan after the Soviet exit. The new political movement was named after the schools themselves. The word *Talib* means 'student.' "

Madrassas also gathered up non-Afghan nationals from Arab states and Pakistan to fight their opposition, known as the Northern Alliance. By the year 2000, the Taliban controlled 90 percent of Afghanistan, with the Northern Alliance mainly cornered in the north, near the Uzbek and Tajik borders. By then the Central Asian countries and Russia were experiencing the spread of Taliban ideals onto their own soil.

Adding to this tragic formula for anarchy was the crumbling of the Soviet Union in 1992, which forced the Central Asian states of Kazakhstan, Kyrgyzstan, Tajikistan, Turkmenistan, and Uzbekistan into sudden independence from Russia. Initially, all the countries floundered in poverty, inflation, unemployment, and social disarray. Tajikistan fell to anarchy, and a five-year civil war began. In Turkmenistan and Uzbekistan secular, Soviet-trained politicians filled the power vacuum. Once elected, these men installed themselves as virtual presidents-for-life and suppressed opposition parties. Uzbekistan's President Karimov tilted away from Islam despite its being the predominant religion of the country—and despite his name. So far as Karimov was concerned, the mosque, the Islamic clergy, and Islamic political organizations were threats to Uzbek security and to his rule, and precursors to the fundamentalist Taliban revolution that was tearing Afghanistan apart. Karimov banned religious organizations and jailed "Islamists" who criticized his regime.

Ever since Stalin's time, traditional Islamic culture in Uzbekistan had been regarded as a threat to Communist control. Mosques—the centers of community life—that had been boarded up or converted to storehouses under Stalin were in some towns closed again under Karimov during the 1990s. Even so, many Uzbeks hungered to reconnect with their traditions, and the practice of Islam grew strong in the region around Juma Namangani's hometown in the Fergana Valley. This once-fertile valley runs for two hundred miles through eastern Uzbekistan and the Batken area of Kyrgyzstan, though today drought and excessive irrigation by government-owned cotton farms have depleted the soil. Its residents are among the poorest people in Uzbekistan. The Fergana Valley is also a centuries-old stronghold of Islamic culture. When mosques started reopening across the border in post-Communist and more lenient southern Kyrgyzstan, Islamic movements began to spring up and seek a voice in politics in Uzbekistan too. To this Karimov said no. Many religious groups were outlawed, and religious leaders began disappearing off the streets, or were thrown in jail for treason. Human-rights groups blamed Uzbek security forces for these disappearances. In retaliation, Islamic extremists murdered Uzbek security personnel suspected of working against them; Namangani is accused of being behind a spate of such killings in Namangan in 1997.

In an August 2000 report on human rights in Uzbekistan, Abdumannob Polat and Nickolai Butkevich wrote:

In today's Uzbekistan, even wearing a beard, a sign of Islamic piety, or religious clothing can lead to arrest if the person is not a member of the official clergy. With no distinction made between truly dangerous Islamic fanatics and peaceful Moslem believers who do not subscribe to the dogma of the country's official religious structures, and with near-total suppression of prodemocratic, secular movements, political Islam is the main viable source of opposition to the government at a time when social pressures are building. The Uzbek government, by seeking to suppress dissent in the name of avoiding an Islamic revolution, may instead be hastening the country toward one.

The United States also criticized Karimov's treatment of the Islamic faithful. During a visit to Tashkent in April 2000, then-secretary of state Madeleine Albright gave a speech in which she seemed to speak to Karimov himself, warning, "Indiscriminate government censorship and repression can cause moderate and peaceful opponents of a regime to resort to violence." Long before Albright made her speech, however, the Uzbek government and Islamic groups had become utterly polarized.

Namangani became involved in Islamic political parties around 1990, with the Saudi-funded Adolat party. Saudi Arab "missionaries" were active in Central Asia then, setting up mosques and helping create covert anti-government groups that believed in strict Islamic doctrines. Throughout his career Namangani would be surrounded by wealthy Arabs who opposed their own monarchy and who funded the radical agenda of Muslim extremists. In 1991 in Namangan, Juma and Takhir Yuldashev, a fiery twenty-two-year-old activist, organized an Islamic political group called Tavba, which means "repentance." Tavba advocated the creation of a breakaway Islamic state in the Fergana Valley, and the movement distributed leaflets that criticized Karimov. Karimov and Yuldashev came face-to-face in Namangan that year when demonstrators seized the Communist headquarters and rallied a crowd of three thousand supporters in the streets. When Karimov flew to Namangan to quiet the unrest he found himself onstage, bickering with Yuldashev, who was calling for an Islamic state in Uzbekistan, over the right to take the microphone and speak to the crowd. Eventually Karimov persuaded the crowd to disperse, but Yuldashev was a marked man after that. Tavba and Adolat were banned, and Yuldashev, Namangani, and thirty followers fled Uzbekistan just ahead of Karimov's security officers, who sought to arrest them. The exiles settled in the Kurgan-Tyube region of Tajikistan in 1992 and were given housing in Kabul by the Taliban in Afghanistan.

Civil war had broken out in Tajikistan immediately after the Soviets left the country, between neo-Communist government forces of the Soviet-style rulers and an opposition force of warlords and Islamic militants. Namangani was a good tactician who knew how to fight in both the Russian and Afghan mujaheddin modes of warfare, and he was welcomed as a field commander by antigovernment forces like the Islamic Renaissance Party (IRP) and the United Tajik Opposition (UTO). While fighting for the Tajik resistance, Namangani and his fellow exiles didn't forget their struggle against the Karimov regime, and the IMU began to take shape. Namangani became its military commander. Yuldashev took on the role of "terrorist diplomat and fund-raiser," traveling to Pakistan, Afghanistan, Iran, Turkey, and the Arab states to seek financial support. Namangani and Yuldashev's patrons and allies came to include Osama bin Laden, Chechen leaders fighting Russia, and wealthy Arabs and Uzbeks living abroad. A third man, Az Zubair Ibn Abdur Raheem, became chairman of their *diwan*, or supreme religious council. He would author the 1999 declaration of jihad aimed against Uzbekistan and Kyrgyzstan and against foreign tourists.

During the latter 1990s, Uzbek dissidents, Arabs, Afghans, Chechens, Kashmiris, Pakistanis, and Uigars from western China joined Namangani's ranks, building up a multinational pan-Islamic force estimated to number between one thousand and three thousand fighters. Namangani's cause attracted disaffected Muslim men for its version of jihad, or holy struggle, which seeks to create a new world order of Islam based on Shari'a (the canon of Islamic law). He also paid them, from thirty dollars per month for new recruits to one hundred and up per month for fighting men. Namangani carved out heavily defended strongholds high in the Karetigin and Tavildara valleys of the Pamir-Alai Mountains, ninety miles northeast of the Tajik capital of Dushanbe and sixty miles south of the Kyrgyz border. His principal haunt became a narrow gorge in the Tavildara valley above the village of Sanguor, where at the height of the Tajik civil war the "Namangani Contingent" fought alongside Tajik opposition forces to smash a government offensive. The dirt roads leading into the Tavildara valley are littered with destroyed tanks and trucks from that battle. In Tavildara, Namangani's garrison and their wives and children mingled with local people, and Namangani was said to visit local mosques and tearooms, where he discussed the plight of Muslims in Uzbekistan, and where he received recruits and the agents who assisted his operations.

Secretive and elusive, Namangani was cloaked in a cult of invincibility before his death in 2001. Reportedly, he was never photographed or interviewed by journalists, though in late 2001 a grainy postcard-sized photo of him, lifted from a videotaped statement by him, began to circulate among his supporters and in the media. In winter 2000 he was rumored to have flown from Pakistan to Bishkek on a chartered plane, then traveled by car from Osh to Tavildara. Though a wanted man in Kyrgyzstan, he was said to have shaved his beard and carried fake ID. Reports say he had two Tajik wives. One, who lived with their daughter in northern Afghanistan, was reported to be the sister of his old wartime ally Mirzo Ziyoev, a former commander in the UTO who became a minister in the Tajik government after the civil war. His second wife was said to be a widow of that war. By marrying her and adopting her two sons, Namangani fulfilled an Islamic tenet to support the widows of jihad, bringing him goodwill from the local Tajik community.

He was less supportive of his own family in Uzbekistan. They were targets of Uzbek security forces since his implication in the 1997 murders of security personnel in Namangan. An interview with Namangani's sister, Makhbuba Akhmedova, by the Uzbek journalist Galima Bukharbaeva, in the Institute for War and Peace newsletter, told a tragic tale of a family persecuted by security officers who frequently detain family members for questioning and who raid the family houses while they are sleeping and jab them with guns, demanding to know the whereabouts of Juma Namangani, even though after the Tashkent bombings the family had publicly disowned him in Namangan's regional assembly. Not all Uzbek Muslims support the strict and militant brand of Islam that Namangani embraced, nor do they support the overthrow of their government. In desperation Makhbuba and her brother, Nasyr Khojaev, traveled to Tajikistan in March 2000 and found their way to Tavildara, where they visited Juma.

"We went to him because we wanted to tell him face-to-face about the suffering he was causing his family," Makhbuba said. Namangani's relatives hoped he would give up his armed struggle and repent his crimes against Uzbekistan. Namangani refused. Instead, he advised them to remain in Tavildara as they would only face persecution at home. Upon their return to Uzbekistan the brother and sister were arrested. The brother was sentenced to fourteen years' imprisonment for traveling to Tavildara; the sister continues to be called in for questioning by Uzbek security agents.

SEVERAL TIMES between 1992 and 1995 Namangani crossed the Panj River into Afghanistan, to train his army in Taliban camps. Taliban leaders granted Namangani bases in Mazar-i-Sharif and in Kunduz, in northern Afghanistan. The bases would eventually become his main strongholds, though Tavildara would remain a springboard for his strikes against Uzbekistan. In Kunduz he reportedly based two Mi8 helicopters, said to have come from Osama bin Laden. Namangani's men would eventually oblige the Taliban and fight against the Northern Alliance armies of Ahmed Shah Massoud. Massoud, who was assassinated in September 2001 by a suicide bomb hidden in a visiting journalist's camcorder, said this about the IMU's relationship with the Taliban in May 1999: "The Taliban will not stop at seizing the whole of Afghanistan! They have plans to move on Samarkand, Bukhara, and beyond. Their plans include creating a supranational radical and extremist Islamic state—the Emirate of Fergana. The leaders of the Uzbek opposition, Takhir Yuldashev and Juma Namangani, are working actively on this at present in Mazar-i-Sharif on Taliban-controlled territory. This is where the threat to Central Asian security is coming from."

Namangani with his few thousand rebels was no match for the forty-thousand-strong Uzbek army, but with the Taliban to back him and bin Laden to fund him he presented a threat to Central Asian security. Supporting a warlord like Juma Namangani in his jihad against Karimov benefited the Taliban; his Uzbek dissidents could fight for them too, while jihad against Uzbekistan could hinder the Northern Alliance's supply of arms from Russia. All this served to destabilize the Central Asian borders and make them more porous for smuggling opium and heroin, which financed the Taliban fighting machine. Under the Taliban, Afghanistan had become a narco-state, producing more opium and heroin than the Golden Triangle and ramping up production in leaps and bounds. In 1997 Afghanistan produced 2,800 metric tons of opium; in 1999, 4,600 metric tons were produced; in 2000 the crop was smaller—3,275 metric tons—but 40 warehouses across Afghanistan were stuffed with the product of past harvests. For Afghan farmers ruined by the war with Russia, opium poppy became a lucrative cash crop, bringing in between thirty and sixty dollars per kilo. Fortunes were being made by the Taliban, who taxed opium-crop sales to Russian, Chinese, Turkish, Chechen, Azeri, and Georgian criminal organizations.

To get the drugs to dealers and addicts in Russia, China, and Europe, they must cross Uzbekistan, Tajikistan, and Kyrgyzstan. Convoys and couriers flaunt those borders, even when the penalty for drug smuggling in some areas is to be shot on sight. The president of Tajikistan, Emomalie Rahmonov, claimed in 1999 that every day a ton of opium and heroin was smuggled across the Tajik border from Afghanistan. In 1998 Kyrgyzstan major general Askarbek Mameyev said that of an estimated 220 pounds of processed opium being smuggled into Kyrgyzstan from Afghanistan every week, border guards were intercepting only 5 percent. In 1999 the United Nations Drug Control Program (UNDCP) identified Juma Namangani's forces as being among the customers who bought up large amounts of refined heroin from a Taliban stockpile of 220 tons warehoused in Kunduz, Afghanistan.

With bases provided by the Taliban, and with money from narcotics and from rich supporters of jihad like bin Laden, Namangani was, by the end of the millennium, a warlord to be reckoned with. Sometime in 1998, after the Tajik civil war had ended, Namangani and Yuldashev named their army the Islamic Movement of Uzbekistan, and they began planning their jihad against Islam Karimov. Unfortunately for Kyrgyzstan, it lay between the IMU and Uzbekistan.

8.

THE FIRST BATKEN CONFLICT

Batken I is the name the Kyrgyz give to the violent incursion in summer 1999 of one thousand IMU rebels into southern Kyrgyzstan. The name *Batken*, when translated from Kyrgyz, means "valley of poison," or, more literally, "place of bat," after the bat plant, which is unique to the area and which gives off a poisonous vapor when it flowers. The Batken region, and the eponymous town, are a part of the Fergana Valley.

The heavily armed IMU fighters, and in some cases their families, too, were on the move toward the mountain passes on the Kyrgyz-Tajik border, seemingly in search of a new base of operations because the Tajik government had ordered them to leave the Tavildara and Karetigin valleys. On the face of it, the IMU's exodus had an appearance of desperation. They were being evicted from Tajikistan because of the outbreak of peace there, and their ally and erstwhile hosts in the UTO were ordering them out. The five-year-long civil war that demolished Tajikistan had been a struggle for control of economic spoils, fought between tribes and clans with centuries-old ethnic differences. The war killed 60,000 people, or 1 percent of the population (48,000 died in one province alone, Khatlon Oblast). It maimed countless people; it displaced a million (many of whom fled to appalling conditions in refugee camps in Afghanistan); and it left 25,000 widows and 55,000 orphans. Tajik society was torn apart by the war's savagery, in which summary executions and the mutilation of opponents were widely reported. The country was bankrupted, and Tajikistan's infrastructure of roads, bridges, factories, hospitals, schools, communications, and cultural objects was destroyed.

Exhausted by war, Tajiks welcomed the peace agreement brokered in 1997 by the United Nations. The Commission on National Reconciliation called for all armed militias to lay down their weapons by August 24, 1999, and either enter civil society or join the Tajik military. The UTO disbanded and became the legal political opposition party standing alongside its old enemy, the government of Emomalie Rahmonov. But Juma Namangani and his IMU fighters refused to disarm, as their argument lay with the Karimov government in Uzbekistan. Tajikistan was merely their base in exile, not their home, and they had no political legitimacy in the Tajik government.

THE APPARENT INTENT of the IMU's march across the border was to cross a thirty-mile strip of Kyrgyz territory and enter the Uzbek enclave of Sokh (which lay just east of the Tajik enclave of Vorukh), then hop again over another short stretch of Kyrgyz land into "mainland" Uzbekistan and the Fergana Valley, where they would join other IMU fighters and begin guerrilla operations against the Karimov regime.

The largest armed group was led by Namangani. During the peace process in Tajikistan in 1997 he had watched quietly from the sidelines as his former allies in the UTO made the transition from being guerrilla warlords hiding in the mountains to politicians holding powerful positions in the Tajik capital of Dushanbe. UTO field commanders he'd fought under, like Said Abdullo Nuri and Mirzo Ziyoev, were now government appointees—Nuri, the legal leader of the opposition party and Ziyoev, the new minister of emergencies. While he sat tight in his base during the peace talks, Namangani is reported to have invested in farmland in Tajikistan and to have started a trucking company with Tajik partners. But the "Kalashnikov culture" of guerrilla war was the only life he and his followers had known, and they would soon take up arms again.

At a high-level conference in Bishkek on August 16, 1999—by which time the IMU was already on the move into Kyrgyzstan—Tajikistan's President Rakhmonov (leader of the government during part of the civil war) was joined by his former enemy Nuri to discuss with Central Asian delegates the presence in Tajikistan of seventeen hundred illegal Uzbek immigrants. Some of those immigrants were ideologues who peacefully opposed Karimov's rule. A great many others were rebels like Namangani who were already wanted for terrorism in Uzbekistan. The immigrants knew they would be jailed or executed if they went home, yet the government conference agreed that they should "voluntarily return" to Uzbekistan and that Tajikistan would no longer accommodate paramilitary groups.

Viewed from one perspective, Namangani's old friends had given him his marching orders because he had become an embarrassment to the Tajik government, which now wanted to establish good peacetime relations with Uzbekistan and Kyrgyzstan, as well as the West. Reports in the Central Asian press around that time also made it seem that elements in Tajikistan were trying to destroy Namangani himself; in June 1999 Namangani's home was reportedly machine-gunned. He survived, but two bodyguards were killed. Around the same time Namangani was said to have ordered the execution of seventeen of his men who planned to surrender to Uzbek authorities and lead peaceful lives. According to reports, they were shot, beheaded, and buried in a mass grave in eastern Tajikistan. It was also reported that clan members of the slain men, also in the IMU, later killed the commander who carried out the executions.

Infighting aside, peace in Tajikistan had put Namangani and his people in a hopeless and homeless situation and was forcing them to make their armed dash across Kyrgyzstan to Uzbekistan.

But other observers believe that elements in the new Tajik government had very different intentions for Namangani, and that his departure from Tajikistan was part of a complex plan. During the civil war the Tajik UTO and its allies had received money, arms, recruits, and training from many sources: the Taliban, Pakistani *madrassas*, and Saudi billionaire Osama bin Laden's terrorist organization, Al Qaeda. Following the end of the civil war the UTO men in the new Tajik government found that the money from sponsors like bin Laden, which had funded the resistance and lined their pockets, was drying up, because peace in Tajikistan was of little use to bin Laden's worldwide jihad against Russian and American influence in Islamic life. With many former UTO field commanders out of work and divorced from the peace dividend, the stability of the Tajik government, and of those UTO men who had received government appointments, depended on being able to spread money around to appease the various warlords in Tajikistan. One way to get more funding was to begin a new jihad on another front. Many UTO men in the new Tajik government were sympathetic to Namangani's stance against the Karimov regime, even though Uzbekistan and Tajikistan officially were on friendly terms. This created a schism within the Tajik government: on the one hand it agreed to evict the Uzbek rebels; on the other it covertly supported a Namangani-led anti-Karimov jihad. Post–civil war Tajikistan had little control of the country outside of the area around its capital, Dushanbe. "While the Tajik government doesn't endorse terrorists on its soil, it doesn't dissuade it either," said a Kyrgyzstan desk officer at the State Department.

Experts point to a revolt against Tajik government forces in November 1998 in the Khujand region by a renegade Tajik colonel as the excuse for Namangani's raids on Kyrgyzstan. The Tajik government believed Uzbekistan had backed the revolt, so in reprisal the anti-Uzbek rebels were gathered for a retaliatory strike. Namangani was brought in from the cold, sent to Dushanbe to meet with opposition leaders, and given the job of spearheading the new jihad. Meanwhile, reports say that Ziyoev enlisted other guerrilla groups like the Uzbek Islamic Resistance (UIR) as well as his former commander-in-arms, Field Commander Abdullo, to join the Namangani-led coalition with 150 of his own Tajik rebels. The proposal of a new jihad brought in money from the old and dependable sponsors of terrorism. While the Tajik government officially claimed that it was ousting Namangani and his band, other ministers were said to be helping Namangani to ferry arms and hundreds of men to the Kyrgyz and Uzbek borders, and positioning helicopters to evacuate his wounded rebels.

The IMU had been planning its move on Kyrgyzstan for some time. In May 1999 representatives from the IMU visited the Kyrgyz villages of Korgon and Zardaly, no more than forty miles from the Karavshin. They introduced themselves to villagers as protectors of the Islamic faith and explained they would return to fight Uzbekistan. They assured villagers they had no argument with Kyrgyzstan, and they gained trust from some of them. Perhaps the agents of unrest had been in the Karavshin even earlier: Ivan Samoilenko, a Russian climber who had spent many summers in the Karavshin, told me that on his way there in the early 1990s, while traversing Tajikistan by truck, a drunken Tajik from a mountain village bragged to him, "We are waiting for the White General to supply us the machine guns. We must kill all the government men." Who the White General was Samoilenko didn't know, but the statement hinted at "the strong resentment under the skin of the mountain people."

The first units of the IMU entered Kyrgyzstan in late July by crossing the mountains south of Batken. Kyrgyzstan's borders there are unmarked and unpatrolled, appearing on maps as a serpentine line along icy mountain crests. While crossing the border the IMU met neither Kyrgyz or Tajik troops, nor Russian border guards. By mutual arrangement between Uzbekistan and Russia, thirty-two thousand soldiers of Russia's 201st Motorized Infantry Brigade police Uzbekistan's borders with Afghanistan and Tajikistan, to fend off drug trafficking and the Taliban. Tajikistan has long hosted Russian soldiers too. Russian troops had participated in the Tajik civil war on the side of the Rakhmonov government, and both countries were staging grounds for the Soviet war in Afghanistan. But Russian soldiers were absent from "peaceful" southern Kyrgyzstan. When the rebels reached Kyrgyzstan's mountain passes they moved through them easily, using local Kyrgyz shepherds as guides. Provisions came from preplaced caches sometimes hidden in abandoned Soviet-era mines dotting the mountains, and from mountain villagers, who sold the rebels food in exchange for American dollars.

The IMU made its first move on August 3, 1999, when twenty-one rebels took control of Zardaly and seized four government and military hostages. The IMU demanded ransom for their release, and freedom for four IMU comrades in Uzbek prisons. The Kyrgyz military rushed into the area, and fighting erupted along the border as troops encountered bands of rebels filtering in across the mountains. In mid-August unmarked Uzbek warplanes flew over Kyrgyzstan to bomb rebel positions in Tajikistan but mistakenly bombed the Kyrgyz village of Kara-Teyit, killing four civilians, injuring sixteen, and destroying thirty-one houses. Further aerial bombardments killed more villagers. The fighting failed to dislodge the IMU, and by August 13, a sum reported to be between $50,000 and $150,000, as well as an amount of food, was paid to the IMU. Some of the hostages were released, and the guerrillas retreated back into Tajikistan.

By August 22 the Kyrgyz minister of defense, General Subanov, declared that the rebels had left, but on the same day a new drama erupted when more rebels said to be led by Vyatcheslav Kim, a field commander affiliated with the IMU and based in Afghanistan, entered Kyrgyzstan and stumbled across four Japanese geologists and their Kyrgyz interpreter. Nobuhisa Nakajima, Hirotaru Fujii, Haruo Harada, and Toshiaki Ariie, whose ages ranged from thirty-eight to fifty-eight, and their Kyrgyz interpreter, Ourbek Janakeev, were captured while gold prospecting in the remote Altyn-Zhylga, an area whose name means "golden vein." The geologists were working for the Japan International Cooperation Agency as part of an economic-aid program for Kyrgyzstan. To the IMU, the foreigners were worth more than their weight in gold.

Up to this time the IMU was largely unknown to the Kyrgyz in cosmopolitan Bishkek, let alone in the West, where news from Central Asia was nearly nonexistent. But the Japanese-hostage crisis changed all that. On September 2 a shepherd-hostage from Zardaly was sent by the IMU to deliver an oral message to Kyrgyz authorities. The rebels demanded one million dollars for each hostage, free passage for the rebels across Kyrgyzstan into Uzbekistan, release of political prisoners from Uzbek and Kyrgyz jails, and a delivery of food. Around the same time, a representative from the IMU phoned and faxed the BBC and Kabar, the state news agency of Kyrgyzstan. In these calls, Az Zubair Ibn Abdur Raheem claimed he was calling from

Afghanistan and declared that the IMU had begun its jihad against Karimov's government.

The international hostage crisis brought the IMU exactly what it wanted: international attention. Within days of the kidnapping, nearly 150 journalists from Japan converged on the Kyrgyz capital, and they assembled every day at the Kabar news agency, waiting for developments. The Japanese government also sent a task force to Kyrgyzstan. Its negotiator, Shegenobu Kato, stressed that Japan would not pay ransom.

"The Japanese journalists who sat here for two months, they were like hostages too," Turat Akimov, a Kabar reporter, told me in March 2001 in Bishkek. "They wrote about the IMU, and this was what the IMU wanted."

Digging into positions around Zardaly, the rebels prepared for a long siege, and the Japanese geologists settled into life as hostages. They played cards, gathered firewood, and cooked, and their captors taught them the Koran and the correct ways of praying, which they were compelled to perform five times each day with the rebels. By early September the rebels in Kyrgyzstan numbered several hundred and occupied a total of five villages around Zardaly. Most of their hostages were Kyrgyz policemen, but to the embarrassment of the Kyrgyz government they had also captured Major General Anarbek Shamkeev, commander of the Kyrgyzstan Interior Ministry troops. About a thousand villagers were trapped as well, told by the rebels they could not leave the area. Reports from Uzbek sources claimed that the rebels themselves were hostages of a sort, as fellow rebels had aimed batteries of heavy weapons at escape routes leading back into Tajikistan and had orders to fire on their men if they tried to retreat. The government restricted journalists from the area, yet reports filtered out of six thousand mountain villagers fleeing their homes and heading to Batken, and of casualties among the Kyrgyz troops trying to encircle the rebels.

While the rebels sat with their hostages, Field Commander Abdullo's rebels broke through into Kyrgyzstan via the Abramov Glacier and began a new attack. They burned down a scientific glaciological station and captured nine Uzbek mountaineers. The Uzbeks were moved around the mountains for several days, then released. In the valley of the Sokh River on September 22 heavy fighting killed eleven Kyrgyz soldiers before two hundred IMU rebels were pushed back from the Uzbek enclave of Sokh. On October 4 slow-flying Uzbek L-39 training jets bombed rebel positions in Tajikistan, while Kyrgyz Mi8 helicopters machine-gunned and dumped unguided bombs on rebel positions. The Zardaly stronghold remained inviolable, behind a human wall of shepherds and VIP hostages. But when winter cold blew into the mountains, one hundred IMU men shifted their hostages from Zardaly to a settlement near an 11,500-foot pass called Kojie Achkan, closer to the Kyrgyz-Tajik border. Installing themselves in a narrow and easily defended gorge, the rebels resumed their demands. With winter coming and little chance to break through the Uzbek troops massed farther north on the edge of the Fergana Valley, the IMU changed its demand: instead of free passage through Kyrgyzstan to Uzbekistan they wanted free passage back through Tajikistan to Afghanistan.

Between October 12 and October 18 several Kyrgyz hostages were set free, including Major General Shamkeev, who was said to be gravely ill. On October 25, with winter snows building on the passes, the IMU released the Japanese hostages, handing them over to a Tajik negotiator of the UTO. The Japanese were unharmed. They were taken to Tajikistan, then flown to a hospital in Kyrgyzstan for medical evaluation. Japanese officials quickly jetted them back to Japan. There were few glimpses of the former hostages after their sixty-four-day ordeal other than brief video footage and photos of them walking across the airport tarmac. Looking dazed and weary, they had heavy beards and were dressed in camouflage uniforms provided by the Kyrgyz army to replace their own worn-out clothes. "No ransom was paid," asserted the chief cabinet secretary of Japan, Mikio Aoki, but off the record, officials in Kyrgyzstan and the U.S. State Department have nodded to the likelihood that millions of dollars were paid to the IMU. Since then, Japanese nationals have been forbidden to travel in southern Kyrgyzstan.

On November 17 the following news item appeared in *Delo Noma*, a Bishkek newspaper: "It is very likely that the Kirghiz and Tadjik officials plundered 3 million USD, which Tokyo has secretly paid in exchange for releasing four Japanese hostages captured by guerrillas in the south of Kirghizia." The source was named as a Tokyo newspaper, *Mainiti*, and the story claimed that the money had disappeared when Namangani switched his demand from cash to the release of his comrades in prison in Uzbekistan.

"Japan secretly transferred $3,000,000 USD to the Kirghiz authorities, hoping that capricious Namangani would take the ransom anyway. The money was disguised as state economic aid to Batken. However, the Japanese were released free of charge, in exchange for promise of Dushanbe to pass Namangani's group to Afghanistan. And where is this money now?"

AFTER RETURNING HOME, many Kyrgyz veterans of Batken I were shocked by their treatment, especially by broken promises of payment. A young private, Egor Nikolaev, speaking with Bishkek journalist Asel Otorbaeva, reported in the newsletter of the Institute for War and Peace Reporting that his promised combat payment of $50 per day shrank to a promise of $6 per day; in the end he got $28 for two months in the mountains. The standard rate of pay for a rookie recruit was, in fact, $14 per month. Lower officers were paid $35 per month.

"They even threatened to charge us for lost spoons and flasks," he said, adding, "I can be honest about the money. We didn't make anything on that war. Don't believe that you can earn any money as a private."

With few journalists allowed into the area to report on the conflict, the Kyrgyz public had made do with government-sanctioned reporting that said little about the realities for the ground troops. Nikolaev's account to Otorbaeva described an unprepared Kyrgyz army up against well-armed and well-trained "Wahhis," which was soldier slang for the Wahhabis, or Muslim extremists.

"What really shocked me in Batken," he said, "was the 'strategy and tactics' of the military leadership. If the rebel fighters had wanted to shoot us all, they could have done it in about five minutes."

Nikolaev had volunteered for service and was sent with eight hundred young soldiers to Koi-Tash in September. He reported that the officers "did not know what to do with such a mass of people." A battalion of 360 men was eventually formed, made up of reserve soldiers, volunteers like him, and Kyrgyz veterans of the Soviet-Afghan war. According to the former soldier, the weapons they were issued were old and in poor condition. A few new sniper rifles were given out, but they lacked telescopic sights. Of nine radios in his battalion, only two worked. No one received flak jackets.

"We'd move out at night," he said. "Towards Shudman, in the direction of the Abramov Glacier, where the Japanese hostages were being held. One hundred twenty-six soldiers for the first time in those mountains, pitch black darkness, the line spread out over two kilometers, with the guides somewhere way out in front—sitting ducks, especially because the fighters didn't have the sort of antique firearms that we were equipped with.

"The only reason we didn't get shot that night was because it wasn't part of the plan of the Wahhabis. And we were literally following right after them. On the way we'd come across pots with the meat in them still hot, and bags of flour. We were lucky because they didn't leave any mines or trip wires after them."

Nikolaev described a battalion stretched beyond its capabilities. His contingent of more than one hundred men was given rations for thirty men for a week. His battalion was forced to hunt mountain goats for food. After he returned to Bishkek he joined a group of young soldiers protesting their treatment outside military headquarters. They were threatened with arrest and dispersed.

"I'm not going to war anymore," he said. "I understand that war is a big political game, where we, the privates, are just cannon fodder."

AFTER THE IMU LEFT Kyrgyzstan they vanished back into Tajikistan and Afghanistan, leaving the Kyrgyz government to take stock of the damage. The war had killed twenty-seven soldiers and a Kyrgyz hostage and had cost the country $3.3 million. Scores of rebels had been killed as well. When mountain villagers returned to their farms they found that rebels had herded seven hundred of their yaks back into Tajikistan—a crippling loss for poor farmers. There was backlash in the corridors of power in Bishkek too. Kyrgyz president Askar Akayev was displeased to find that his country's borders were poorly defended, and he was uncomfortable that the conflict had forced him to request military aid from Russia, placing Kyrgyzstan in the position of showing dependence on its old master. The affair led to the dismissal of General Subanov as minister of defense. His replacement, General Esen Topoev, was handed the unenviable job of fending off the next IMU incursion.

In the span of time between Batken I and the next assault by the IMU, in August 2000, the Central Asian governments met at conferences like the "Shanghai Five" summit and signed treaties to stamp out the Islamic militants. Appealing for international military aid, the Kyrgyz and Uzbek armies received help from Russia and China in the form of arms and ammunition, and communications equipment and training from the U.S. military. Privately, the Central Asian countries blamed one another for the conflict. Karimov's repressive policies had helped start it all, some officials argued. At the same time Uzbek and Kyrgyz ministers bickered with their Tajik counterparts, claiming they had proof that IMU training camps existed on Tajik soil. Publicly, the Tajik president denied the existence of terrorists in his country and said he knew nothing of Namangani's whereabouts. Privately, he pressured Namangani's old friend Mirzo Ziyoev to get the IMU out of the country or lose his government post. Shortly afterward the IMU began to move.

9.

ONTO THE YELLOW WALL

When Kate Dooley visited the American base camp on August 5 she warned Smith and Dickey about the three thieves. While the Australians had been climbing on the cliffs above their camp, a trio of local shepherds had been pilfering their tents. Dooley's red-handled Swiss Army knife had been among the several small items stolen, and when she mentioned this to Smith he told her about a trio of seedy-looking men who had recently dropped by their camp. One of them had proudly flashed a knife just like Dooley's. When Smith described the man, Dooley recognized the description immediately. It was Murat Kalnarazov, a.k.a. Homer Simpson.

On August 8 Rodden and Caldwell are back up on the Yellow Wall several hundred feet above the ground, working on a difficult 5.12 pitch, and Smith and Dickey are about to leave camp to climb Asan when the three thieves make an appearance at their camp. After making small talk in broken English the shepherds follow the two Americans out of camp and up the trail toward Asan, then a quarter mile from camp one of the three men slips away. When Smith sees the man heading back toward the base camp, he suspects a setup.

"I just know he's gone back to camp to steal our stuff," he tells Dickey.

"Where has your friend gone?" Dickey asks the remaining two shepherds.

"Home. Sleep," one of them indicates, using hand signs.

Neither Smith nor Dickey believes the shepherd, so Dickey marches back down the trail to base camp. While Smith sits waiting, the other two shepherds try to cajole his "compact disketta" from him.

"We friend, yes?" Homer asks. He points to the CD player and says, "You many. Give me!"

Smith says no. Then Homer indicates that he wants Smith's watch. Again Smith turns him down. When Dickey returns, he reports that no one is at camp, but right then Homer and his friend suddenly stand and walk toward the American camp. Smith and Dickey realize that they are unlikely to get any climbing done today, as they feel sure that the men will rob their tents if they don't stay with them. So they follow the shepherds at a distance. Sure enough, when they arrive at base camp they find the three shepherds creeping around, inspecting the items the Americans left out in the open.

"I thought you went home to go to sleep?" Smith asks the man who had disappeared earlier.

"You give?" the man says, pointing to a carabiner clipped to Smith's pack.

The men loiter around till they see that Smith and Dickey are not leaving, then they head off down the valley. By this time it's too late for the Americans to hike to Asan, so they walk over to the Yellow Wall and join Rodden and Caldwell on their climb for the remainder of the day.

HEAVY RAIN FALLS in the valley the next day, August 9, and the four climbers sit in the large yellow tent playing cards. On August 10 Dickey and Smith finally do some climbing on the tower of Asan. Afterward, on the way back to base camp, they encounter a bear and a cub ambling across the meadows.

That night in camp the climbers discuss what to do with the remainder of their time in the mountains and they agree to join forces on the Yellow Wall. On the morning of August 11 they pack food, portaledges, and equipment into two large haul bags that they'll drag up the wall. It's a bluebird day, approximately noon, and as they get ready for the climb Dickey, as expedition photographer, snaps photos of them packing. Their eyes turn skyward when the buzz of an Mi8 drifts up the valley, but no chopper appears and the noise subsides, suggesting a flight path to the Ak Su or somewhere down the valley, near Kurbaka.

While Caldwell, Dickey, and Smith stand among the tents, loading up the haul bags, Rodden walks to the spring and sits down to pump water through a purification filter into plastic bottles, which they'll haul up the wall. Rocks and low brush surround the spring, concealing her position. A few feet away is the foot trail used by everyone who walks along the Kara Su. When Rodden glances up from the bubbling spring, her heart skips a beat at the unexpected sight of two men sitting on an embankment, two hundred feet from the trail. They wear camouflage vests and pants and hold rifles in their laps, and they are watching the activity in base camp. They cannot see her. She crouches low and waves at her companions, quietly directing their attention toward the men.

"Whoa, who are those guys?" Dickey asks, surprised.

"Soldiers?" suggests Caldwell.

"I guess so," Dickey replies.

"They don't look like soldiers to me," Smith says warily.

The men sit with expressionless faces and make no move to visit their camp. The mottled green camouflage of their vests is different in pattern from the uniforms of the Kyrgyz soldiers they've grown used to seeing, and these men have thick beards and long hair, whereas the Kyrgyz soldiers they've met have nearly always been neat and clean-shaven. More than anything, it is the reticence of these men that the Americans find odd. Everyone they've met to this point has been friendly, smiling, even chatty. Soldiers are always quick to ask to see their passports and frontier permit, and shepherds inevitably want to inspect their CD players. Smith, for one, has often asked soldiers and shepherds to let him examine their rifles, as nearly all the passersby are armed. He notes that the weapons that the two men on the embankment carry are military-style "automats."

"Maybe it's a good idea to pretend we haven't seen these guys," suggests Smith, acting on an impulse. The unblinking gazes coming from the men make the climbers a little uneasy. They continue packing without overtly reacting to the men, who sit still as stones. But after a few minutes it proves impossible for the Americans to avoid looking up, and the two groups lock eyes. Dickey waves a greeting, and the men wave back. Then the visitors stand and walk away. The Americans never see them again.

"That was strange, huh?" Rodden says to Caldwell after she joins the group.

The climbers don't give the encounter another thought. They've grown used to seeing armed men—both soldiers and shepherds—and if they regard the visitors as potential trouble, it is to the same extent that they regard the three thieves as trouble. That the two men might be terrorists does not occur to the climbers. Yet, there had been much weirdness these past few days that the Americans cannot fathom. The eviction of the Australians was just the beginning of it. While hiking back from the Ak Su on August 6, after their attempt to connect with Dooley and buy her fuel bottle, Rodden and Caldwell met a leather-faced shepherd they had never seen before. He "really creeped me out," Caldwell would say of the man. "He stared at us and said just one word: '*Cuidado.*' " Then he walked away.

Back at base camp they told Dickey and Smith about the encounter. Dickey, who speaks a little Spanish, confirmed what Caldwell and Rodden had thought—that *cuidado* means "Be careful."

"What's a Kyrgyz shepherd doing talking in Spanish?" Rodden said. "I wonder what he meant."

Also strange was an encounter a week before the expedition left America, when a family friend of the Caldwells' had visited Mike Caldwell, expressing an urge to talk to Tommy. Sitting down with Caldwell, he had described an occasion in Mexico when he'd stumbled into a violent situation. His life was in danger, he'd had to flee, and in the process he'd run his car over one of the attackers. He escaped, and his message to Caldwell seemed to be that saving yourself was right even at the cost of a human life.

He didn't explain why he'd felt compelled to tell Caldwell and his parents this story. His need to talk with Tommy seemed to have come from someplace deep inside him.

AT 1 P.M. all four climbers leave camp with heavy haul bags on their backs. At the foot of the Yellow Wall they find the dangling ropes that Rodden and Caldwell had previously set up, and they head up the cliff using the ropes and ascender clamps. At the anchors where the ends of each two-hundred-foot rope are secured, they pause to winch their seventy-pound bags of gear up the cliff on another rope through a small pulley-and-ratchet system. The process of traveling up the ropes one at a time, hauling the loads, and then removing the line of ropes from below them so they can use them on the wall above takes till sundown. At the top of the ropes they hang just under a thousand feet above the foot of the cliff, dangling from a web of slings, cams, and wedges slotted into cracks under a projection of rock that juts out over their heads like a roof. Figuring this overhang will protect them from falling stones, they snap together the metal frames of their two portaledges and suspend the bunklike contraptions side by side. By the time they're lying in the portaledges, it's midnight. They snack on freeze-dried dinners, and Rodden sings "Happy Birthday" to Caldwell in one portaledge, while in the other Dickey and Smith listen to heavy metal on their CD player.

10.

SLAUGHTER

ORTOCHASHMA RIVER AND CLIMBERS' BASE CAMPS

AUGUST 9-12

"I don't think the soldiers had any inkling of what was coming," Kate Dooley would write of her last meeting with Ruslan Samsakov and his men. "They were very relaxed in the base, nothing was said to make us think they were anything but bored."

It is August 10, the night before the Americans head up on the Yellow Wall. Rain pelted the mountains the previous day, but the storm has blown through, leaving a sky pockmarked with stars. In the predawn hours Dooley and her companions are safely sleeping in a hotel in Osh, the climbers in the Karavshin are slumbering in their base camps, and the Kyrgyz soldiers stationed at Kurbaka and the surrounding outposts await the dawn and the beginning of another day of patrolling the mountains. Unbeknownst to them all, twenty-eight IMU rebels have infiltrated the valleys of the Karavshin. On August 9, far up the Ortochashma River, they ambush a three-man army patrol. Two Kyrgyz soldiers are killed and one is captured.

The prisoner is Sergeant Turat Osmanov. He's been patrolling the shepherd trails crisscrossing these mountains for weeks, though for Osmanov to be on patrol right then and there would appear to be a matter of fate. He had postponed his scheduled leave to take on another tour of duty in the mountains to earn more money, and on this particular patrol toward the Turo Pass he was covering for a fellow soldier who had injured his knee. Even being in uniform smacked of destiny for Osmanov, as twice during 1999 he had, said his mother, bribed his way out of calls to return to service. When the army sent him a third call-up notice in summer 2000, he had decided to report for duty.

The rebels take Osmanov farther down the Ortochashma valley. On the evening of August 10 they ambush a second patrol of seven men, three miles downstream. In a brief exchange of fire four soldiers are killed; three are taken prisoner. They are unable to send a Mayday message to Kurbaka, as their radio is out of range. Disarmed and stunned, the soldiers stand with their hands raised, looking into the faces of the enemy their training warned them about. Most of the rebels holding the soldiers at gunpoint are young. Some are bearded, like Afghan Taliban, but others are smooth-faced, like the Kyrgyz. A few have the hardened look of war veterans, but others seem edgy, as if they're newcomers to this way of life. They finger their rifle stocks and dart their eyes around nervously.

The rebels are led by two Uzbeks. One will be known to the Americans as Abdul, but his real name is Sabir. He is reportedly from Namangan. The other goes by the name Abdurahman. They bark questions at the most senior officer, a lieutenant named Bakyt Almbekov. They demand to know the location and strength of the block post down the valley, and they ask about foreigners in the area. To get the information they want, the rebels beat Almbekov and his men and slash at their bodies with knives. Even as they suffer, the soldiers hold out hope that the torture will stop, and that their lot will in the end be no worse than to become the first hostages of Batken II. When the soldiers give up the information the rebels are after, the killing begins. Kyrgyz soldiers will find Almbekov's corpse half-naked, mutilated, and dumped in a gully.

The rebels form two groups. The most heavily armed group numbers twenty, and they head down the valley to hit the base at Kurbaka. A second group of eight, led by Abdul, forces Osmanov to guide them over a shepherd's path known to locals as Kugai Bulak. The path leads steeply uphill for three thousand feet and crosses the divide separating the Ortochashma River from the upper Karavshin Valley. It empties the rebels at the farms of Karavshy. From there it is a few easy miles to the climbers' camps in the Kara Su and Ak Su valleys. The two rebels who watch the four Americans packing their haul bags on the morning of August 11 are part of Abdul's group. They keep an eye on the Americans until they set off up the Yellow Wall. Meanwhile, Abdul heads toward the camps of the Germans and the Ukrainians.

When Almbekov's patrol is noted as being overdue by the soldiers at Kurbaka, ten men march up to look for them. Ruslan Samsakov is among the men who hurry along the trail early on the morning of August 11. They know nothing of the murder of their comrades a few hours earlier, and as they enter the narrow canyon on the Karavshin just below the bridge at Mazar they have no idea that they are walking into a trap. The narrow defile gives no cover from the crossfire of Abdurahman's snipers when they fire down from the canyon rim. Within minutes, the canyon is running with blood. A handful of soldiers surrender and are dragged back to the ibex skull–festooned shrine at Mazar.

But the tables quickly turn. The alarm is raised down the valley, and later that morning three Kyrgyz patrols converge on the rebels. Heavy fighting pushes the rebels back up valley. They retreat to Mazar, where they execute their Kyrgyz prisoners by slitting their throats or shooting them, leaving the bodies in the graveyard of the shrine. The Kyrgyz attackers continue to gain ground all day, fighting from rock to rock. By dusk the shooting has killed eleven of the twenty rebels. The rest flee up the Ortochashma valley. Kyrgyz soldiers will report seeing wounded rebels shot by their own and tossed in the river, to prevent capture and identification. By the time the Kyrgyz soldiers fend off the attack, nineteen of their own are dead—many of them executed while unarmed. It is the first battle of Batken II.

Many of the soldiers who had visited the Australians are among the dead. Major Djizelbek Subanbekov and Captain Ruslan Samsakov are two of them. Two weeks after this battle the Kyrgyz newspaper *Vechernii Bishkek* runs a story about three of the men killed at Mazar. One photograph, of a uniformed, ruggedly handsome, and confident-looking young man— Samsakov—stares off the page at the reader. "Doctor is a very peaceful profession," wrote the journalist when describing Samsakov. "But he was not hiding behind the soldiers. He was at the front, holding a gun to defend his motherland, and he was among the first to die in this struggle. In a house in Bishkek on the day of his death, his relatives had gathered to celebrate the 30th anniversary of his parents' wedding. But instead the holiday became a funeral. Ruslan was 29, and he was married."

RIVER NOISE AND granite walls mask the gunfire from the climbers sleeping in the base camps ten miles from Kurbaka. Only Stefan Hiermaier, a thirty-two-year-old German, hears a faraway burst of machine-gunning wafting in on the breeze, at 10 A.M. on August 11, while he is walking up the glacier at the head of the Ak Su valley, toward the Tajik border. "I used to live near an American military base in Germany, and I was used to hearing guns," he said later. "I was certain that I heard the rat-a-tat of a machine gun. But my friends said no, you're crazy, it was only the sound of a boulder rolling along the river."

In addition to Hiermaier the German team in the Ak Su comprise Robert Lange, twenty-eight, Wentzel Lutz, thirty-seven, Mike Meyer, forty-one, Roland Laemmermann, twenty-four, and Radan Svec, twenty-eight. The group all hail from in and around the city of Nuremberg. Two Uzbeks, Andre Karnienko and Mischa Volosovitch, are with them also; Asia Travel, the Tashkent-based company that has arranged the German expedition, has provided the Uzbeks as travel guide and cook. Karnienko has already led a French trekking group through the area earlier in the summer. Since reaching base camp on August 1 the group has amassed an impressive list of ascents, including a thirty-seven-pitch climb on a tawny rock pyramid named by the Soviets 1000 Years of Russian Christendom, and the fabled Perestroika Crack on Russian Tower.

Waking to clear skies on the morning of August 11, Hiermaier, Svec, and Meyer left base camp to make the five-mile hike up the Ak Su glacier toward a slender spire known to Russian climbers as Ptitsa, to English speakers as the Bird. Its needle-sharp summit stands at 14,730 feet. Lutz and Lange and Karnienko also leave camp, but they choose a shorter climb closer to base camp. Only Laemmermann and the cook, Volosovitch, remain in camp. A few yards away, in the Ukrainian camp, the mood is relaxed. The sunny weather persuades the Ukrainians, Igor Chaplinsky, forty-two, Viktor Nikitenko, thirty-six, and Vasili Kolysnik and his wife, Natasha, both thirty-six, to rest a day longer before beginning any climbing. The Kolysniks and Chaplinsky are fabric importers; Nikitenko is a rigger on high-rise buildings. Their climbing adventures have taken them from the Caucasus and Pamir Mountains to the Himalayas, and the Karavshin is to them what the playground of Yosemite is to the Americans.

Laemmermann and Volosovitch stroll over to the Ukrainian camp for lunch. They all lie on the meadow, sunbathing and eating sliced watermelon, a luxury that the Ukrainians brought in on the helicopter. Inspired by the view of the massive triangular cliff of Peak 4810 across the river, they discuss the routes they plan to climb in the days ahead. Talk of climbing often has the effect of making a climber's hands sweat with anticipation, but at 2 P.M., the sound of two shots fired into the air jars these climbers into a different reality.

"Everyone lies down, hands stretching forward!" a voice calls loudly in Russian.

When Chaplinsky looks up from his position on the ground he sees a crowd of men toting automatic weapons, striding toward him. Smoke rises from the barrel of one of the rifles, which is pointed in his direction. "The first thought occurring to me was that someone got an idea to joke," Chaplinsky would comment later. "But it was not funny, because these brave fellows were well equipped and were not in an amusing mood."

Laemmermann is dumbfounded by the intrusion. "They didn't look like terrorists to me," he said of the men, whom he described as wearing a mix of camo clothing and sportswear. But the Ukrainians know the look of Islamic guerrillas when they see them. Wars in Chechnya and Dagestan and even terrorist bombings in their hometown of Rostov-on-Don have educated them well in this respect. More than their Kalashnikovs, it is the fibrous black beards on most of the men that identify them as "Talibs."

The climbers are ordered to their feet and told to raise their hands. The gunmen are filthy, their clothes soiled and rank. One of them—Abdul—struts around the camp, checking the tents for additional occupants and inspecting bits of gear. He moves quickly, Chaplinsky notes, "with a jumping motion, like an animal," and he speaks through a clean-faced young rebel who knows good Russian. Through the interpreter, Abdul makes it clear that he is in command and that everyone must obey him.

Before they traveled, the Germans had checked the Web sites of the Uzbek embassy and the German Foreign Office about the region, but they'd seen nothing about potential guerrilla activity. The management of Asia Travel in Tashkent had offered no warnings either, and the Germans were allowed to pass all army checkpoints. But the warnings of the border guards who stopped the Ukrainians from entering the Karavshin ring in their ears. Natasha Kolysnik and her group had dismissed the warning. "If the mujaheddin were going to go after anyone, we figured it'd be the Americans," she said, thinking back on their reasoning at the border.

Noting the way Chaplinsky is studying him, Abdul stares back at the Ukrainian from close range. Chaplinsky shrinks from the man's piercing gaze. As Abdul raises his hand toward Chaplinsky's face, the Ukrainian notes the man's slender, clean fingers and the fashionably modern, yet unfunctioning, watch around his wrist. Abdul removes the designer sunglasses from Chaplinsky's head and pockets them.

"Bitch," the Ukrainian mutters.

The rebels ransack the camp, taking food, gear, and clothing. Then they sit down to the melons laid out on the grass.

"Do not look," one of the rebels orders, and they noisily devour the melons.

While the rebels eat, Laemmermann and Volosovitch see that the seventh man is Turat Osmanov. They know him well. He and his soldiers made several friendly visits to their camp while on patrol. A couple of days earlier, Osmanov shot a yak and brought the meat to the Germans for a birthday feast for Andre Karnienko. He and another soldier, who had introduced himself as Wolfgang, a nickname probably, joined the visitors around a bonfire, and they drank a good amount of vodka. For as much time as the Germans have spent around Osmanov, they have never heard the soldier warn of danger in the Ak Su, though when Hiermaier asked Osmanov why so many soldiers were in the area, he'd told the Germans in halting English, "Not good people come here."

Osmanov's face is ashen with worry. While the rebels loot the camp, he lies down apart from the climbers and tries to sleep. As the afternoon cools down, the rebels order the climbers to put on their shirts and long pants. The German, the Uzbek, and the four Ukrainians are in no doubt that they are hostages.

"Where are your weapons?" Abdul demands.

The Ukrainians tell him they have none. Then Abdul makes a decree, which the Russian-speaking rebel delivers to the hostages.

"From now on no alcohol, no drugs, no cigarettes. And you cannot listen to music of any kind."

His order is an echo from Taliban-controlled Afghanistan, where edicts handed down by the general presidency of the ruling clergy and enforced by the ubiquitous religious police control every aspect of life. The decree "to prevent music" states: "In shops, hotels, vehicles and rickshaws cassettes and music are prohibited," under penalty of prison. Music and dancing are banned at weddings too. The heads of the families are jailed if they violate this law. Other decrees imposed since the Taliban took control of Kabul in 1996 include the decree "to prevent beard shaving and its cutting," which orders that anyone who has shaved "should be arrested and imprisoned until their beard gets bushy." The decree "to prevent keeping pigeons and playing with birds" orders pet birds to be killed. Kite flying and the selling of kites are forbidden. Hanging pictures and portraits in public buildings and in homes is considered idolatry; the religious police are expected to tear up all pictures. Under the edict "to prevent the British and American hairstyle," people with long hair are arrested and taken to the religious police for a head shaving. "The criminal has to pay the barber." Gambling is banned. Drinking alcohol brings jail time and a flogging. Drug addicts are imprisoned.

ABDUL WAS, in fact, more interested in the Americans than in the German and Ukrainian climbers, but the shepherd Kalnarazov had inadvertently directed him to the Ak Su when he and his rebels passed through

Karavshy. So in the early afternoon Abdul picks four rebels and they leave for the Kara Su, marching Osmanov ahead to guide them. At six-fifteen the next morning, Abdul and his men will take potshots at the Americans and force them down from the Yellow Wall.

The remaining three rebels make their hostages pack light rucksacks with food and clothing. The rebels watch carefully, making sure no one slips in a knife or a weapon, and they order the Ukrainians to read aloud the contents of every can. The youngest rebel helps them pack. The men he's with call him Hamsa, and they badger him not to let any alcohol or pork slip into their loads. To Natasha Kolysnik, this clean-faced, handsome kid looks to be as scared as she is. When he speaks, he speaks in educated Russian; when he asks her to pass something, he says "please."

The packing done, the rebels demolish the camp, smashing the tents down into heaps and cramming the wreckage under boulders and bushes. Within minutes, the camp has disappeared. During the destruction, the rebels take the passports of the climbers. Then they wait, while mountain shadows fill the valley and the evening sets in. With the menacing Abdul gone, Chaplinsky ventures a few questions.

"What are you going to do with us?" he asks.

"Don't worry," one of the rebels answers. "We are not going to kill you. We want you only as hostages."

Chaplinsky asks how long they will be kept as prisoners. The rebel replies, "For a month."

"God, I won't last that long," Natasha Kolysnik says in despair.

The group of nine leave base camp at 6 P.M. on August 11. They move down the canyon for an hour, stopping to hide in a grove of pine trees. Night falls. Laemmermann sits quietly. He speaks no Russian. "I did what I was told, I did what I had to do to stay alive," he said later of the conversational blackout and the uncertainty that surrounded him. But the other hostages communicate readily with the rebels.

The oldest of the trio is about twenty-five. He wears a black scarf over his skull and carries a rifle with the Russian word for "wolf"—*volk*—carved into the wooden stock. To Chaplinsky, this rebel even resembles a wolf, with his lean, hunched stature, his sparse Asiatic beard, and his eyes that reveal "a mixture of cruelty and pain." "If you needed a killer, he was the one to ask," Chaplinsky would note. Beside Wolf sits an equally lean man, also in his mid-twenties, whose body odor is overpowering. He is bearded, and he too has the narrow eyes of an animal. These two have a hardness about them, as if they have hijacked people before. The third one—Hamsa—is the youngest. Wolf orders him around as if he is a new recruit.

Natasha knows that talking to her captors will humanize her and make it harder for them to harm her. She focuses on Hamsa. They quickly develop an affinity. "You talk with someone, and they can't remain a wild animal for you," she said later of the young rebel.

She asks him where he is from and he tells her he is Bashkir. It's far away, a part of the Caucasus Mountains of Russia, located on the fringe of Asia and Siberia. Hamsa addresses her in the grammatically formal way of speaking to a woman in Russian, suggesting he's educated and from a good family. It occurs to her that his rougher, less sensitive comrades-in-arms may call him Hamsa as a nickname, after Hamsa Hakimazdeniyazi, a famous Uzbek poet of the Russian Revolution.

While night birds and crickets sing in the dark, the Ukrainians use conversation to enter the world of the rebels. Wolf stares into the distance, saying barely a word; Hamsa fiddles nervously; the third rebel is more talkative.

He tells them he'd lived in Tashkent before he took up arms eight years earlier. He'd been an artist and a *mancurt*—a Tajik term for a religious prophet—but he ended up a warrior. The Ukrainians call him "the Artist."

"Most of the time they talked about religion," said Natasha. "They wanted to impress us with the strength of their faith. Allah had forgiven them from on high for their killing. He'd sent them to cleanse their Muslim world from the unfaithful. They said it was a sin not to fight. They were fanatics."

When Natasha asks the Artist, "Why can't you just live in peace? Isn't there room for all of us on this earth?" he speaks wistfully of the home and the life he left behind, but he checks himself and slouches back into the language of the fanatic: "Our goal is to establish a state where God's will is law. Democracy, communism, capitalism—those are all nonsense. The highest truth is the Koran."

He continues proselytizing. He and his men have no fear of death; to die for such a holy cause is to become a saint. The Artist then brags of fighting in Chechnya and hints that he has met the Chechen rebel leader Shamil Basayev.

The name is familiar to the Ukrainians gathered under the trees. Basayev is the Chechen field commander who proclaimed a jihad to rid the Caucasus nations of the Russian army. Commander of eleven thousand Chechen troops in his heyday during the mid-nineties, he led his army through the bloody fight for the city of Grozny, expelling the Russians in the first Chechen war but ultimately being driven out by another Russian offensive. He has fought in Tajikistan, Afghanistan, and Nagorno-Karabakh, and now he hides in the mountains of Dagestan, where he plots spectacular displays of terrorism aimed at taking the Chechen war onto Russian soil. He is blamed for blowing up two apartment buildings that killed three hundred civilians in Moscow in 1999, and he led the second-largest mass hostage-taking ever organized when, in 1995, he crept through heavily guarded Russian lines with one hundred men and took fifteen hundred people hostage in a hospital in southern Russia. His demand: that Russia end its war with Chechnya. One hundred twenty people died in that hostage crisis, half of them killed in Basayev's initial attack, the others when Russian troops stormed the hospital. An even larger hostage crisis came a year later, when three hundred rebels commanded by Basayev's comrade-in-arms, Salman Raduyev, infiltrated Dagestan (which was fighting a war of independence with Russia) and took control of a Russian hospital containing thirty-four hundred people. And it was Basayev's men who planted a container filled with radioactive cesium-137 in a Moscow park and informed Russian television journalists of its location. Had the container been armed with an explosive device and detonated, radioactive material would have showered the city.

If it is the school for terrorism of Shamil Basayev that these rebels are graduates of, Chaplinsky and his fellow hostages think to themselves, then they are in the hands of dangerous men. One by one, the hostages fall into a fitful sleep. Whenever one of them lifts an eyelid to see if their guards are napping, they see a rebel peering back.

———

THE NEXT MORNING, at six o'clock on August 12, the group continues down the canyon. The Artist leads the way, moving stealthily ahead of the hostages, while Wolf and Hamsa walk in the rear. The shepherds' huts appear deserted, though they sense the presence of the Kyrgyz families inside, hiding in fear. At an abandoned *khosh* not far above the junction of the Kara Su and Ak Su Rivers, they stop to rest. Inside, the rebels heap up a pile of kindling and light a small fire. In a tin pot they make tea, which they pass around to one another and their captives. They snack on food they have brought from base camp. Chaplinsky again makes conversation with his captors.

"Where are you from?" he asks Wolf.

Like the Artist, he's an Uzbek, and an eight-year veteran of the jihad. The rebel tells Chaplinsky that the Taliban has established the right kind of state, and that he and his fellow rebels are bringing that way of life to Uzbekistan. He talks of their band of rebels as if they are a tribe, and he makes it clear that no one ever leaves the tribe—except in death.

"Do you have a wife?" Chaplinsky asks.

"No," he says in a tone of resignation. "I have never known anything but ploughs and guns."

Wolf sees Chaplinsky eyeing his weapon.

"Kalashnikov," he says proudly. "Reliable. American weapons are just for one fight, then throw them away." He laughs.

Chaplinsky checks his watch: noon. They have been inside the hut for four hours, waiting, he assumes, for the other rebels to return with the Americans. He suddenly hears the thunder of a helicopter echoing off the canyon walls.

Wolf shouts, "Don't move! Just sit!"

The machine hovers a couple of hundred feet above them. The noise rattles the old *khosh*. Years of dust and soot caked onto the walls and rafters shake to the floor. The three rebels peep at the helicopter through cracks in the clay walls. It lands on the hillside somewhere above them.

"Maybe it's the army," Natasha Kolysnik whispers to her husband. She is right. Helicopters are deploying detachments of Spetsnaz—special forces—as well as Skorpion commandos and border guards. By day's end 130 Kyrgyz soldiers will surround the rebels. The helicopters depart after a few minutes, and the rebels hustle the hostages out of the hut.

"Hurry!" Wolf orders in a hushed voice, ushering the hostages down the trail. The rebels are twitchy, nervous. They peer through the brush toward the hillsides, looking for soldiers but seeing none. They march less than a mile, then hide everyone among a tangle of trees growing beside the river. They sit quietly, then at 2 P.M. the eruption of distant gunfire startles them all. The shooting is heavy, and it comes from the river junction two hours beyond their hiding spot. One moment it seems that dozens of guns are firing at once; the next moment all is quiet. For the remainder of the daylight hours of August 12 the six hostages and the three rebels huddle in the riverside hideout, listening to the ebb and flow of a violent firefight. With darkness, the shooting fades to occasional single shots.

LATER IN THE NIGHT Natasha Kolysnik sees Wolf and the Artist creep out of camp. Before they leave she hears Wolf order Hamsa to guard the hostages until they return.

"What if you don't come back?" Hamsa asks him.

Wolf replies in Uzbek, but there is no ambiguity about his meaning.

"If we don't return in two hours," Wolf says, then he makes the sign of the slit throat.

Natasha said later, "Hamsa's face went pale, and we became very scared. It was clear to me right then that he didn't know how to kill."

Wolf and the Artist leave. Hamsa sits alone, several feet from the hostages, with his weapon on his lap. He stares at them with what looks like anger, perhaps because it is easier to kill people you despise. Wolf and the Artist have remained distant throughout, machines of the jihad who eat, sleep, fight, and kill. But Hamsa seems different to Natasha. She edges toward him.

"I just wanted to sit next to you and your gun so it wouldn't be so frightening."

"How is it possible to shoot a person?" Hamsa asks.

"It's all right," she tells him comfortingly. "You won't have to kill any-one."

THEIR SURVIVAL DEPENDS on the bridge she is building between her-self and the rebel. She tells him stories about their lives in Rostov-on-Don, and about her and Vasili's teenage daughter, Golya. Then she asks Hamsa about his family. His eyes gloss at the thought. He talks like a boy who wants nothing more than to go home, who misses his parents, who is as afraid of Wolf and the Artist as he is of the Kyrgyz soldiers who are hunting him. Yet the fanatic in Hamsa is never far below the surface. He wipes his eyes and steels himself with a lecture to Natasha about his jihad. She has no idea that only a few hours earlier he had been present at the torture and execu-tion of Kyrgyz soldiers in the Ortochashma valley.

11.

UNDER FIRE

———

KARA SU AND KARAVSHIN VALLEYS

AUGUST 12-13

In the Kara Su valley, at around 11 A.M. on August 12, Abdul orders his American prisoners to dismantle base camp. They pull tent stakes out of the ground, slide poles from the tents, and start bundling everything into duffel bags. When Osmanov tugs one of the long aluminum tent stakes out of the ground, he taps the pointed end with his fingertip. Catching Smith's eye, he makes a stabbing motion with the stake. The soldier wears a look of desperation. Smith can see that he's suggesting they use the slivers of aluminum as daggers. He scans the ransacked camp. The odds are not very good. The three men carrying assault rifles are alert and wary, trained killers besides. Violence and hand-to-hand combat using flimsy tent stakes are not among the skills that climbing has taught Smith or his friends.

"No way," Smith whispers, shaking his head. "No way."

"Passporty!" Abdul shouts.

The climbers retrieve their passports from their scattered belongings. Certain now that they are going on a long walk, they round up anything they can fit in their pockets that may be useful to them: Smith takes his credit card; Rodden stuffs her pockets with PowerBars; Caldwell grabs a credit card and a bottle of antibiotics and furtively slips a wad of cash—two hundred dollars in twenties—into his sock. They make no mention of another wad of cash stashed in the camp; it will remain there, like buried treasure. Yet the rebels have not asked for money. They seem interested only in food and supplies.

They offer the passports to Abdul, but he shakes his head and points to the chest pocket in Dickey's shirt, so they tuck their passports into their own pockets. Dickey turns to Rodden.

"That's a good sign, Beth," he tells her. "It means they want us alive."

Rodden nods. She is trembling. The events unfolding around her are incomprehensible. She knows nothing of Islam, let alone militant Islam. She has never heard of the Taliban or Osama bin Laden. The one thing she does understand—that she is the sole woman among these men—makes her particularly apprehensive. *What'll these guys do to me?* her racing mind asks. A year earlier, on her first trip to the Third World, to Madagascar, she was emotionally overwhelmed by the constant attention of the Malagasy children who, laughing and jostling, had surrounded her to touch her golden blond hair. Now, on her second expedition abroad, she is in the hands of kidnappers.

As they dismantle the large yellow tent, Abdul sorts through the personal belongings of the four climbers that lay strewn on the ground. Among the pile of things from Rodden and Caldwell's tent is a tampon packet. Abdul peels the wrapping from it, sniffs it, and thrusts it toward them. He seems to be asking if it is food. Rodden shakes her head. Abdul tosses the tampon aside. Then the rebel finds a Polaroid photo of the couple, smiling, arm in arm. Abdul shows the photo to Obid and Su, and they all examine it. Abdul has been studying the couple's every move, as if trying to figure out the state of their relationship. When Rodden gets the message across to Abdul that she needs to move away from the group to relieve herself, Caldwell accompanies her to the edge of the camp and stands watch while she urinates behind a rock. Abdul gapes at this display of familiarity between her and Caldwell. Turning to his hostages, he points to his finger and makes the sign of a wedding ring, then he points to the couple.

"Yes—married," Dickey loudly interjects as soon as he understands Abdul's question. If these men think the two are married, Rodden, he reasons, may be safer.

Abdul, who lives in an archly conservative moral universe of Taliban thinking, is accustomed to a world in which unchaperoned relations between couples is forbidden. Adulterers are stoned to death. Western dress is considered sinful; Afghan women wear, by decree, the all-enveloping head-to-toe veil called the *burkha.* Education and employment are forbidden to women. Even in the case of illness, male doctors are forbidden from touching or seeing anything but the "affected parts" of a woman patient.

A directive for women issued by the Taliban's leadership and the religious police reads in part:

> Women you should not step out of your residence. If you go outside the house you should not be like women who used to go with fashionable clothes wearing much cosmetics and appearing in front of every man before the coming of Islam. . . . Women should not create the opportunity to attract the attention of useless people who will not look at them with a good eye. . . . In case women are required to go outside the residence for the purposes of education, social needs or social services they should cover themselves in accordance with Islamic Shari'a regulation. If women are going outside with fashionable, ornamental, tight and charming clothes to show themselves, they will be cursed by the Islamic Shari'a and should never expect to go to heaven. . . . We request all family elders to keep tight control over their families and avoid these social problems. Otherwise these women will be threatened, investigated and severely punished as well as the family elders by the forces of the Religious Police. The Religious Police have the responsibility and duty to struggle against these social problems and will continue their effort until evil is finished.

By noon the camp is packed into duffels and the rebels order their captives to help them hide the brightly colored bags under the stunted trees surrounding the campsite. Their large dining tent has left a pale imprint of dead grass where it stood. Although their tents have vanished, the yellow patch on the meadow makes the campsite plainly visible.

Su, by now, has marched down the valley a few hundred yards, taking one of the Motorolas owned by the Americans. Abdul holds the other radio, and it squawks to life with a message from Su. The news sends Abdul into a frenzy. He runs to Obid, who these past few minutes has flopped out under the shade of a tree and fallen soundly asleep. Shouting wildly, Abdul kicks him in the leg to wake him, while simultaneously hurling a ski pole at Osmanov and ordering him to his feet. Abdul motions for everyone to crawl under the sparse greenery fringing the camp.

Seconds later the cause of Abdul's tantrum becomes apparent when the windy roar of an Mi8 helicopter gunship fills the valley. The climbers watch through branches as the dronelike machine flies up the river, several hundred feet off the ground. As it carves a wide, slow turn in the air over the edge of camp, the climbers and their captors see that one last orange duffel bag has been unintentionally left in the open. Abdul's eyes alternate between the duffel and the chopper, and he keeps his finger on the trigger of his rifle. When he sees that Rodden, crouched beside him, is distraught, an unexpected smile cracks his face. Like a father soothing a scared child, he shakes his finger at her. "Don't cry," he signs, pointing at her tears.

A minute later the helicopter leans its nose into the air and flies back down the valley, veering over the ridge toward the Ak Su. Abdul rouses everyone out from the bushes. They shoulder the heavy rucksacks and quit camp at a brisk pace.

"Where are we going?" Caldwell asks Osmanov, with a series of shrugs and pointing gestures.

Osmanov shakes his head. He points downriver, the direction in which they are heading. "Uzbekistan," he says. Then he points the other way, toward the snowcapped peaks at the head of the Kara Su valley. "Tajikistan," he adds. Then Osmanov stumbles forward along the well-worn cattle trail. The former country is fifty miles to the north, the latter's border seven miles to the south. Osmanov does not know where they are going, but for some of them, judging by their well-stocked rucksacks, a long walk is planned.

They are only three hundred yards from camp when the helicopter makes another sweep. Abdul rounds up the captives, pushing those nearest him under a thorny thicket of wild-rose and juniper brush. Dickey takes to the cover too slowly for Abdul's liking, and in an instant he finds the rebel's face inches from his own, shouting hysterically. His eyes are wide and white-rimmed, saliva sprays from his lips, his breath is bitter. Leveling his weapon point-blank at Dickey's head, Abdul leaves no doubt as to his meaning: move toward that helicopter and you're dead. Dickey backs into the greenery. This is a madman, he thinks, as the noise of the helicopter becomes a roar.

The Mi8 heads directly to the Yellow Wall, where it circles to gain height till it is level with the deserted portaledge camp. It hovers long enough to see that the platforms on the cliff are abandoned, then it flies off again. They resume their march. Scouting for soldiers, the rebels creep from boulder to bush along the riverside trail, keeping a watchful eye on their captives, who follow a few steps behind them.

They pass the homes of Kyrgyz families who supplied them with yogurt and bread during better days. At the house of the young shepherd Ulan, Abdul pauses and calls out. Ulan's elderly father appears in the doorway, looking tense. Fortunately for Ulan, who told the Americans he was in the army, he left for Osh several days earlier. Frightened women and children huddle inside his house, peering at the Americans from behind the old man. Abdul questions Ulan's father. The elder raises his hand and points northward, down the river. He directs the rebels to the trail that cuts over the hill, to the Ak Su. The old man glances quickly at the Americans before turning back into his house.

While they walk, Smith tries to reassure Rodden. "Beth, listen up," he tells her. "Your concern is no longer Beth. I'm thinking about Beth from now on. All you are thinking about is whatever these men tell you to do. If you see a helicopter, I want you to play James Bond and jump headfirst into whatever tree these guys tell you to jump into. This is just a big giant video game, and we are gonna turn it off in a couple of hours. Okay?"

Rodden nods. She is, by nature, quiet, a listener; Smith is a talker. He is, however, no less terrified than she is.

By early afternoon they have cut across the hill between the two rivers, and they stand looking down on the hamlet of Karavshy. Below them the trail crosses the Ak Su by a log footbridge. Abdul pulls a pair of binoculars from his battle vest and trains them on the hillside opposite. He waves to someone on the other side, suggesting to the Americans that more rebels are waiting there. Then Abdul turns the binoculars on a farmhouse three hundred yards below them. Among a clutter of fences, goats, and cows, he sees a green army tent and two Kyrgyz soldiers at the rear of the house, talking to a shepherd. The rebels become agitated, whispering and pointing at the soldiers. Easing back from their positions and treading carefully so as not to dislodge rocks or snap branches, they order the prisoners to creep farther uphill. When they are out of sight of the farmhouse, Abdul makes everyone break into a run.

"Oh, fuck, these guys are gonna start shooting any minute," Smith whispers to Dickey as they move.

Dickey's teeth chatter and his flesh twitches with involuntary spasms. He has noticed the way that they all speak in fits and stutters. Climbing is a field in which keeping a lid on an array of fears is key to success and survival. Between the four Americans they have experienced enough storm and steepness to cope with almost anything a mountain of rock can throw at them. But being menaced by murderous outlaws with uncertain intentions is beyond their ken. Dickey, for one, comprehends that on this day he has topped his personal Richter scale of fear.

The heavy rucksacks press into their backs, and their lungs burn as they climb the hill. When Rodden lags behind, Smith grabs her rucksack from her back and drags it up the hill along with his own. Hers is bright orange. A sure target, he thinks to himself.

Ten minutes later they stop below the hillcrest. The footbridge over the Ak Su is directly beneath them. They lie sweating and gasping amid long yellow grass and wildflowers. Smith returns Rodden's rucksack to her. When they hear Abdul shouting at Osmanov in a threatening tone they look up. The rebel points to his gun, points to Osmanov, and waves his hand about. The Americans get the sense that Abdul is warning Osmanov that he'll shoot him if he alerts the soldiers. The Kyrgyz soldier stares back at Abdul with a stony expression. Before they can regain their breath they set off again, skirting farther around the hill into the Ak Su valley. After a few hundred yards they stop among some bushes. Abdul moves off to scout the path, leaving Obid stationed a few feet away.

When the climbers look at Osmanov they see a face seething with anger. He makes a motion with his hands of throttling their guards. It seems to Smith that he is inciting them to fight their captors. Obid looks on, unmoved, panting, his rifle ready. The Americans stare at Osmanov in confusion. If they offer any resistance, Obid will surely cut them down with his weapon.

"Listen, everyone," Dickey says, sensing the tension pumping through the air. "They obviously want us alive. That's why we're carrying all this food and clothing and our passports."

Eventually Osmanov becomes quiet. He scratches in the sand at his feet with a twig, then looks up. "Over there," he says in Russian, pointing to the hill above the footbridge, then sweeping his fingertips across his throat and pointing to himself. "Over there they kill me."

Caldwell and Smith stare incredulously back at the soldier. Osmanov's meaning is crystal clear.

"*Nyet, nyet,*" the Americans reply, shaking their heads. "You'll be okay."

Abdul returns and herds them straight down the hill to the river. They pass the crumbling walls of an old farm building, then they cross the log-and-plank footbridge over the Ak Su, one by one. There is no chance to try to escape, as they move under the guns of Obid and Abdul, who stand on either side of the river. On the east side of the Ak Su they leave the trail and scramble up a brush-covered hillside for a few hundred feet. At a wooded, rocky area they halt. The rebels divide the hostages into two groups. Smith and Dickey occupy a depression, while Rodden, Caldwell, and Osmanov sit fifteen feet away and slightly below them, among low rocks and tree branches. Abdul crouches behind a lump of granite between the two groups, while Obid moves off several dozen yards to their side. They wait quietly. Rocks and tree roots dig into their backs uncomfortably. Smith and Osmanov sleep. Caldwell and Rodden hug each other.

"We're going to be okay," Caldwell tells Rodden repeatedly. "I'm going to look after you."

Dickey lies listening to the whisper of unfamiliar voices coming from the small boulders dotting the hillside behind him. More rebels, he thinks. It dawns on him that Abdul's men may be laying an ambush for the Kyrgyz soldiers who must have arrived on the helicopter. The footbridge is fifteen hundred feet away, and the rebel position overlooks it. Any soldier crossing it will be in the line of fire.

On the west bank of the Ak Su thirty-eight soldiers of the Border Patrol of the Southern Army Group—Pogranichky, as locals call the border guards—have taken up positions among the ruined buildings and rocks around Karavshy. Shepherds have tipped the army off to the rebel position and have told them that foreigners are among them. The soldiers know about their murdered comrades at Mazar. They want the rebels dead, but they cannot see them. At 2 P.M. they send three men toward the footbridge.

The ear-splitting crack of more than forty weapons firing thousands of rounds in concert jars the climbers to attention. The Kyrgyz soldiers have sniper rifles with telescopic sights, RPK machine guns, and AK-74 rifles firing 7.62-by-54-millimeter rounds. The soldiers also have carted in a heavy weapon—an SPG-9 antitank gun that fires an armor-piercing shell. The smell of spent rounds, the ping of ejected shell casings, and ricochets of incoming fire are everywhere. The climbers draw in their limbs and crunch into the smallest shapes they can make. A fine sliver of hot metal flies down Caldwell's back, burning his skin. When Rodden glances up, she sees a Kyrgyz soldier near the bridge. He drops to the ground, then rolls downhill for ten feet, killed or wounded, she cannot tell. Simultaneously, another soldier goes down beside him. Meanwhile, inside a farmhouse several yards downstream, Murat Kalnarazov huddles with his family. His four children scream and cry as stray bullets hit the clay walls. As the shooting grows more intense he becomes certain that they'll all be killed, so he kicks a hole through the rear of his house and the family runs. Kalnarazov—Homer Simpson to the Americans—has had more than enough violence in recent days. The previous morning Abdul had barged into his hut, held a rifle to the shepherd's head, and threatened to kill him and his family unless he revealed the way to the climbers' camps.

The weapon firing behind Dickey and Smith is Abdul's, and it sounds like a cannon. It's the long-barreled gun that Obid had been holding at the base of the Yellow Wall. A fast action RPK-74 light machine gun, it is a longer-range, higher-velocity weapon than the Kalashnikovs the other rebels shoulder. Abdul fires bursts of three and four shots from it, sighting his targets with the steady hand of a hunter of men. He captured the weapon from the Kyrgyz patrol he had ambushed two days earlier. A half hour into the firefight Dickey turns his head toward Abdul's position and their eyes connect. The rebel orders him to leave his shelter and join him behind the boulder he's firing from. Dickey crawls toward Abdul on his hands and knees and crouches next to him behind the insubstantial cover. Then Abdul does something so inexplicable that even today it puzzles Dickey: he drops the weapon from his shoulder and lays it on the ground in front of Dickey. He looks into the American's eyes, then to the weapon, then back to the American. The gun is inches from Dickey's hands. Is he suggesting Dickey should shoot back at the Kyrgyz soldiers, like a prisoner conscript? Does he want the border guards to think that Dickey is another rebel, bluffing them into believing that the rebel force is stronger? Or could Abdul be testing Dickey—he alone among the Americans has a beard—to see if he'll willingly join his cause?

Dickey looks back and forth between Abdul and the weapon. He does not fathom the workings of this man's mind. For all he knows, the offer to take up the rifle might be some perverse trick: touch the weapon and Abdul might draw his side arm and waste him right there. Whatever Abdul's game may be, Dickey doesn't play. A bullet glances off the boulder they huddle behind, then the rebel sends Dickey back to his shelter. Smith is hyperventilating when his friend crawls back to his spot beside him; he'd felt sure Abdul was going to execute Dickey.

Shooting continues sporadically for several more minutes. During a lull, Abdul slides into the shelter where Rodden, Caldwell, and Osmanov hide. They are curled into balls, sheltering their faces with their hands from rock chips thrown up by incoming bullets. Caldwell has his arms wrapped around Rodden. When Abdul utters a monosyllabic grunt at Osmanov, Caldwell detects a tone of finality to the order. The rebel commander has told the soldier to move to the low, car-sized boulder two hundred feet up the hill. Caldwell shifts his eyes from man to man. Their two faces are locked in hatred. A pivotal moment has arrived for Osmanov, but if he is scared, he shows no sign of it. Weeks later Caldwell will remember this moment. "The toughest man I've ever seen," he'll say of the soldier. When Osmanov stands to leave, Rodden weeps and shakes inconsolably.

Osmanov turns to her. He takes a piece of candy from his pocket and presses it into her hand. In the mix of words and gestures with which they have learned to communicate, he makes clear the message: "You, don't cry. I don't cry, and I am the one who will die." He stands and runs through gunfire, disappearing behind the boulder where the other rebels are firing. Abdul follows seconds later. A minute passes, then Caldwell and Rodden hear two pistol shots.

BY LATE AFTERNOON the fire from the border guards starts homing in on them with greater accuracy as men who have somehow crossed the river begin to outflank the rebel positions. Abdul reappears in Dickey and Smith's shelter. He announces with a flurry of shouts and pointing that everyone must move to the boulder where Osmanov had been sent.

"To *soldat:* Go," Abdul orders, pushing Dickey out of the shelter. *Soldat* means "soldier"—in this case, one of the rebels.

Dickey's rucksack is the heaviest, and it slows him down as he runs uphill for two hundred feet. Uncertain at this point whether the running figure is a rebel or a hostage, the Kyrgyz soldiers draw a bead on Dickey. Puffs of dirt fly up where bullets strike the ground around him. A rebel behind the boulder shouts and motions at him to hurry. Dickey dives behind a three-foot-tall rock halfway to the boulder, sloughs off the rucksack and ditches it. While he covers the final few yards, the rucksack takes a direct hit. Days later, the rucksack will be recovered by Kyrgyz soldiers, and they'll see a bullet hole in its waistband.

At the boulder Dickey recoils from the sight of Osmanov's corpse, lying facedown right in front of him. Dickey, with his head down low in his own shelter, has been unaware of the execution. Now he wonders if they'll all be shot behind the boulder, but Su reappears, along with a rebel they have not met before, and the two men pull Dickey to a safe position. Smith runs to the boulder next, then Rodden. When she arrives Smith twists her head away from the body.

"Listen to me!" Smith shouts. "You are not going to look over to the left. You are just going to sit here and watch Tommy as he comes in."

Caldwell arrives, chased by bullets. He latches on to Rodden reflexively, wrapping himself around her. Finally, Abdul runs in, crouching beside them all. Obid is nowhere to be seen, having been dispatched to a position farther uphill at the beginning of the battle.

Lying low, the Americans barricade themselves behind their three remaining rucksacks as an upsurge of shooting begins. Behind the boulder the rebels move around freely, leveling their weapons over their heads from behind their cover, firing off short bursts. They seem to have no fear of being hit. A rebel they have not met before laughs when he sees the Americans cowering from the rock chips that spray out whenever a Kyrgyz bullet strikes the edge of the boulder. Crouching in front of them and smiling, he holds up a small granite flake, then he points to the clip on his rifle and shakes his head. Don't be scared, he is telling them; the air is full of rocks, not bullets. He catches Smith's eye and extends his hand.

"Abdullah," he says, introducing himself. He's heavily bearded, like Abdul, and he shakes their hands vigorously, smiling as if it's just another day. The Americans clasp his hand with limp-wristed grips. "I kept saying to myself, 'This isn't happening, this is a dream,' " Caldwell recalls later.

Abdullah reaches into his pocket and pulls out an apple, which he throws to Abdul. The rebel commander crunches into it. Then Abdullah leans against Osmanov's corpse, as if it's a piece of furniture. With zero visible emotion he picks up the dead soldier's arm and lets it drop. Abdul laughs, then he too sidles up to the corpse and kicks at Osmanov's legs. When he has cleared enough room, he removes a prayer mat, one foot square, from his gear-laden battle vest, lays it on the ground, kneels, and begins his evening prayer. Rodden is no longer crying. Like the rest of her companions she stares blankly at the madness surrounding them. After Abdul has finished praying, Obid, Abdullah, and Su take their turns. They kneel toward Mecca, beside a dead man, with bullets flying over their heads. Smith sits staring at Osmanov's body. The soldier lies facedown with his arms flat against his sides. The left side of his head is turned upward, showing a pulpy, mashed-in dent. Blood is pooled around him, saturating his black hair.

"I realized that we might be seeing a lot of that sort of thing before this was over, and I had to know how I would react to it," Smith would later say. "I stared at Turat for nearly an hour. Eventually, it didn't affect me anymore, and that was good." The climbers will never know for certain which one of the mujaheddin murdered Turat Osmanov.

Near sundown an antitank round explodes in front of the boulder. A shudder vibrates the ground like an earthquake, and a wave of dirt sprays over onto everyone behind it. The climbers huddle together in a ball of arms and legs, and the rebels crouch low, shooting blindly over the top of the boulder at the border guards, who seem to be getting closer. The sound of a helicopter, spotting high overhead, adds to the chaos. The Mi8 is packed with rockets and machine guns, but seeing the Americans, it does not fire. Looking for shelter, Smith crouches over Osmanov, practically sitting on his legs. He considers pulling the body around him and his friends as cover, but the head wound is grotesque. Despite all the blood and noise, hunger overcomes the hostages' fear and revulsion. They numbly devour a packet of cookies.

At about 6 P.M. Abdul gives another order to change positions. He makes the Americans shoulder the three remaining rucksacks and sends them running to a small tree twenty feet away, but the rifle fire is so heavy that they dump two of the rucksacks near the tree and retreat to the boulder. Bullets chip away at the tree, then they hear another antitank round ripping through the air. It sounds like an angry hornet and demolishes the tree.

"I don't know whose side I'm on in this fight!" Smith shouts. Like all of them, he's trying to think the situation through. Do the Kyrgyz know they're there, or not? Given the intense fire all around them, he concludes that the soldiers either don't realize or don't care, that they are among the rebels. If the Kyrgyz close in on them, laying down fire as they approach, the Americans will be shot full of holes; if the rebels escape the shoot-out, they'll remain hostages. Either way, he decides, he and his friends lose.

With everyone now behind the boulder, Abdul prepares them to make a break into the hills. He empties out the climbers' last rucksack, dumping heavy cans and packets of food, reducing the load to an odd array of items that they divide among them: Dickey is handed Osmanov's sleeping bag in its green sack, and Caldwell takes charge of a small zippered toiletry kit bag containing a dozen PowerBars, a candy bar, and a bottle of his contact lens solution. Caldwell and Smith wear insulated jackets, but Dickey and Rodden have lost their warm clothes in the abandoned rucksacks. The other rebels carry nothing except ammunition. When Abdul indicates that they are about to leave, Dickey points to his friends, to the ground they stand on, and clasps his hands.

"Please," he implores, "leave us here. We'll only slow you down. You can get away without us." They all join in, begging for freedom. The cacophony of pleading angers Abdul. When they see him winding up for another tirade, they shut up and prepare to move.

At dusk a third projectile blasts the hillside eighty feet above them. Then, a few minutes later, night surrounds them and Abdul sends the Americans running uphill. Occasional bursts of fire ring out as they move from tree to tree. Everyone, rebels and prisoners alike, staggers with fatigue. It has been hours since they've had a drop of water. Dehydration makes their leg muscles cramp.

Rodden and Smith run up the rear. When she lags behind, he grabs her by the collar and propels her toward the cover of a tree. Behind it he lies over her, protectively. Twenty days earlier and a world away at San Francisco International Airport, Smith told Rodden's father that he'd look after his daughter and "absolutely one hundred percent make sure nothing happened to her." He also fired off a glib, tongue-in-cheek, yet prescient e-mail on the eve of their departure: "Dear Friends: Tommy Caldwell, Beth Rodden, John Dickey and myself are headed for the mountains of Kyrgyzstan for some fun in the sun. I wish you all happy and safe travels this summer and I pledge to do the same. After all, I don't have to be able to outrun AK-47–toting terrorists—just Beth."

They gain thirteen hundred feet of elevation on the hillside, then moonlight paints the ground silver. Shunning the light and possible detection, the group traverses the hillside sideways. As they move, Caldwell and Rodden see a red light blinking brightly on the Motorola in Abdul's hand, indicating a low battery. It flashes all night. They wonder how their captor can ignore it, and they worry that it might attract a Kyrgyz sniper. At about eleven o'clock they round a ridge crest and stand above the valley of the

Jopaiya River. The four Americans, plus four rebels, rest on the ridge, among boulders and trees. Abdul broods quietly, Su falls asleep, and Obid brushes his teeth with a toothbrush stolen from the German camp. He turns to the Americans and produces five pieces of hard candy from his pocket. Holding them in his palm, he takes one for himself and hands a piece to each hostage. The gesture surprises Smith, as the rebel offers nothing to his comrades, but he takes the candy and pops it into his mouth. Smith pulls his passport from his pocket, opens it, and points out his birth date to the young rebel.

"Twenty-two," he tells him. "I am twenty-two years old." He writes the number with his finger in the air. "Twenty-two. You, how old?" He points to Obid.

Obid replies by inscribing the number 19 in the air. Smith points to himself again. "California. I live in California."

"Caleeforneeya." The rebel mouths the word and nods. It seems a familiar-sounding place to him, one he may have heard mentioned on a radio station. Obid points to himself. "Tashkent," he replies. So, the man is an Uzbek.

The group steals an hour of sleep, then at around midnight the rebels begin chattering, planning. Obid and Abdullah march off across the hillside, heading south. Abdul and Su rouse the hostages and march them downhill. They stumble through the dark morning, down rubble-filled gullies and grassy slopes crisscrossed by goat paths. At about 3 A.M. on August 13 the ground levels out and they arrive at the Jopaiya River. They have been moving for eighteen hours, and it seems that no one can walk any farther. Abdul scouts around the bank of the crashing river as if looking for something, then after a few minutes he returns and separates the Americans into pairs. Abdul urges Dickey and Rodden to move in one direction; Su takes Smith and Caldwell in the other. The parting is sudden and distressing.

Abdul and his prisoners march to an elbow in the river where water action has carved a small cave out of the dirt and rounded stones of the embankment. The hole is mud-floored and cramped, more a shelter for a water rat than for a human. At first Dickey cannot believe that Abdul is serious when he motions them to crawl inside it.

"You must be kidding!" he says.

"What is he saying? Are we supposed to get in there?" Rodden asks, incredulous.

"Impossible! We won't fit in that small-ass little hole," Dickey tells Abdul, shaking his head. But Abdul presses Dickey forward with a suggestive touch of his rifle butt.

The cave is eighteen inches tall at its highest point. It is cramped for Rodden, who is five-feet-one, but Dickey, at six feet, must lie with his knees to his chest. Abdul badgers them to crawl in deeper till their feet are out of sight of the entrance, then he covers the cave with reeds and broadleaf plants. He stations himself at the opening and camouflages his own body with more greenery. There they lie, through the dawn and the daylight of August 13.

12.

THE CROSSING

JOPAIYA RIVER

AUGUST 13–14

I t is something of a point of pride among mountaineers to be able to suffer through any sort of uncomfortable or frigid bivouac in the name of getting to the top of a peak, but the riverside cave that Rodden and Dickey occupy for seventeen hours on August 13 is more torture than bivy. Dickey lies on his side, with his knees raised against his torso, his head jammed into an alcove of dirt, and his cheek pressed against a cold, rounded stone. He's also lying on Abdul's weapon, which the rebel has slid into the hole. The cold metal barrel digs into Dickey's back. Rodden occupies a smaller cavity, with Dickey spooned around her. "We had to get extremely intimate on a right-now basis," he'd later say of the experience.

The river they are beside, the Jopaiya, is fed by a glacier three miles upstream. The water pouring from its icy snout at 11,500 feet above sea level is frigid, and the wind that rips down the canyon chills everything in its path. Dickey and Rodden are dressed in summer-weight thermal shirts and nylon trousers. With daylight comes a hint of sun-warmed air, but as the sun melts the glacial ice, so swells the river. At 1 P.M., water starts welling up through the ground. When inch-deep rivulets begin trickling around their legs and hips, they scoop together tiny dams of rocks and dirt, but the barriers wash away.

"I'm getting wet," Rodden says. "How long do you figure we're going to be in here?"

"All day, I think," Dickey says. "I'm guessing they only want to travel at night, to hide from the soldiers."

"That asshole. He's got a space four times bigger than us, and he's dry." Rodden gestures angrily at Abdul, who sits at the mouth of the cave on a patch of sand, elevated above the rising water.

Dickey tries to get Abdul's attention. "Hey, it's getting wet in here. Hello? Water. Getting wet."

Abdul looks in the cave and responds to their plight by passing in a few flat stones. Rodden and Dickey squirm about, sliding the stones under their feet, knees, and hips to raise themselves above the water. By noon the puddle under them is four inches deep and water is soaking into their clothing. Dickey also notices the delicate structural nature of their cave. Rocks of all sizes are held in place by sand and dirt; dampen that matrix and the whole cave could collapse. As the day wears on, erosion sets to work and sodden flakes of dirt begin peeling off the walls.

"Holy shit, this boulder above us could drop onto our heads if this keeps up," Dickey says.

He reaches down and shakes Abdul's foot. When Abdul peers into the hole again, Dickey points to the decaying walls and the water, but Abdul shakes his head as if to tell them, "It is not important." When the shivering sets in it does not stop. Rodden cries softly on and off throughout the day. Her ears still ring from the firefight, and her thoughts replay an endless round of violent scenes: the shot Kyrgyz soldiers collapsing by the bridge; Turat Osmanov lying dead behind the boulder. Much later she will learn that one of the soldiers felled by the bullet, a thirty-seven-year-old captain named Beishen Raimbekov, died on the spot.

"Beth, I know this is awful, but somehow I know we're going to be okay," Dickey says through his chattering teeth when he hears her whimpering.

"They're not going to kill us?"

"No, I really don't think so."

"Why aren't they going to kill us? They killed Turat."

"Turat wasn't of use to them any longer. We are. They want us for ransom."

Rodden worries aloud: Where are Caldwell and Smith? Does anyone know where they are? Will the marines come to rescue them? Dickey comforts her as best he can.

"John, what did you know about this place before we left?" Rodden asks. "Did you know anything about a war or these guys with the guns?"

"I had no idea this shit could come down on us. I would never have come if I did."

Dickey strokes Rodden's forehead and her shoulders. He'll liken their state that day to that of two newborn monkeys he once saw in a zoo, wide-eyed and trembling, huddled together in a fetal curl, clutching at each other out of fear of the unknown. For Rodden and himself, the unknown is all they are certain of. The motives of their captors are a mystery. They don't know whether yesterday's firefight was a rescue mission or a clash between the army and the invaders. Given the intensity and closeness of the fighting, they hold little hope that the Kyrgyz army knows they are prisoners.

When they are not in a trancelike stupor and wracked by shivering, they pass the hours that day, and every day from then on, by talking about their lives back in America. They talk about their parents and grandparents, brothers and sisters, pets, childhoods, and schools. Tracing the arcs of their lives keeps them sane, and it draws the contrasts of their histories: Dickey, the teen hellion rebelling from his staid, religious parents; Rodden, the straight-A student who'd stay home to study or train in the gym for her climbing competitions rather than go to teen parties.

"Why is this happening to us, John?" she asks at one point during the interminable day.

"I guess we were in the wrong place at the wrong time."

"But why us? Did we do something wrong? I keep going over this again and again in my head, trying to figure out what we did wrong. We aren't bad people, are we?"

"No, you are not a bad person, Beth. We did nothing to deserve this. How can you think like that?"

"Everything happens for a reason, right? So I'm trying to figure out what I did wrong, to make this happen. But I can't figure it out. I haven't hurt anyone. I never lied to my parents about anything I've done. I worked hard at school."

In her world there is moral cause and effect. A terrible thing is happening to her, and she cannot figure out what she did to trigger it. "I was trying to justify myself to God, trying to believe that I was a good person," she later explained. "If I could convince myself that we weren't evil, then I could believe in our survival."

THE WATER in their cave recedes with the approach of night and the cooling of the glacier. At 9 P.M. Abdul taps Dickey's leg. It is time to leave. The Americans reverse out of the cave slowly, like two old arthritics. Standing in the dark, Dickey stretches his limbs and manages a few sluggish jumping jacks to get his blood flowing. When Caldwell and Smith appear beside the rumbling river a minute later both groups realize they have been bivouacked no more than a few dozen feet apart. Caldwell and Rodden embrace.

"We had the most heinous bivy," Rodden tells her companions.

"Ours wasn't so bad," Smith says.

Caldwell and Smith, with Su, bivouacked beside the river under an overhang of dirt shrouded by brush; they remained dry and were able to stretch out. They wore their insulated jackets and covered themselves with Osmanov's sleeping bag.

Abdul prays, then when he is finished he presses Su to do the same. The climbers get the impression that Su cares little for the ritual. Prayers finished, all thoughts turn to food. What little nourishment was in their stomachs is long gone, replaced by lonely cramps; their captors are as hungry as they are. The Americans huddle together by the riverbank and divide two Power-

Bars between the four of them. Rodden's jaw muscles lock up when she bites into her chunk, cramping from her incessant, molar-grinding shivering. The sight of the Americans eating attracts Su. He sidles up to them and points to the small wads of food they are stuffing into their mouths.

"Not now," Caldwell says, without thinking that he is stiffing their captor. Su accepts the rebuffing and turns away without a word. The Americans look on, surprised at the rebel's meekness. Abdul is not so meek; he reaches into the sack of food and takes an energy bar. He breaks off a small chunk and passes it to Su, then he munches down the larger portion. A minute later Abdul orders them to move. They walk upstream searching for a place to cross, but the current is strong and the water deep. When they find a log on the riverbank the two rebels begin manhandling it into position, to try to span the river.

The climbers are unaware that on the other side of the Jopaiya is a path that leads upstream past farms to a series of passes. They are unaware even of the river's name, let alone that the passes at the head of the valley connect to the 12,500-foot Tamangan Pass, which leads back toward Tajikistan. Seventy miles from there lies Tavildara, and the stronghold of Juma Namangani.

Abdul enlists the climbers to help shove the log into position. It is large and waterlogged, with a thick mass of gnarled roots that make one end heavier than the other. The engineering problem needs no translation: use the weight of the roots to stand the log upright on the riverbank, rock it into position, then let it fall across the stream and form a bridge. But Abdul and Su tackle the problem in the most illogical manner: they lift the heavy end and throw it out into the stream. The log barely makes it halfway across before the roots snag on a boulder. Standing in the river up to their knees, Abdul and Su jostle and push the log, trying to span the gap. They get nowhere. The fast-flowing water has brought out a timid side of their characters. It is evident that they cannot swim.

"These guys aren't very bright, are they?" Caldwell says. The Americans discuss going over to help them solve the problem, but Dickey laughs unkindly at the idea.

"Ah, let them have at it," he says. "Maybe the bastards will fuck themselves and drown."

Smith, though, has been thinking hard to himself these past few hours, and he has an idea. He removes his shoes and wades into the hip-deep frigid water. When Abdul sees Smith thigh-deep in the river, he beckons him back, shouting and making gestures to say, "Danger, danger, too fast, too fast." Smith ignores him.

Reaching the end of the log, Smith works like a man possessed, muscling it toward the center of the river where the water is deeper and the current can do the work. Near the opposite side of the Jopaiya his feet slip on polished rocks and he drops into a waist-deep hole in the riverbed. He is pushed backward a few yards, but he claws his way back upstream and resumes his work. With a final heave he rolls the wad of roots over a boulder beside the riverbank, then he braces himself between the rock and the wobbling log. Shouting above the river's roar, he motions for everyone to cross. Dickey goes first.

"What the hell was with that?" Dickey asks Smith of his seemingly pro-rebel heroics, when he reaches the other side.

"We gotta get out of here," Smith says.

Watching the rebels bungle the river crossing, Smith realized that there are a lot of things that he and his friends can do to help themselves set the scene for an escape. As Smith will put it later, "One: They should think we were one hundred percent behind their cause. Two: We should show them we were tough as nails because for all we knew they might eliminate the weak; somebody twists an ankle, they would kill them. Three: It would help if we were supercool and helpful to them, because that would lead to . . . Four: They could trust us."

Caldwell runs across the log, carrying Smith's boots, followed by Rodden. When Abdul balances across he pauses at a final hop from the log onto a slippery boulder. Smith sees through the night that Abdul is uncomfortable, even fearful, of the precarious position he's in. Smith extends his hand, and to his astonishment Abdul hands over the long-barreled weapon. Smith passes the gun to Dickey, then grips Abdul's hand. If they are going to seize this moment, there is little time to react: Smith must kick the log out from under Abdul and push him backward into the river, and Dickey must flip the safety on the automatic weapon and shoot both Abdul and Su. If the current overpowers Abdul and he does not catch himself in the river and pull out his pistol, and if Dickey knows where to find the safety release on the trigger box and is willing to kill, they are free. If not, Su and Abdul will kill them all. But they have no plan. The notion of escape is just a wild, spur-of-the-moment thought that they have arrived at as if through telepathy. The moment boils down to kill, or be killed. Or do nothing.

Abdul reaches the bank and plucks his weapon out of Dickey's hands, then he pats Smith on the shoulder. "You *soldat?*" he asks, praising Smith's courage in the river.

On the east side of the river they step across a well-traveled dirt path. Abdul makes a show of teaching the climbers to walk not on the path but on the grass beside it, to leave no footprints. But they only walk a few yards upstream before they head up steep grassy slopes into an area of thick, sharp brush.

Sometime after the night of August 13 has rolled into the early morning of August 14, Abdul orders them to halt.

"Why are we stopping again so soon?" Rodden asks. They are not more than a few hundred yards from the river and their previous hideout. After the confinement of the riverside cave, she dreads the idea of another bivouac.

"I think they're trying to let Abdullah and Obid catch up," Dickey guesses. Regardless of what sort of bivouac is in store for them, he and Smith are glad to sit and rest. Their short journey has seemed like miles. They break out Osmanov's sleeping bag and huddle under it for an hour. Abdul listens to his FM radio. Tribal-sounding music plays faintly from it. Then he switches on the small Motorola and mumbles into it: "Abdullah, Abdullah, Abdullah." After repeating the chant several times, he looks up from the radio and gets the message across to the Americans that they are indeed waiting for the other rebels, to bring food. With hand signs and grunts he depicts a goat, and the act of eating, then he turns his palms and his eyes skyward and invokes the name of Allah. "Allah willing, my men will return with food," the Americans interpret him as saying.

"Yeah, barbecued goat burgers, I'm sure," Dickey remarks. "Singer, rack up the coals and crack me a beer."

"If we're eating goat, it'll be raw," Caldwell says dourly.

"I can't eat raw meat!" Rodden says. "I'll throw up my half of that PowerBar."

Abdul tries the radio again. When there is no reply his optimism becomes a scowling silence. He switches off the Motorola, then takes out the larger black radio that he keeps in his battle vest. He walks a few feet away from the group and whispers into it for several minutes. Whoever he is contacting, he is secretive about it. Even Su doesn't get to hear the conversation.

After his calls, Abdul scours the hilly surroundings for another hiding spot. When he returns he splits the climbers into the same pairs as the previous night and directs them to a snarl of brush growing out of the hillside. He makes them break off branches from the surrounding greenery for additional cover, then orders them to tunnel into the thicket. They occupy a pair of sloping, dusty depressions that appear to have been dug out by animals. Separated by forty feet, and with their captors stationed an arm's length away, they entwine themselves around tree roots and settle in. This time, though, Dickey and Rodden drape Osmanov's sleeping bag over them. The covering makes the cold less penetrating than it was during the dark hours beside the Jopaiya River, but now the discomfort is from within their bodies. With only the brown water of the Jopaiya to drink, the Americans feel their stomachs churn and gurgle from the fine silt—so fine that geologists call such cloudy mountain-born water glacial flour.

SUNRISE BRINGS the distant crack of automatic fire and the sound of helicopters welling over the ridges.

"You know what I think, Tommy?" Smith says when they wake. "I think Obid and Abdullah have snuffed it. I think all that shooting is the end of them."

"Maybe so." Caldwell nods.

Both Americans look over at Su. He sits a couple of feet to their side, sleeping hard. The same thought passes through each of their minds: reach over and take his gun. But then what? Neither of them has ever fired such a weapon, and Rodden and Dickey are out of sight, guarded by a more ruthless man. At the first shot or sound of a struggle, the lives of their companions will be threatened. Separate the man from his woman, and separate both pairs from each other. Abdul keeps his hostages passive not so much by the power of his weaponry but by using their love and friendship for one another against them.

While Su sleeps, the noise of another helicopter rumbles up the valley. Smith reaches over and shakes their supine captor awake.

"Hey, Su, wake up. Here they come." He points skyward.

Smith helps Su add more greenery to camouflage their position. The helicopter passes over the top of them, flying high, then moves on. When it is gone, Smith gives Su a thumbs-up sign and cuts him a big smile.

"Why did you do that?" Caldwell asks.

"I want these guys to think we're all for them. If they trust us, maybe they'll relax and we can get away."

After the helicopter sweep, everyone quietly dozes. But during the afternoon Rodden and Dickey's hearts jump-start when they hear boots crackling over grass and sticks. The footsteps are yards away, though Caldwell and Smith hear nothing. Abdul, sitting a few feet to the left of Dickey, leans over and gently adds more branches to cover his hostages, then brings his weapon close to his chest. The footsteps stop, and two men talk softly at the rear of the hideout. Abdul holds his breath. Dickey and Rodden sit silent, then Rodden hears a faint metallic ping. For one moment she's certain that it's the pin being pulled on the grenade that Abdul carries on his waist. She is about to leap up and run, but she knows if she does, Abdul will shoot her.

But there is no explosion, and the unseen presence evaporates. They stay stone-still for an hour longer, then Abdul starts breathing again.

Rodden whispers to Dickey: "I couldn't see them, but I think they were soldiers. And I think they saw me."

She points to the sunlight falling on her yellow-blond hair. The top of her head is plainly visible through a break in the bushes.

"IN FACT, my soldiers saw the Americans every day," Lieutenant Colonel Akyl Dononbaev would tell me in Bishkek months after the operation had ended. "We had a very strong instruction from our superiors: if you meet the rebels with the hostages, do not fire."

Built like a small sumo wrestler and with a youthful Eurasian face, Dononbaev wears the blue-and-white striped T-shirt and the mottled forest camouflage of Kyrgyzstan's elite Skorpion commandos. When he and his men of the Second Separate Motorized Brigade stepped off the helicopter at Kurbaka on August 11, the smell of death wafting down from Mazar was already strong in the summer heat. Clashing with rebels that morning his brigade would take casualties, and they'd wound a rebel whom they would finish off on the spot. The same day, helicopters would install a radio command post—Mountain One—on an 11,050-foot summit directly above Kurbaka. Detachments of fifteen soldiers would be airlifted to the high ground above the valleys and passes to set up ambushes and block the rebels from escaping. The day following the August 12 firefight between the border guards and the rebels at the Ak Su bridge, Dononbaev's Skorpions would find the body of Turat Osmanov. Nearby, they'd find a dead rebel— one of Abdul's band but one the Americans did not meet. Shepherds would tell Dononbaev that the rebels had marched the Americans down the Kara Su valley. The same shepherds would escort the Skorpions to the American base camp. There the soldiers will find the airline tickets, driver's licenses, bank cards, and a journal of Smith, Dickey, Rodden, and Caldwell. They'll also find the Polaroid photo of the couple in the base camp.

There is sorrow in Dononbaev's voice when he tells me that of the soldiers found slaughtered at Mazar and Kurbaka, he had known eight. When he flew in, their bodies were being bagged for removal.

"I cried all night after I came to that place. I found the body of a friend I had studied with in military school. Both our families were friends, his wife and my wife were friends. He was lying among some stones, and his finger was stuck to the trigger of his gun. There were no more bullets left in his weapon.

"You can imagine the mood of my men when we reached Kurbaka," Dononbaev added. "We were surrounded by the bodies of our soldiers. It brought us all to such a state that we cared about absolutely nothing and were ready to kill the first rebel we met. If there had been no instructions from headquarters to control the fighting around the hostages, we would have shot down everyone—Americans, rebels, all. We were not angry with the Americans, but we felt such frustration that we cared about nothing."

General Bolot Januzakov, secretary of the Kyrgyz Security Council, said that it was around that time that the military intercepted a radio message from Abdul to his base: "We have goods in our hands." By that time, though, Kyrgyz soldiers were tightening their circle around the rebels.

13.

TALKING KILLING

KARAVSHIN VALLEY

AUGUST 14–15

The moon has just passed its fullest stage when the Americans emerge from their hideouts at about 9 P.M. on August 14. Climbers and captors gather together before they begin their third night of wandering, and they divide up another ration of PowerBars. Again, Abdul takes a larger portion for himself. Caldwell and Smith are intrigued when Dickey tells them about the unseen visitors at their bivouac.

"They must have been soldiers," Dickey explains. "But they couldn't do anything because they knew that these guys are sitting right next to us with their guns."

They watch Abdul pull out the Motorola and try again to make contact with Abdullah. By now his dronelike chant is getting to Smith, who is tired and irritable.

"You moron," he mutters, "Abdullah is probably dead and so are the batteries in that radio." The radio barely crackles and the red light flashes like a beacon, but Abdul continues chanting Abdullah's name anyway. Protected by the veil of language, Smith asks Abdul how it feels to be speaking to a dead man.

Their route that night continues uphill, to around ninety-five hundred feet. All the while they look for water. Although they follow the bed of a gully and mountain streams rush loudly in the valley below, the landscape is dry. Hours have passed since their last drink, and their thirst is painfully acute. They follow Abdul on a zigzag course across the hillside. He pauses in spots, laying the palm of his hand flat against the ground and picking sprigs of plants that he holds to his face so he can inhale the scent. He appears to be divining for water, but the ground looks dry and unpromising. But in a grassy depression Abdul stops and waves the group over. When they arrive, he points to a shallow pond no bigger than a soup bowl. He's smirking, as if proud of his find. He scoops aside leaves and dead beetles floating on the surface, and they take turns bending down and slurping their fill from the spring.

"I've never seen anyone who could sniff out water like that," Smith says. "This guy is one awesome survivor." The arid landscapes of Tajikistan and Afghanistan have trained Abdul well.

Caldwell takes his empty contact-lens solution bottle and fills it from the pond, ladling the spring water into it with his hand. His contacts have not been out of his eyes for three days, and his vision is cloudy from the protein-covered lenses. When he blinks, his eyelids grate against his reddened eyeballs. They feel as if they are filled with sand. During a parched moment the previous night he and his companions drank the remainder of the salty lens solution straight out of the bottle.

Dickey and Smith stagger as they thrash through the clinging bushes.

"I'm bogging," Smith tells Rodden, who is right behind him. Bogging—a slang term—is his way of saying that he's stepped over the edge of his physical endurance. Dickey is feeling the effects of their meager diet too. The journey over the pass to Kit Kim Saray burned off what little excess fat had been on their bones. Smith, with his boyish physique, weighs in at just 130 pounds, and with the starvation diet of the past three days, their bodies move as slowly as if they are reaching the summit of Mount Everest without oxygen. With no idea how long they will be wandering through the hills, they have set their ration of half a PowerBar per person, or about one hundred calories, per day.

Smith groans while stepping up a rocky incline. Caldwell reaches back, grabs his hand, and pulls him over it. Moments later Smith flops onto the ground and curls up onto his side. "I can't keep my eyes open," he slurs. He's on the verge of sobbing.

"Jason, eat this," Rodden says, shaking him out of his narcolepsy. She crumbles up their sole candy bar and pushes small chunks of it into his mouth. It's a Three Musketeers bar—how fitting, she thinks. The infusion of calories gets Smith moving again, though he still stops every few paces to regain his breath.

The rebels stash their hostages among another knot of bushes in the predawn hours of August 15. No sooner does Rodden pull the sleeping bag from its stuff sack and drape it over her and Dickey than Abdul drags it away to cover his own legs. The hostages sleep fitfully. Roots and stones dig into their backs, and the cooler air of the higher elevation nips at them. Before sunrise, a bout of irregular breathing coming from Abdul makes Dickey and Rodden each cast an eye toward their captor. He is kneeling with his back to his hostages. His feet are jammed against Dickey's legs. At first the two Americans think Abdul is praying, then they assume he is urinating, something they have gotten used to doing around one another of late.

"John, I think he's . . ." Rodden whispers.

"Just go to sleep," Dickey says abruptly.

Abdul is masturbating. The hostages lay their heads on the dirt, close their eyes, and try to blot out the strangeness.

EARLY ON THE MORNING of August 15 Dickey and Rodden wake to the chatter of small birds flitting among the branches around them. The birds seem to be driving one of their kind from their flock. They screech and peck at the outsider until it flees. Beyond the cage of brush, it's another clear day. The morning hours pass quietly, save for the murmured snatches of song from Dickey and Smith. Music lifts them out of their doldrums. This time it's a Bob Marley song they sing: "Cold ground was my bed last night and rock was my pillow too. . . . Everything's gonna be all right . . ."

There are no sounds of battle this day, but a helicopter passes their hillside bivy at eye level. At nine o'clock Abdul tunes into the news on his FM radio receiver. Among the chatter coming over the airwaves is a familiar name: President Clinton. Whatever the news story is about, it prompts a bellicose laugh from Abdul. He leans toward Dickey and Rodden and babbles at them, as if trying to explain the joke. They understand nothing. But President Clinton's name gives Rodden a ray of hope.

"That was about us!" she says excitedly, while Abdul chuckles in the background. "President Clinton is trying to get us out of here!" In her mind she builds a scenario of high-level discussions and rescue missions by U.S. Marines. She envisions Clinton in Bishkek, and satellites scanning the mountains searching for them with infrared sensors.

Dickey isn't so optimistic. He doubts that America has the slightest idea about their plight, or even that the Kyrgyz army knows they are among these men. At the firefight bullets flew at random, as close to captives as to captors. As hostages, the four Americans exist in an informational vacuum. In that shadowy world, the unseen visitors who passed by their bivy above the Jopaiya River might have been soldiers, or they might have been shepherds being evacuated from the fighting; the helicopter flybys might be a search mission, or they might be the army hunting down rebels. The circuitous path Abdul is leading them on suggests that soldiers are tracking them and turning them away from the passes, yet he's certain of nothing. He worries that if there is another firefight, they'll be shot in the crossfire.

Snatches of sleep during the morning give them reprieve from the uncertainty. When they wake they step back into a nightmare world that they tame with talk. That third morning of their captivity, Dickey tells Rodden about the way he met his girlfriend, Rita Di Lorenzo, a fiery artist and fashion designer of Italian descent.

"We both worked in the same part of San Francisco. I used to see her on the bus. Eventually I got the guts to talk to her. It came out that she had a boyfriend and they were planning to go to Canada. But something clicked between us, and pretty soon she's not going to Canada with this guy, and we're living together in this roach-infested hotel in the middle of all the strip joints of North Beach. The Golden Eagle Hotel. What a dump! Anyway, Rita and I have come up in the world since then, better apartment and all that. We even got married, sort of."

Rodden laughs. "Sort of married?"

"Well, two years ago we were sitting in a seedy old bar in North Beach called Specs, having a few glasses of Scotch, when we suddenly got the idea to get married. The bartender was our man of the cloth. The whole thing was a joke, but we kind of took it seriously at the same time. In fact, we told quite a few people that we were married."

"Maybe you will marry her," Rodden says.

"I'd like to. I really would. I just hope this crazy situation here doesn't screw things up for us, or scare her away."

OVER AT THE BIVOUAC of Smith and Caldwell, killing and escaping are the main topics of conversation. Smith talks; Caldwell listens.

"We've gotta take these guys out somehow, Tommy. If they take us to wherever-the-fuckistan, we could be there for months."

"I don't see how we can."

"All it takes is a rock to the head. It's gotta be a rock just a bit bigger than fist size. Because you've gotta swing fast. The first three blows are the key. First blow they're stunned, second blow they're trying to defend themselves, third blow they go down. Or punch them in the throat and break their larynx. Nobody can take that. It hurts like hell. That could be an option."

"Yeah, I suppose," Caldwell says. Smith has been chewing Caldwell's ear about killing all day. Caldwell isn't comfortable with the line of thought.

"Have you noticed Abdul's holster for his pistol?" Smith continues. "It has a snap on the cover. It'd be easy to get that thing out of the holster if you and John had a hold of him. Wait till his back is turned and get him in a choke hold. Wrap your arm around his neck, and flex your forearm muscles and squeeze."

In Smith's mind, he is trying to turn the strengths they have as climbers to their advantage. He's convinced that Su can be outwitted, and he's certain they can outrun and outclimb the rebels. Now he envisions taking the immense physical strength that allows Caldwell to do a one-armed pull-up from the tips of his fingers and turning it against their captors. But Caldwell isn't so sure.

"Wrestle with Abdul? I don't think so. That guy is a nightmare."

"Yeah . . . he does have that knife on his chest, and that hand grenade pinned to his belt. Maybe the grenade is wired on. First sign of trouble, he pulls the pin and bang, we all go up with him. No, that's too dicey. It has to be quick and quiet, whatever we do."

"How do you know all this shit about killing?" Caldwell asks.

"I hung out with thugs at school. I read *The Anarchist Cookbook*," comes the glib reply. Then Smith pauses and thinks about what is happening to his mind.

"Tommy, when I woke up today I realized that something was different inside me, and I just figured it out. I have lost all compassion for these men. I don't hate them. But I'm ready to do whatever it takes to get out of here."

Smith has already gone far with Su toward laying the groundwork for an escape, by "cracking his icy exterior" and gaining his trust. Although the young rebel's angry-looking demeanor initially intimidated Smith, Su has now warmed to him and Caldwell. While Abdul forces Dickey and Rodden to bivouac in the most confined spaces he can find, as if to break their will, Su lets his charges occasionally sit outside their hideouts and bask in the sun. The Americans have made no move to escape, and Smith always warns Su of the helicopters that fly by three times a day, every day. The Americans are pliant and obedient prisoners. Smith has even gotten Su to call him by his first name, and they've made primitive conversation about matters like their ages and their home countries; Su claims he is nineteen and that he came here from Tashkent (which turns out to be a lie). The trio even share the occasional laugh. In the days ahead, Smith will make a point of offering Su a helping hand to surmount boulders and steep bits of terrain. "Good *alpinista*; good climber, Su," Smith will say, laying on the compliments thick and rich to the tired and clumsy rebel, praising his climbing skills and patting him on the back. Smith regards Su as a slow-witted bumpkin who believes that his prisoners are too weak-willed and scared to try an escape.

As the day wears on, boredom and depression assail everyone as they sit under the canopy of branches. Smith finds a short, sharp stick and repeatedly jams it into the trunk of a tree, seeing how deep he can penetrate the soft wood before it snaps. It must be clear to the rebel what Smith is thinking: the stick is a weapon, and Su's neck or eyeball is the target. But Su doesn't make the connection. He laughs and shakes his head at Smith's obsessive jabbing, and he puts his finger to his lips and says, "Jason, shhh!"

"What do you think, Tommy, should we crack his head in with a rock right now?" Smith asks calmly, while looking directly at Su. "Or should we wait till he falls asleep and we'll wrap my shoelaces around his neck?"

Caldwell doesn't reply. He's unsure who scares him more, Su or Smith. He's seen his share of killing, and he doesn't want any more.

Later, in a moment when Caldwell is alone with Rodden, he quietly voices his concern over Smith's plan to try to "take out" their captors: "He keeps talking about killing these guys. I don't think it's right. Even if we tried, I don't see that we can pull it off."

"John is starting to say the same crazy stuff," Rodden says. "He was lying on Abdul's rifle today while Abdul was right next to us, and he started talking about grabbing it and shooting the guy. These guys will kill us before we'll ever kill them. I want no part of their plan. You stay out of it too, Tommy."

AS THEY CONTOUR AROUND the hillsides high above the river Karavshin on the night of August 15—their fourth night on the run—they compare notes about the hours cooped up in their bivouacs.

"Abdul was full-on choking the chicken," Dickey tells his companions. "He was practically sitting on my legs, beating off. It was so surreal it barely registered with us."

"What did you do when you figured out what he was doing?" Smith asks.

"We just tried to sleep through it. What else can you do when a madman with a gun is whacking off nextdoor?"

At eleven o'clock they arrive at a steep-sided bluff of rock high on a hillside overlooking the Karavshin and Jopaiya Rivers. Here they sit, at around

Tommy Caldwell

TOPHER DONAHUE

Beth Rodden

TOPHER DONAHUE

Jason "Singer" Smith

JOHN DICKEY

John Dickey

JOHN DICKEY

John Bouchard and
Michael Dmitri at the
foot of the Yellow
Wall, November 2000.
Arrow indicates
location of the
portaledges 1,000
feet up the wall.

GARTH WILLIS

The Russian Tower, also called
Slesov Peak, in the Ak Su
valley. German and Australian
climbers scaled this peak prior
to the invasion of IMU rebels
in August 2000.

GREG CHILD

A view down the Ak Su valley glacier from the vicinity of the Boz Toz pass and the peak known as the Bird. At the end of the valley, Peak 4810 rises on the left, and the Russian Tower stands on the right. Rebels of the Islamic Movement of Uzbekistan traveled over this terrain while trying to escape Kyrgyz forces in August 2000. GREG CHILD

Kurbaka, in the Karavshin valley, the army camp where fighting took place in August 2000. GARTH WILLIS

Murat Kalnarazov and his family. This shepherd from the hamlet of Karavshy befriended many climbers during their visits to the Kara Su and Ak Su valleys.
GREG CHILD

Turat Akimov (left) and Lt. Col. Akyl Dononbaev at Dononbaev's Skorpion Base outside Bishkek in March 2001. The memorial is in honor of fallen soldiers of the Batken campaign of August 2000. GREG CHILD

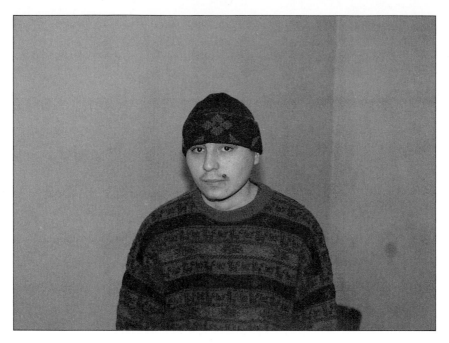

Ravshan Sharipov, KGB prison, Bishkek, March 2001. GREG CHILD

Ruslan Abdullin, KGB prison, Bishkek, March 2001. GREG CHILD

Grave of Turat Osmanov, Tuz Village, March 2001. GREG CHILD

Jason and John speak to reporters in Batken on August 19, 2000.

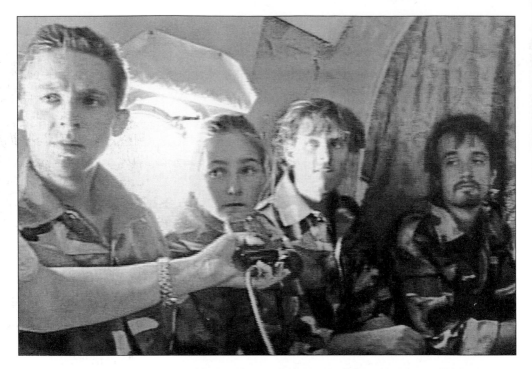

A shell-shocked and exhausted Tommy, Beth, Jason, and John in a helicopter leaving Batken Mobile anti-terrorism base. AP/WIDE WORLD PHOTOS

Tommy and Beth smile when asked if they are happy to be home during a news conference held in Davis, California, on August 24, 2000. AP/WIDE WORLD PHOTOS

ninety-eight hundred feet of altitude, while Abdul performs another of his nightly rituals.

"Abdullah, Abdullah, Abdullah," he intones into the Motorola. The radio remains mute, then he pulls out his little FM radio and switches it on. The reception is crackly and fluctuating, but a foreign voice delivers the news. Perhaps the station originates in Tajikistan, or maybe it's Radio Shari'a in Afghanistan, or from even farther away. Ever since the Tajik civil war, *The Voice of Horasan*, broadcasting from southern Iran, has served as an information link to the forces of jihad. Abdul's devotion to the nightly and morning news suggests to the climbers that he is learning more from it than just current affairs; the broadcast might contain coded messages for the commanders of the IMU.

The Americans huddle under the sleeping bag while Abdul sits several feet away, perched near the edge of the cliff with the radio close to his ear. Su sits beside the Americans. Far below them, moonlight glints off the river's sinuous braids. Smith looks across at Dickey. They have been whispering about trying to escape, and now they see an opportunity. Speaking nonchalantly so as not to arouse the suspicions of the rebels, Smith suggests that the moment might be right to make a move. He calmly hypothesizes that if Caldwell and Rodden were to tackle "Little Dog" and pin him down, Dickey and Smith could rush "Big Dog" and send him over the edge. They had started using pseudonyms when speaking about the rebels. Abdul was Big Dog, or sometimes Number One; Su was Little Dog, or Number Two.

"You guys are nuts," Rodden protests. "This isn't even a very big cliff. He might just get up and walk away, and then there'll be a shoot-out and we're dead."

The dilemma—whether to take action to free themselves, and risk the wrath of Abdul if they fail, or be led into captivity and depend on a rescue—produces heated whispering among the Americans. Rodden feels sure that the Kyrgyz army will help them, but Smith shakes his head. "What if the soldiers don't come, Beth? What do we do then? How long can we wander around like this before someone gets hurt? Maybe we have to take matters into our own hands."

The tone of the debate does attract Abdul's attention. He stares at the Americans and orders Su to move.

"Okay, cool it," Smith says. "Big Dog is on to us."

Su seems oblivious to their scheming. He relocates to a rock fifteen feet away, leans against it, and goes to sleep until Abdul rouses them all and they continue their nocturnal wandering. As the crow flies, the distance they travel across the hilltops above the Karavshin that night is just a couple of miles, but the landscape is deeply corrugated by dry gullies filled with unconsolidated rubble, on which they slip and slide. At about 3 A.M. on the morning of August 16 they come to an area of steep, slippery grass slopes, then they arrive at a huge boulder on a hillside. In the cavity beneath it the ground has been flattened out and lined with straw, and walls have been built around it to fend off the wind. It's a shepherd's dwelling. It would be a comfortable place for a bivouac, but it's on a beaten path and Abdul makes them leave it quickly.

They head north, contouring in and out of another major streambed, and cross a meadow where fresh dung piles indicate the recent passing of farm animals. They leave the pasture and grope their way downhill through dark shadows to the base of a tall limestone cliff. In a maze of boulders and brush, they bed down. While inspecting the hideouts, Abdul pauses before Smith. He takes off his camouflage cap and puts it on Smith's head, to better conceal Smith's crop of straw-colored hair. He doesn't want a repeat of the last bivouac, where soldiers had seen Rodden's golden hair.

"Cool," Smith boasts to Caldwell. "Now I've got a terrorist cap."

14.

ON THE RUN

AK SU VALLEY

AUGUST 15-17

By August 15 the fight has gone against the rebels. They are surrounded, and Kyrgyz snipers are picking them off one by one. More than
half the IMU men are dead. The two rebels the Americans met, Abdullah
and Obid, have been shot beside the Karavshin River on the afternoon of
August 13 while pausing for a drink of water. Abdurahman, however, is
still on the run, racing up the Ortochashma valley with his last four men.
They're trying to get back to the Turo Pass.

On other fronts, bands of the IMU have invaded Kyrgyzstan and Uzbekistan, and fighting is heavy there as well. The Kyrgyz government places
the rebel body count in Kyrgyzstan at forty, while in Uzbekistan the dead
number thirty. At a press interview in Bishkek the secretary of the Kyrgyz
Security Council, General Bolot Januzakov, announces that Kyrgyzstan,
Tajikistan, and Uzbekistan have agreed to work together to fight the IMU:

"With our joint forces we will annihilate the rebels, and we will take measures to annihilate them wherever they gather," he tells reporters. The strategy in the first Batken conflict was to negotiate for the release of hostages and drive the rebels out of Kyrgyzstan. Now the general is saying that the policy is to confront them and "wipe them out completely from the territory of the Commonwealth of Independent States." The Kyrgyz press will call the IMU mujaheddin "the disposable rebels" and "the rebels for one use" when Kyrgyz soldiers report the way that wounded IMU men are shot by their own, rather than allowed to be taken alive.

Since the afternoon firefight of August 12, the Ukrainian, German, and Uzbek hostages in the Ak Su valley have lain "like mice," to quote Igor Chaplinsky, under the guns of their three captors. That afternoon they shift their hideout from the riverside to a spot under a tousle of pink-blossomed wild rose growing a few feet from the abandoned hut in which they were sitting when the helicopter flew in. The rebels build a wall of rocks on one side of the hideout and position the hostages on the other side, like a human wall.

As with the Americans, soldiers come to within a few dozen yards of the hostages on the Ak Su. The rebels stare their captives down and emphatically shake their heads, warning them to be still, or die. The soldiers do not detect the hideout. "Thanks to the mujaheddin's skill in hiding, we were not shredded like cabbages," said Chaplinsky. There is another close encounter on the next day, August 13, in broad daylight when Mischa Volosovitch is ordered by the rebels to go to a stream seventy feet away and fetch water. At the stream he finds fresh boot prints; he's an ex-soldier, and he knows an army boot sole when he sees one. But no soldiers are about, and he returns to his companions.

The night of August 13 is bright with stars and moonlight, and the hostages on the Ak Su sleep to the sound of stones clacking together, rolling over and over in the river current. When the first fingers of sunlight slant through the branches of the wild-rose bush the next morning, August 14, Roland Laemmermann wakes and sees a pile of passports stacked neatly on a rock beside his head. The sight is strange because the rebels were carrying them. When Laemmermann raises his head he sees that Hamsa, Wolf, and the Artist are gone. Outnumbered by the Kyrgyz troops, they have fled. Laemmermann notes that the rebels have taken several items of the climbers' warm clothing, indicating that they are headed back over the mountains to Tajikistan. But Wolf and the Artist will not live through the day.

The abandoned hostages emerge from their hideout and test their freedom carefully. When they are certain that the rebels are gone, they discuss what to do next. Though they hear no sounds of battle, they fear downstream as a no-man's-land of fighting. So they head back upriver to their destroyed camp, in the hope that their uncaptured friends have returned from their climbs and are waiting for them.

THE DISAPPEARANCES of Laemmermann, the Uzbek cook, and the Ukrainians come as a chilling, *Twilight Zone* shock to Lutz Wentzel, Robert Lange, and the Uzbek base-camp manager, Andre Karnienko, when they return to the base camp on the evening of August 12, after climbing a smaller peak in the south end of the valley. Everything in their campsite, from people to tents to matchsticks, is gone. They scour the woods for signs of their missing friends, even wondering for a while if they are at the right campsite. Finding nothing, they accept foul play as the only explanation and split up into two groups: Karnienko will remain hiding in the woods around the camp, in case someone returns, while Lutz and Lange will hike the five miles up the Ak Su Glacier to the Bird to look for Stefan Hiermaier, Michael Meyer, and Radan Svec.

The Bird stands like a sentinel above the Ak Su Glacier, on the border between Kyrgyzstan and Tajikistan. The glacier at that point is a flattish, mile-wide expanse of snow, ice, and crevasses at an elevation of 12,600 feet. It is also an old trade route between Kyrgyzstan and Tajikistan, via the 14,114-foot Boz Toz Pass, which cuts across the range two miles west of the Bird. Hiermaier, Meyer, and Svec are camped on a strip of glacial rubble in front of the Bird, sleeping after they have spent the day fixing their ropes over the first couple of hundred feet of their intended climb, when they hear Wentzel and Lange calling their names in the frosty night. They shout back and guide them to their camp by waving their headlamps.

"What's wrong?" Hiermaier asks his breathless companions when they reach the bivouac.

"Roland is gone," Wentzel blurts out. "Mischa is gone. The camp is gone. Everyone else down there is gone."

"Gone? Gone where?"

"No idea. Maybe bandits took them."

The news is surreal, but it is too late to hike back to base camp, so the five men sleep until first light. Meanwhile, down at the camp, Karnienko does some detective work on his own. Creeping for two miles down the moonlit valley that same night, he makes his way to a shepherd's hut. After the shepherd in the hut calms down from the shock of Karnienko's intrusion, he reveals that in the afternoon he heard two shots, then in the evening he saw three terrorists marching the climbers away. The shepherd warns him that the valleys are full of rebels and that fighting has broken out between them and the army. Karnienko hikes back to the base camp and searches till he finds some of his team's gear and food hidden among trees and rocks. He carts some of it up the hill behind the camp to a glade of huge boulders and prepares a bivouac.

On the morning of August 13 the five Germans assemble at the base camp and Karnienko confirms what they fear the most: their friends have been kidnapped. They retire to the hideout among the boulders and discuss what to do next. The only decision that makes sense is to keep a low profile. They assume that whatever trouble is brewing, the soldiers at Kurbaka will settle it, and a Kyrgyz helicopter will soon fly up the valley to rescue them. But August 13 passes and no helicopter appears. While they bide their time, they unearth more of their gear. Buried in a shallow pit and trampled by yaks they find their smashed tents; hidden among rocks they find the climbing gear of the Ukrainians, still packed in duffel bags. Whoever dismantled their camp has hidden it well, and this makes the motives of the kidnappers all the more sinister. The temptation to hike down the valley to alert authorities about their friends is high, but the fear of encountering the kidnappers holds them back. Then at noon on August 13 they see a helicopter.

They run into the open meadow, waving their arms. One of the men holds up a red bivouac sack and waves it like a flag. The Mi8 is several hundred feet above them. It makes a wide circle around the valley, then flies away. They assume it did not see them.

Two hours later they hear jet engines. Again they run into the open. This time they see a plane, following the valley downstream. When it nears the confluence of the Ak Su and Kara Su, two bombs drop from its wings. The thud of the explosions echoes up the canyon. The staccato of machine gunning soon follows. The men stare at one another in fear. Somewhere down in that war zone is Laemmermann, the Uzbek cook, and the Ukrainians. While they stand in the open, searching for the smoke of battle, a high-flying helicopter appears, heading straight for them. Since the first helicopter ignored them, they have fashioned a sign with the word HELP written in English, made from silver duct tape stuck to the brightly colored nylon floor of a portaledge. They've positioned the sign on top of a boulder, and they wave the red bivy sack while they jump and shout. This time the pilots see them— small figures scurrying on a hillside—but the pilots are not thinking of climbers; they're thinking of rebels. The HELP sign means nothing to the pilots. They don't read English, and they're flying too high to read it. They are keeping out of range of rocket-propelled grenades and their greatest fear, Stinger ground-to-air missiles.

The United States had given the Afghan mujaheddin nine hundred Stingers in 1986 during the Afghan-Soviet war, and the mujaheddin used them to blow 333 helicopter gunships out of the sky. Hundreds of the missiles were never used and still remain unaccounted for, despite a secret CIA buyback operation in 1992. The Kyrgyz pilots had every reason to believe that the IMU had gotten their hands on such weapons via the Taliban.

When the helicopter is several hundred yards from the climbers, the pilot releases four S-5 rockets. They launch with a hiss and a white flash out of pods mounted on the side of the helicopter.

The sight of the rockets streaking through the air sends the men running into the boulders. Two rockets explode on the far side of the Ak Su, five hundred feet from them. The other two go over their heads and explode at the spring where they gather water, sixteen hundred feet upstream. The helicopter heads away.

"These idiots think we're terrorists!" Svec yells, picking himself up from the dirt. "Get the sign off that boulder!"

The boundaries of their world are suddenly more narrowly defined: they are certain the army will not rescue them; they are targets for helicopters or rebels if they stay in their base camp; their food will run out soon; helping the hostages is impossible.

"We weren't even sure they were alive," Svec would recall later of their missing friends. But the men can help themselves. After the rocket attack, they pore over their Russian-made map of the area looking at escape routes.

Getting out of the Ak Su valley by hiking down toward the area that has been bombed seems an invitation for ambush, so they plot a route that avoids Kurbaka altogether and takes in the Tamangan Pass and the Kundik River, and an 11,300-foot pass that leads out of the mountains. It is long—fifty miles at least—and they'll have to cross glaciers. Terrorists or trigger-happy soldiers might lurk along the way too.

Karnienko persuades them to give him one more chance to go down the valley to gather information from the shepherds. He trusts the country folk; they'll know if the fighting has finished and if it's safe to pass. He'll then return to their hideout with the news, and they'll either head out via the five-hour walk to Kurbaka or cross the mountains.

As Karnienko leaves camp on the afternoon of August 14 to head back down the Karavshin River, he warns his clients, "If I am not back by midnight, go the other way, without me."

The farther down the Ak Su he walks, the more like a ghost town it becomes. The shepherd he met the previous day has left. *Khoshes* are abandoned. Cattle, udders heavy with milk, stand around the empty farms. A dog standing outside its owner's home barks wildly as he passes. Everyone has gone. There are no sounds of battle. Karnienko returns and tells the Germans of his findings.

They leave for Kurbaka at 4 A.M. on August 15. Traveling light, with only one small pack, their map, and a compass, they head downstream. Far down the Ak Su, at around eleven o'clock, near a tall granite boulder ornately etched with the signatures and graffiti of two decades of explorers and climbers, Karnienko pauses and stares at the dirt on the path.

"These footprints," he says, "they are not like the boots of soldiers. They are the terrorists."

WHILE KARNIENKO and the Germans examine the footprints, one of the rebels who has been holding Laemmermann and the others at gunpoint sits hidden in a bush, watching them. It is Hamsa. He's running for his life. His companions are dead, and he's ready to pull the trigger of his AK-47 if the men detect him. Nobody sees him though, and the climbers continue on their way.

Hamsa's former captives—Laemmermann, Volosovitch, and the Ukrainians—are not far in front of the Germans. They were heading back up the Ak Su valley to their base camp, but a shepherd told them that Kyrgyz soldiers had set up an outpost in the Kara Su valley. Hearing this, Laemmermann and the rest of them had cut across the hill between the two valleys to head for the soldiers. The two groups will narrowly miss running into each other.

The Skorpions on the Kara Su are surprised by the appearance of the German-Ukrainian-Uzbek group. They escort them back over the ridge to their base camp on the Ak Su. The camp is empty, but the gear of the Ukrainians and the HELP sign lay where the Germans dumped them. A radio call brings an Mi8 to the camp, and the former hostages are whisked to Kurbaka. At one end of the large helicopter's fuselage is a stretcher. On it is a body under a sheet. It's Turat Osmanov.

ABOUT THE SAME TIME, Wentzel, Lange, Meyer, Hiermaier, Svec, and Karnienko hit the bridge near Mazar at a run. They fly a flag: a white T-shirt tied to a stick. The moment they cross the bridge Kyrgyz soldiers spring up from behind rocks and brush, leveling their weapons at them.

"Don't shoot!"

"Who are you?" a soldier demands in Russian.

"We're the German expedition," Karnienko says.

The soldiers hustle them into a sheltered area, where they frisk them. Karnienko tells the soldiers their story. Hiermaier said later, "It looked like these soldiers didn't know we were up there, in the Ak Su. We asked about our captured friends, and they didn't know what we were talking about. When they saw we had a map they were surprised; they had no map, so we gave them ours. They asked if we had any batteries to give them, so we gave them what we had. We had been in the Ak Su for ten days; we had passed the outpost of Kurbaka and met patrols of soldiers. These guys didn't know anything about that."

Nearly all the soldiers they have met at Kurbaka and in the Ak Su, however, are dead.

ON THE AFTERNOON of August 15 both groups of climbers reach Kurbaka. The reunion is emotional, then they're all airlifted to the mobile antiterrorist base at Batken. At the far end of this helicopter there's a bundle on the floor. This one is alive though. It's a man. His hands are cuffed behind his back and a hood covers his head. Every few minutes a soldier in the helicopter kicks the prisoner. The man on the floor groans in a spasm of pain. Lying beside him is a Kalashnikov rifle with a distinct scar on the barrel. Laemmermann recognizes the weapon. It belongs to Hamsa. He's been captured.

On the night of August 16 an official of the Ministry of Internal Affairs interviews the climbers at the Batken base, but the Ukrainians have gotten their hands on several bottles of vodka and the interview turns into a drunken farce. The Internal Affairs man throws up his hands in exasperation. "I can't do anything with these people," he says of the reveling climbers.

When the Germans relate their experience of being fired at by the Kyrgyz helicopter to the officers at the base, they are met with restrained yet polite laughter. The soldiers tell the climbers that they had been expecting an invasion for months. They don't understand how the climbers got into the area. They should never have been let past the checkpoints, they say. None of the men seem aware that the Karavshin has been attracting foreigners for decades.

The Germans have lost everything they brought to Kyrgyzstan. The Ukrainians are luckier—their gear is retrieved from base camp. Both teams leave Batken by car on the night of August 16 and are in Tashkent the next morning. The Kyrgyz and Uzbek media speak with them briefly before they fly home. Little news of their ordeal appears in the local press. Even in Germany there is scant mention of the drama, as the media are preoccupied with another hostage crisis, this one concerning a German family kidnapped by Islamic rebels in the Philippines.

Kabar, the government press agency of Kyrgyzstan, issues a press release titled "Kyrgyz Troops Free German Hostages," after the climbers leave the country. The report says that Kyrgyz troops "released" eight German mountaineers taken hostage by the Islamists. Reacting to the report, Hiermaier will say, "It seemed nothing like a rescue, but if the soldiers had not come, we would have been sitting in Dushanbe still waiting for ransom to be paid."

But there is no mention in the Kyrgyz or Uzbek media of the missing Americans. This raises the question: who knew about the American kidnapping, and when did they know it? The Kyrgyz military says they knew at all times about the foreign hostages; but did they? The Germans, the Ukrainians, and the Americans have all wondered about that, saying that the Kyrgyz soldiers who intercepted them invariably seemed shocked by their sudden appearances. The firefights at the bridge on the Ak Su and the rocket attack raise questions too. Because the U.S. embassy in Bishkek has maintained a policy of no-comment on this crisis, it is hard to know when and from whom they learned about the Americans' situation. Most likely, they heard about it sometime after the Germans' return to Tashkent and their visit to the German embassy on August 16. The German embassy most certainly communicated with the American embassy after the German team told them that Americans were in trouble too. In an amusing aside confirming this, Stefan Hiermaier had become mixed up over the identities of the Americans—Caldwell and Rodden—who passed through his base camp on August 7. He'd thought that Caldwell resembled a U.S. climber named Jared Ogden, whose photo he'd seen in a magazine, and he gave that name to German officials. Having obtained Ogden's name from the German embassy, a confused U.S. official would later ask the Americans, "Where is Jared Ogden?"

The Kyrgyz army has not revealed when or if they informed the U.S. embassy about the American hostages either. Perhaps it was a coincidence when the U.S. State Department on August 17 advised Americans planning to visit Uzbekistan "to remain vigilant to their personal security in connection with intensive clashes" along the Uzbek-Tajik border areas. But there was no new warning to Americans about Kyrgyzstan.

Nevertheless, Elena Kalashnikova of Ak Sai Travel was worried about the Americans. According to her, she flew to Batken on August 15 and met the German climbers and helicopter pilots, who told her of "rumors—nothing confirmed or official—that there were Americans in there, among the fighting." Kalashnikova says she "informed the minister of defense by letter that her clients might be in trouble" on about August 16. Back in Bishkek she faxed the U.S. embassy about the Americans on August 18. The same day a female official from the embassy called Kalashnikova. "She was very upset and excited by the fax," Kalashnikova recalled.

15.
LAST CHANCE

"Strangely enough, there were moments when the time between us was sober, even friendly," John Dickey said later of his interactions with Abdul.

As the night of August 16 forms around their bivouac under the limestone cliff above the Karavshin, Dickey and Rodden mentally prepare themselves for another miserable nocturnal journey, while Abdul kneels on his mat and performs his evening prayer. When Dickey sees Abdul slip a small book into his vest after his prayers, he points to it and says, "Koran."

Abdul nods. He takes the pocket-sized collection of Islamic canons from his vest and holds it reverently in his palm. The Koran is the backbone of Abdul's faith. Abdul's Koran is made of well-thumbed, tissue-thin paper. He opens it and pages through, pointing at lines of minute and ornate script, reading aloud. Dickey hears the names of Allah, Muhammad, and Jesus. Being the son of a Church of Christ deacon, Dickey knows preaching when he hears it. Abdul scratches a Christian cross in the sand at their feet and continues speaking, pointing from the Koran to the cross. For a moment it looks like Abdul is trying to build a spiritual bridge between them, but the rebel abruptly changes the course of the discussion by erasing the cross in the sand with an abrupt sweep of his hand and by pointing decisively at his Koran. Dickey and Rodden lean back into their bivouac, chilled.

"Does his religion allow people to kill each other?" Rodden asks later.

"No," Dickey answers. "But men like Abdul twist their religions around until they believe that killing is God's work."

"Do you believe in God?"

"Not anymore. Not since I was a kid. I think it gives you a false sense of security. I believe in life, though, and I believe there is something good in everyone." He pauses a minute, then changes the direction of the conversation. "I'm starting to believe that we are going to have to do something drastic to get ourselves out of here."

"Don't you think someone will rescue us?" Rodden says. "The Marines or the Kyrgyz soldiers?"

"Forget the Marines. Or anyone."

"I know Singer keeps talking about killing these guys, but how can we possibly kill anyone?"

"We may have to learn. Beth, don't you want to go home?"

"God, yes. I want to see my mom and my dad and my brother so much. I want to sleep in my own bed. I want someone to help us."

"We might have to help ourselves."

THAT NIGHT they travel down the broad gully of a stream that shepherds call the Azhankain, which takes them to the Karavshin River. Along the way they find a deserted hut standing on a knoll. The rebels gently kick open the door and slip inside. They look for food, but the hut is devoid of even a crust of bread, though the lingering smell of baking tells them that the residents left in a hurry. At a clear spring beside the hut the hostages and their captors gorge themselves; the water fills their bellies and staves off their nagging hunger.

They hit the Karavshin a mile and a quarter north of the junction of the Ak Su and Kara Su Rivers. On the trail beside the Karavshin, Abdul orders the Americans to keep off the path. Then, to their amazement, he leads them upstream.

"What the fuck are we doing?" Smith exclaims in a hoarse whisper. "We're heading back toward the scene of the battle. It's got to be crawling with soldiers up there."

"These guys are lost," Caldwell says.

"No, they know exactly where they're going," Dickey replies. He is sure that Abdul has been trying to lead them back into either Uzbekistan or Tajikistan, but at every turn the rebels have caught wind of soldiers. The convoluted loop they are now starting to close is a function of the tightening noose the soldiers have drawn around the invaders.

The two rebels shift into battle mode and fan out ahead of the climbers. They creep from rock to tree, keeping a watchful eye on their captives, who lag fifty feet behind. The Americans whisper openly about trying to escape while the rebels are preoccupied with scouting the path. But the four hostages hesitate. There are too many uncertainties. They worry that in their weakened conditions they will be easy targets. Dickey moves especially slowly, limping with a swollen knee from the pounding descent of the gully and from his cramped bivouacs.

Then Smith hears Caldwell behind him, whispering his nickname.

"Hey, Singer. Turn your jacket inside out so the soldiers will see us." Nights earlier, when the Americans had been climbing the hillside trying to evade the friendly fire of Kyrgyz troops, Caldwell had come up with the idea that he and Smith should turn their insulated jackets inside out, switching the light blue outer fabric for the drab black inner lining—the camouflage of night. Smith praised it as a wise move. Now Caldwell has turned the light blue shell back toward the outside. It shines like neon in the moonlight.

"What the hell are you doing?" Smith hisses angrily, pointing to Abdul. "Do you realize you're still a hostage here? Do you want to piss those guys off?"

"Okay, okay." Caldwell turns the jacket back to black. Their minds are filled with fear and a confusion of choices as they traverse the riverside meadow. Should they sprint off into the night and hope that Abdul will not shoot them? Should they stand up and scream for help to the Kyrgyz soldiers who may or may not lurk in the shadows? Instead, they play it safe, following their captors from one rock to another, until they reach the Jopaiya River. They crossed this river on Smith's log bridge a mile and a half upstream on the second night of their captivity.

The Jopaiya at this lower level, though, is spanned by a shepherd's bridge. They cross it, returning to the hamlet of Karavshy. Here they scour more huts for food, but there is nothing. Half a mile upstream, at 1 A.M., the rebels sit the hostages under a tree fifty feet from the Karavshin River. The river roars here, misting and chilling the climbers. Abdul informs the Americans that he is heading upriver, and that Su will stay put and keep watch over them. Abdul delivers his message using three signs: the Russian word *soldat*, meaning soldier; the sign of the slit throat; and a mime show of spooning food into his mouth. To some of the hostages the message means he is heading off to kill soldiers and steal food; to others he is warning them that Su, his soldier, will kill them if they try to escape. Abdul bids them good-bye with an earnest handshake.

An hour later the hostages are dozing under Osmanov's sleeping bag when Abdul shakes them awake and tells them to pack up and move. Su is nowhere to be seen, though. They find him on a floodplain of round white river stones a quarter mile upstream, standing like a zombie, half-asleep on his feet. Beside him are two stinking, greasy, and heavy sacks. One contains a large slab of salted yak butter, the other a Kyrgyz snack called *qurut*, dried yogurt balls. Abdul has stolen them from a hut. The food excites the hostages until they try to eat it. The white yogurt balls are half the size of a walnut and nearly as hard, and they taste moldy; when the shell is cracked and the soft core spills onto the tongue, the flavor is as bitter as sour cream. They each force down half a dozen of them, then they dig their fingers into the rancid butter. It hits their stomachs hard. They nearly vomit. While he eats, Smith realizes that the rebels' mission to get the sacks of food represents another missed opportunity to escape. The whole time they were sleeping beside the river believing that Su was guarding them, he was, in fact, helping Abdul fetch the food. Smith chides himself for not checking to see if Su was really guarding them. He has begun to realize, these past days, the role that complacency plays in their captivity, and the way Abdul uses it to his advantage.

Back on their feet they shuffle upriver. They are all weak, getting weaker. Abdul, weighed down by his heavy battle vest as well as his fifteen-pound weapon, stops every thirty feet to sit on a rock. Su and Smith are hurting too, creeping along together. Caldwell and Rodden and the limping Dickey still maintain a decent pace, though the heavy sacks of food burden the two men.

They pass under the hill where Osmanov was murdered, cross the footbridge spanning the Ak Su where the Kyrgyz captain was gunned down, and reenter the Kara Su valley.

"We are headed back to base camp!" Caldwell whispers to Rodden.

The same thought warms all their minds: at base camp there are duffel bags stuffed with the remnants of their food and with warm clothing. But they walk only a few hundred yards before the first hint of morning prompts Abdul to search for another bivouac, like a vampire shunning the dawn. At a cluster of boulders Abdul hops into a pitlike recess among the rocks and noses around for a cave. After finding no suitable bivouac, he gesticulates at Caldwell to pull him back out of the pit. When Caldwell reaches out he is shocked to receive Abdul's weapon instead of his hand. He holds the long gun, as they've taken to calling the machine gun, feeling the weight of it in his hand. Abdul jabbers at Caldwell while trying to clamber out of the pit. The rebel's feet slip and slide, but Caldwell makes no move to help him. His eyes are glued to the weapon. The thought of shooting the man occurs to him, but he cannot consider it. He knows nothing of guns, and he doesn't doubt that Abdul would beat him to the draw with his pistol. Even if Caldwell was a crack shot, would he be able to aim the weapon at Abdul, look him in the eye, and pull the trigger? Caldwell knows himself, and he knows he is not like these men.

A moment later Su appears and helps his commander out of the pit. Knowing nothing of what has passed through Caldwell's mind, Abdul takes the gun and continues searching for a bivouac.

They find two dark nooks beside a large boulder. Again, the rebels set the climbers to work gathering branches for camouflage. All except for Rodden. He lets her gather grass to line the caves, but he refuses to let her toil alongside the men. They eat the last of their precious PowerBars then. Abdul pairs them off as usual, and they squeeze into the holes. Cooled by the breeze skating over the river, the caves are cold as meat lockers. The endless marching and cold have whittled their body fat to nearly nothing, and they shiver constantly. Smith sits on the suitcase-sized slab of butter. It affords some insulation from the cold rocks. Hunched over and with arms folded, he pulls his jacket over his head like a monk's cowl. Under the hood he savors the warmth of his breath blowing against his wrist. He concentrates on that sensation, trying to ignore the rest of his body, which rattles convulsively. Caldwell sits beside him, shivering and shifting against the rocks that jam into his buttocks.

"I'm so sick of this," Smith says angrily, "so fucking sick of this." He repeats variations of this mantra over and over for the rest of the day. Mostly, he is talking to himself. For the first time in a long time, Caldwell prays.

Peering through the mouth of the cave, Caldwell watches the sky. Clouds are building. He senses that the mountains are due for a storm. He's been studying his partners and the rebels the past couple of days, wondering who will be the first to shut down from exhaustion. He knows his body and his capacity for endurance well enough to know that he can outlast the rebels, and probably his teammates. If need be, he feels he could carry Rodden through the mountains, though her body seems to be able to run on empty. Her days of ruthless dieting during her time as a competition climber are serving her well. At ninety pounds, she has little weight to lose, but she also needs little fuel to run. But the darkening clouds worry Caldwell. No one, no matter how strong, is immune to hypothermia.

Storms in the Pamir-Alai Range can be fierce. I learned that the hard way on my 1995 trip to the Karavshin. I was near the summit of the Bird—that very peak the Germans had been about to ascend—with Lynn Hill, Alex Lowe, Conrad Anker, Chris Noble, and Dan Osman, when a gray cloud crackling with electricity and booming with thunder enveloped us. The cloud had crept in from Tajikistan, and we hadn't seen it coming. Within seconds the atmospheric electricity had us tingling with the skin-crawling sensation one feels when standing under high-tension power lines. A loud buzz, like a swarm of bees, filled the air. Dan Osman, who had never experienced an electrical storm, began scratching his scalp, complaining of bugs in his hair.

"Sit the hell down!" Lowe shouted. "This is electricity, not bugs!"

Electrical storms in the mountains are unpredictable. At their most harmless they'll set your hair on end and make your ice ax hum like a tuning fork; at their worst you can be struck by a heart-stopping discharge of electricity and blasted out of your mountain boots. The most dangerous place in an electrical storm is on the summit, and the top of the Bird is as sharp as a lightning rod, so we rappelled down fast. But even two hundred feet below the summit, where we crouched down on a ledge to dissuade a lightning strike, the air crackled loud as a campfire. To minimize the likelihood of a strike, we dumped everything metal—carabiners, pitons, and ice axes—on a ledge ten feet away.

After a few minutes the buzz and thunder died down and we raised our heads. What I did next was probably foolish, but instinct made me raise my arm into the invisible halo of energy and wave my hand across the sky. The action produced another loud noise, identical in tone to the light saber that Luke Skywalker wields in *Star Wars*. When I did it again, another major chord sounded out. Lowe yelled at me to quit it.

The electricity passed by long enough for us to descend to our camp on a snowy pass. We stuffed our tents into our rucksacks and loped down the snowy ridge that separated Kyrgyzstan from Tajikistan. Partway down, snowflakes started falling. Electrical current ran down the strips of aluminum that formed the back supports in our rucksacks, tickling our spines.

By the time we were down on the glacier, I looked back toward the Bird to see it truncated by a cloud the color of a bruise. To the right of the mountain I saw a saddle leading back into Tajikistan: the Boz Toz Pass. In the summer of 2000, bullets would be flying up there.

That night the storm spewed four feet of snow, burying our tents on the glacier below the Bird. All night we dug away the building snow with our hands to prevent the walls of our shelters from caving in. By morning it was raining, turning the snow into slush. By the time we got back to base camp on the Ak Su, clear skies were returning to the Karavshin. Our Uzbek base-camp keeper, Slava (an ethnic Russian built like a bouncer, who distilled "vodka" from a mix of aftershave, rubbing alcohol, and Alka Seltzer), told us that while we'd been in the mountains, the cliffs above base camp had turned into curtains of water, and mudslides roared down hillsides. Slava called it a "hundred-year storm," but when we asked him if he had seen storms like it before in these ranges, he replied, "Every year."

IN THEIR CAVE beside the Kara Su, Smith suddenly breaks the moody silence between him and Caldwell.

"Did I ever tell you I was a professional clown?"

The non sequitur catches Caldwell off guard. He encourages Smith to tell his story.

"When I was about eleven I decided I wanted to be a clown. My inspiration was a clown named Happy. She was an older woman who I met doing tricks at the grand opening of a local gas station. I became her sidekick. We did magic tricks and balloon sculpturing at store openings and birthday parties. I called myself Scrimples the Clown. By the time I was thirteen I had my own business card and was getting thirty bucks a day for doing kids' parties. I had a suitcase full of makeup, goofy clothes, floppy shoes, and fright wigs. I wish I could show you some of my magic tricks. I had one bitchin' trick where I made a playing card disappear, then I'd slice open an orange and pull the card out from inside it."

"I'd eat the orange," Caldwell says.

"I'd fight you for it."

"How long did you do this clowning stuff?"

"Till I was sixteen. At the Utah State Clown Convention I took second place in balloon sculpturing. Youngest recipient of the award, ever. My folks were stoked."

"Awesome."

"We gotta get out of here, Tommy."

Home. Childhood. The future. The story transports them out of themselves only for as long as it takes Smith to tell it. Then the shivering and misery continues.

"I know," Caldwell answers.

———

IN THE ANNALS of hostage dramas, escape is rarely attempted and is seldom successful. Everything weighs against the hostage: the terror of being shot in the back while on the run; the consequences of angering the captors and being punished; and the uncertain landscape into which an escaping hostage flees. Rarely has a hostage escaped from a kidnapper's stronghold.

It is hard not to draw comparisons between the four Americans in Kyrgyzstan and the experience of a group of trekkers kidnapped in Kashmir, India, in July 1995, by a violent band of Islamic separatists called Al-Faran. Kashmir lies in the mountainous border region between Muslim Pakistan and Hindu India, and it has been a contested and war-ravaged area ever since the partition of the two countries in 1948. In 1989 Muslim separatists began a concerted guerrilla campaign against Indian rule and the 300,000 Indian soldiers stationed in Kashmir. The ensuing fighting claimed 20,000 lives and shut down Kashmir's tourism business. But by the mid-1990s a lull in hostilities brought tourists back to trek around the lakes and passes of this Himalayan paradise. Even though tourism companies in Delhi and Srinagar encouraged customers to sign up for their treks, the Indian government and the U.S. State Department issued warnings that foreign tourists were at risk of being kidnapped. Terrorists had taken hostages before in Kashmir. In each case, the hostages had been released after ransom was paid or the demands of the kidnappers were met. There was one exception, however, when an American hostage had been executed.

On July 4, 1995, some sixty trekkers from Europe and the United States were camped in groups along the Lidda River near the mountain village of Aru when twelve armed men began rounding up foreigners and looting the camps. They checked the passports of the trekkers and separated six men from the foreigners they held at gunpoint: two Americans, two British, a German, and a Norwegian. To the horror of the wives, girlfriends, and friends of these men, the guerrillas then marched them into the hills.

Al-Faran is a wing of a larger Islamic terrorist group called Harkat ul-Ansar (HUA), which commands several thousand fighters and which is believed to be based in Muzaffarabad, Pakistan. Like the IMU, Al-Faran and HUA are pan-Islamic, multinational, cross-border guerrilla forces, comprising mainly Pakistanis, Kashmiris, and Afghans. They are funded by Islamists in Iran, Saudi Arabia, and other Arab nations. Prior to the kidnappings, Al-Faran was unknown, though HUA members had fought on the side of Muslim antigovernment groups in Myanmar, Bosnia, Kashmir, and Tajikistan.

One of the men kidnapped by Al-Faran was an American tourist named John Childs (no relation to the author of this book). While the men were being led into the mountains that first night, Childs conceived an escape plan. Reports say that he deliberately drank from a stream that gave him diarrhea, and he turned the symptoms to his advantage by immodestly defecating along the trail. The kidnappers found his habits disgusting and ordered him to relieve himself in places away from them. Childs's illness required him to make several toilet visits per day, and each time he tested his guards' vigilance by walking farther away from them. He also pretended to be sicker than he really was, and he lagged wearily behind everyone on the trail, though he always caught up with the group in the end.

When Childs saw a village he had visited during his trek, he realized that he could navigate his way out of the mountains. To prepare for his escape he hoarded morsels of food from each meal and hid them in his pocket. By the fourth day of his abduction, Childs's guards were accustomed to his long toilet visits. Before dawn, he rolled his bedding into a bundle to make it appear that he was sleeping and walked out of camp as if to defecate. He squatted, waited till he felt sure no one had noticed that he was missing, then he kept walking, all night and all the next day, until Indian soldiers found him.

After Childs's escape, Indian negotiators dealt by radio with a hostile band of extremists who frequently threatened to kill the prisoners unless several Al-Faran prisoners were freed from Indian jails. The Indian government refused to give in to Al-Faran's demands, and their negotiators stalled for time. On August 13, 1995, the drama took a gruesome turn when the decapitated body of the Norwegian hostage, Hans-Christian Ostro, was found by a group of village women who were gathering firewood. Forensic experts would later say that Ostro's throat had been cut before his head was hacked from his body. Ostro's chest was covered in a bloody hatchwork of knife wounds. The cuts were deciphered to read "Al-Faran." The corpse also had a note pinned to the shirt. It read, "We have killed the hostage because the government has failed to accept our demands. In 48 hours, if our demands are not met, the other hostages will meet the same fate."

Indian negotiators continued to stall, refusing to give in to the guerrillas' demands. "Proof of life" photos of the remaining hostages that Al-Faran sent to Indian authorities showed Donald Hutchings (U.S.), Paul Wells and Keith Mangan (U.K.), and Dirk Hasert (Germany), looking weary, terrified, and gaunt. Some photos showed guns pointed at the hostages. Messages from the terrorists warned of the hostages' failing health. By November 1995 negotiations broke down and nothing more was heard from the terrorists. Then in May 1996 Indian soldiers arrested a man named Naser Mohammed. He was a ringleader of Harkat-ul-Ansar, the parent group of Al-Faran, and although he had never met the hostages, he confessed to their fate. The kidnappers had been taking their prisoners into Pakistan, he said, over a mountain range, when a fierce, cold, Karakoram storm blew in. The guerrillas had killed the weakened hostages right then because they were slowing down the terrorists' escape. The men were buried in unmarked graves. Mohammed also claimed that Ostro had been beheaded because he had repeatedly tried to escape, and because one of the kidnappers "got a message from Allah" in the form of a vision that reportedly told the kidnapper that the death of Ostro would help achieve Al-Faran's goals. There's been no news in five years of the missing men, and no bodies have been recovered.

LATE AFTERNOON HAS ARRIVED, and in the hole adjacent to Caldwell and Smith, Rodden and Dickey feign sleep while Abdul masturbates. After Abdul finishes, he crawls outside the shelter. Dickey opens his eyes and sees him standing, looking down at Dickey's unlaced boots. Abdul tugs a boot off Dickey's foot as roughly as if he were dead, then tries the boot on. It is too large, so he tosses it back into the cave.

"You fucker," Dickey sneers.

They lie silent for a while longer, then Dickey broaches the subject of food. For him and Rodden, talk of eating has become a constant source of diversion. Dickey asks which restaurant Rodden will go to when she gets home.

"I'm going straight to this place called Dos Coyotes. It's a southwestern-style restaurant in Davis. The servings are huge. My favorite is the chicken Caesar salad. It's like no other Caesar salad you've ever had. It's smothered in beans and chips and salsa. I'm going to tell Mum and Dad to bring us a take-away when they meet us at the airport. What are you gonna order, John?"

"Hamburgers. And steak. What about dessert?"

"Definitely not ice cream. I'm too cold for that. Maybe just a big mug of hot chocolate. How about you?"

"Pizza."

"For dessert?"

"Yeah. Pizza. For breakfast too."

16.

THE CLIFF

The moon is waning, two-thirds full, when the hostages crawl out of their caves at nightfall on August 17. It is their sixth night of captivity. The breeze is moist. A halo around the moon and scudding clouds confirm that the weather is changing. They force a few yogurt balls down their throats and drink a few palmfuls of brown, bitter water from an algae-covered pool beside the river, then they move upstream. They avoid the trail by walking across a floodplain of loose rounded stones. When the flat ground ends they sidle across a steep riverbank. Movement has become a dream. There seems no end to the drudgery of their journey. Half of their steps along the shadowy riverbank are stumbles; the other half consist of picking themselves up off the ground. Thorny brush and sharp twigs scratch at them, tearing at their dry, parchmentlike skin.

Up in front, Abdul searches for a way across the Kara Su. For reasons the Americans don't understand right then, he wants to cross to the west side of the river. The realization that they are not heading to their base camp, which is on the river's east bank, hits the hostages with disappointment and anger. There will be no food, no warm clothes, only more aimless wandering.

They find a point on the Kara Su where a tree trunk leaning over the river lets them gain a trio of enormous boulders jammed across a narrows. White water seethes through the gaps between the boulders, which serve as stepping-stones to the other side. Abdul sends Rodden and Caldwell across first. The couple assist each other, passing the sack of butter between them as they cross. They wait on the far side of the river while both rebels position themselves on a rock midway across. When Smith crosses he finds himself on a smooth, round-topped boulder in the center of the river, right between his captors. The thought crosses his mind: *if I had a like-minded partner right here, we could push these bastards in.*

He looks around for support. Dickey is just stepping off the tree trunk behind them; Rodden and Caldwell sit twenty feet away. Smith's hands sweat as he contemplates tackling the maneuver alone. Even if he sends both rebels into the foaming pool below, it's not a drowning situation and chances are they will claw their way out of the current and onto the bank. Maybe their rifles will still be slung over their shoulders. The four climbers are strung out all over the place, easy targets if Abdul starts spraying bullets. Smith feels torn between acting now and waiting for a better opportunity. His chance evaporates when Abdul steps onto the next rock.

OVER THE DAYS they have learned to interpret the mannerisms, hand gestures, and a few of the guttural words used by the rebels, so when Abdul launches into an explanation of his intentions for them that evening, the Americans quickly get the rebel's drift. It is ten o'clock on the night of August 17, and they are on the west bank of the Kara Su. The Yellow Wall, where their nightmare began, lies south by three miles. In front of them is a craggy, brushy hillside banded with slopes of loose rubble and the humps of steeper metamorphic cliffs. Abdul announces that they must climb this hillside and wait for Abdullah and Obid on top of the ridge. The Americans do not know it, but on the other side of that ridge is the Ortochashma River, and the trail to the Turo Pass. Nor do they know that in either direction are trails that cross the ridge. Abdul has chosen a route more suited to mountain goats than people because he fears an ambush on the trails.

Abdul takes Su aside. For ten minutes the commander lectures the younger man, telling him that their position is desperate. The time may be near to make the ultimate sacrifice. When the rebels return to the Americans, Abdul explains that he will meet them on top of the ridge after he heads up to the Americans' base camp to fetch more food and clothing.

"He's going back for batteries for the Motorola, that's what he is doing," Smith guesses aloud.

Abdul solemnly shakes each of their hands, as if they are friends sharing some great adventure. As a parting gesture, though, he makes Smith hand over his insulated coat, leaving him in a T-shirt. When Smith protests, Abdul indicates that he can wear Osmanov's sleeping bag as a shawl. Smith, freezing cold and twisted with anger, stares at the rebel. But what catches Smith's ear is Abdul's final message—a mix of words and gestures that Smith deciphers to mean, "Su will protect you." It's as if they've all slipped over some edge in which the difference between prisoner, captor, and companion has become blurred. Indeed, the Americans have been model hostages, never resisting Abdul's will. Smith feels more certain than ever that their captors do not imagine they have the guts to try to escape. He sees that his gambit is working. The rebels trust them. They will be alone with the dimwitted Su for the rest of the night.

"John, this is it," Smith says. "It's our fucking chance, dude."

"Right. We gotta whack this guy, tonight."

From where they stand beside the Kara Su the luminous but waning moon defines a three-thousand-foot hillside comprising high-angle brush and rubble, then intermittent cliffs. It is the sort of terrain that skilled climbers commonly tackle without ropes but that nonclimbers find unnerving and impossible. While Caldwell and Rodden stumble up the initial rubble slope with Su, Smith and Dickey come up the rear, scheming and calculating.

"It'll take Abdul half an hour to get to base camp and half an hour to walk back to the start of this climb," Smith says. "Add an hour for him to climb up the slope and catch up with us. That means we have two hours be-fore we see him again. It's ten o'clock now. We have to get rid of Su and be on the run by midnight at the latest."

"Exactly," Dickey replies. "So how are we gonna do this?"

"How the fuck should I know? I've never snuffed anyone. We could all grab him and huck him off one of those cliffs up there, I guess."

Rodden overhears their planning and faces Smith and Dickey. "I don't like this at all," she says. "I'd rather be sitting in a hut, starving for months in some village, than watch Su shoot you guys full of holes. I'd rather be suf-fering and alive than take that chance."

"Okay," Smith says abruptly. "Beth, you don't have to have any part of this at all. Tommy, you can be in it if you want."

Caldwell's voice falters as he struggles to decide what course to take. He wants out of the situation as much as anyone, but the idea of killing is anathema to him. He sees clouds, and he smells rain. Since they emerged from their bivouac, he has been fretting about how they will survive a storm in their weakened condition without any protective rain gear, and he has been worrying about Rodden. What will happen to her when they get to the rebels' final destination? Will she be treated with respect, or set upon by thugs? "We had all been talking about killing someone for days," Caldwell will later remember, uncomfortable with the thought, "but Beth had said to me she just didn't think I could emotionally handle it. So I had been keeping out of it." Torn between committing one way or the other, Caldwell cannot give Smith an answer.

"Singer, if you and John are going to do this, it is your decision," Rod-den says, answering for Caldwell.

"Fine," Smith says curtly. "You two go ahead, so you don't get hit by Little Dog when we huck him."

DESPITE ALL THE CHATTER about killing, Su is oblivious to the Ameri-cans' intentions. Smith and Dickey march past Caldwell and Rodden and begin shadowing Su up the slope. A thousand feet above the river the ter-rain begins to steepen from a hillside to a layer cake of cliffs and ledges. They scramble up small, low, angled cliffs that are ten, twenty, and thirty feet high. Brushy terraces break up the vertical rise, but the cliffs mount up, one atop the other, creating a precipitous drop. Smith and Dickey discuss the merits of each cliff as a place to hurl Su.

"It's gotta be far enough so he isn't gonna come looking for us," Smith says, peering over one drop.

But their movements are awkward on the slope. Dickey is burdened by the sack of yogurt balls, and Smith carries Osmanov's sleeping bag in its sack. Behind them, Caldwell carries the butter. Rodden has the black kit bag crammed with yogurt balls. Caldwell had earlier tried to abandon the bag beside the river, in the hope that soldiers would spot it, but Abdul noticed Caldwell's ploy and sent Su running back to retrieve it.

"Alpinista!" Su orders Smith to the front. He waves his hand at a cliff, as if to ask, "Which way?"

Smith points to a path leading straight up. The climbing will involve nothing more than beginner-level moves—about 5.5 in climbers' ratings— but Su looks worried. Rodden and Caldwell move past him, to get in front. Su points at Rodden and points to the cliff, then shakes his head. "Surely the girl cannot climb this cliff," he seems to say.

Smith waves aside Su's protest. "She's cool with it," he says, letting Rodden pass them; then he heads up the thirty-foot rock step too. He pauses near the top to show Su the way. The outcrop is angled at an easy sixty de-grees and peppered with large slots and edges for the hands and feet, yet it challenges Su. Smith points out the holds, urging Su on as if he were a pay-ing client. The rebel's movements are shaky. From his stance at the top of the cliff Smith sees that Su's rifle is slung over his shoulder, safely out of the way. A shove here could be fatal, or knock Su senseless at the very least. Smith steps into position on the ledge to body-slam Su off the top of the out-crop. His heart is thumping as he waits for the precise moment to wedge his hip against Su. But the rebel walks across the ledge in the opposite direction. Under a more gentle slab of rock he sits and rests. When Smith joins him, the rebel smiles at his guide.

"Good *alpinista,* Su," Smith tells him cheerily.

Smith thinks about picking up a rock and battering Su's skull, or wait-ing for Dickey to arrive so they can hold the rebel down and choke the life out of him, but something holds him back. They climb on, and then a hundred feet higher another opportunity presents itself when Su makes a precarious balance move off the terrace to begin another rock step.

"Okay, this is it," Dickey says in a trembling voice. He whispers to Caldwell to take the sack of yogurt balls from him.

"Careful," Smith warns. "If he sees you up there without the bag, he'll think something is up." They've been juggling the heavy bags all night, trying not to raise the rebel's suspicions.

Dickey moves into position just below Su. "Come on, do it, John" comes a collective murmur out of the night. He's ready to grab the rebel by the ankle and pull him backward, but Su lifts his foot onto a higher edge, evading Dickey's grasp. Above the short cliff, on a ledge, Dickey notices that Su steps away from him and casts him a leery stare. "I think Little Dog is wising up to us, Singer," he whispers.

Twice more in the next half hour Su slips out of their reach. For all the discussions of how to edge the rebel into eternity, they find that doing the deed is no easy business. They miss their chances for many reasons. If they attack him and he eludes their grasp, he might swing his rifle around on them; if they manage to knock him over an edge, Su might grab a handful of shirt as he topples backward, taking the pusher with the pushed. Their hesitations are rooted in an amalgam of fears and abstractions, but they are easy enough to understand: they are not killers.

Rodden and Caldwell stay a few feet ahead of the others. Although they have opted out of ambushing Su, they keep looking behind them, hoping to see their captor tumbling down a cliff. While they wait for the others to catch up, Caldwell sees that Rodden is shivering. He puts his jacket around her and looks at the threatening sky.

"Beth, these clouds are coming in fast. We're gonna be dead if it starts storming."

"I know. We may not make it. Oh, I want to go home so bad," she replies, nearly in tears.

At midnight they stand under the last section of cliff. Above it, they can see the top of the ridge. For all they know, more rebels may wait for them there. Caldwell has begun to think that his friends might not push Su after all. They've been trying for over an hour, to no avail. Now Smith and

Dickey are out of position, below the ledge on which he, Rodden, and Su have gathered.

Caldwell looks at the clouds, and he thinks about the speed at which hypothermia will set into their bodies during a storm at ten thousand feet if it rains. Somebody has to do something. Caldwell watches Su stand up and walk across a ledge toward the final cliff. The rebel peers up, trying to decide which path to take up the jumble of ledges and slabs in front of him. The slope has steepened to an exposed rib that drops away sharply below. A person could fall far from this place, Caldwell thinks to himself.

He turns to Rodden. "Jason and John aren't gonna do it. That's obvious. We need to get out of here. Do you want me to do it?"

When she doesn't say anything, he drops the sack of butter and starts moving toward Su.

17.

NO-MAN'S-LAND

Caldwell knows what he must do. He sprints across the ledge, then steps onto the cliff and climbs up into position right beside his captor. Su is feeling out the moves in front of him and barely seems to register Caldwell's presence. Smith's coaching has lured the rebel higher and higher, and Smith and Dickey have again moved to stances a few feet below the rebel. Minutes earlier, Su encouraged the Americans with a smiling series of gestures that seemed to say, "Don't worry, we are nearly on top." Su suspects nothing, and he doesn't notice Caldwell's hand stretching out toward him.

"Tommy made up his mind and bounded across that ledge and up that cliff with incredible speed," Dickey said later of Caldwell's actions. "It was speed climbing at its most aggressive." Dickey and Smith freeze when they see that Caldwell has committed himself. Below them all and off to the side, Rodden sits on a gnarled, wind-twisted tree growing out of the end of the ledge. The moon has emerged from behind a cloud, highlighting every-thing.

"Come on, Tommy," they all say under their breath. "End it. Now."

Caldwell grabs the barrel of the Kalashnikov slung across Su's back and gives it a single, strong, outward tug. The force makes the rebel lose his bal-ance. Su's torso arches backward, and his hands part from the holds he's clinging to. A faint breath of surprise, a sound like *whaaa*, escapes his lips as he falls. A second later everyone hears a fleshy crunch as he collides with a sloping rock ledge thirty feet below them. Dickey hears the groan of wind forced out of lungs, and a sliding sound as Su keeps going.

"I watched him arc right through the moon, from my view," Smith would later recall. "He was looking over his left shoulder. It was bright enough I could see his facial expression. He was pedaling in the air with his feet, and, like, rolling up the windows with both hands. He was in a flat, level position, with his back to the ground. He hit the ledge flat, then rolled off."

Caldwell watches the rebel fall too. He sees that beyond the edge of that ledge is an inky void of slabs and cliffs. With enough momentum he will keep tumbling for hundreds of feet. Caldwell has just bought their freedom, but the realization of what he has done forces a wail from deep inside him.

"My God, what have I done?"

He claws his way up the final few feet of the cliff onto flatter ground and runs a few paces along it.

"What have I done?" He drops to the ground. He's done the worst thing he can imagine.

Below, Smith peers over the ledge, searching for a trace of Su. He sees nothing, hears nothing. So far as he can tell in the murky light, Su has fallen hundreds of feet. "He's gone! Go! Go! Go!"

They pick up the sacks of butter and yogurt balls on the ledge and Os-manov's sleeping bag, and they fling them into the void after the rebel. Dickey and Smith are conscious that they don't want to leave any signs for Abdul to pick up. Shaking with fear, they scramble up the cliff. Dickey reaches Caldwell first. He finds him curled into a ball. "Holy shit, I killed a guy!" he wails. Next Smith arrives, then Rodden.

"How could I have done that?" Caldwell shouts. "What is wrong with me?"

Caldwell is the considerate, deferential, and gentle kid who'd never hurt a fly, the kid who in teenage wrestling and swimming contests would deliberately lose so his competitors would feel better about themselves. Dickey and Smith's incessant talk of killing repelled him, yet in the end they didn't carry it through; their inability to kill seems right and normal. Caldwell is horrified that he was able to succeed where his friends did not. He feels that some terrible flaw must exist deep inside him.

"Did you see him go?" Caldwell sobs.

"He's gone. Tommy, you did it!" Smith roars.

Caldwell wails in reply. Dickey and Smith try to console him by telling him that what he has done is right. Rodden embraces him and rocks him from side to side. He buries his head in her shoulder and cries.

"How can you love me now?" he sobs to her. "After I did this?"

"You just saved my life, Tommy," she answers. "I couldn't love you more."

"Let's go! Let's go!" Dickey shouts. "Before Abdul gets here!"

Caldwell knows there isn't a second to lose, but his body won't move. He gets to his feet, but a moment later he sits back down and resumes sobbing.

"Are you sure he's gone?" he asks. "Are you sure?"

"I saw him go over the ledge," Dickey answers. "He went the distance. I'm sure."

"Tommy, listen to me!" Smith shouts at Caldwell. "We did nothing wrong. We saved our lives. YOU didn't do it; WE did, understand? But right now—listen up—we have to get the fuck out of here. Go!"

They are amped. Their fingers and lips tingle from fear-driven, rapid breathing. They take off along the ridge at a frantic pace, moving away from the cliffs and putting as much distance as possible between them and the man they fear most: Abdul. Said Dickey later, "My view of that man was of a stalker, a killer. I knew that if he could find us, he would, and if he did, it wouldn't be pretty."

During the climb up the side of the valley, Dickey and Smith explained their escape plan to the other two: set off across the hillside the moment they push Su, make their way down to the river, and go as fast as their legs can take them toward the soldiers at Kurbaka. But every few hundred yards Caldwell stops. His mind is wandering. He's thinking of Su, a man he spent days sleeping beside—a terrorist, true, but a living, breathing man, nonetheless. "Just keep moving, Tommy," Dickey says.

Later, thinking back on his emotional state up there, the twenty-two-year-old Caldwell would say, "I was mixed up. I didn't know whether to be proud that I had been strong enough to push Su, or horrified because I was evil. I wasn't scared that I had broken a law because I had seen these guys kill, but I worried that my parents and my friends would think I had done a terrible thing. And I worried that Beth would change her mind about me after everything was over. Even though she was telling me she loved me right then, I worried that she'd go away from me when she had time to think about it."

They run across a steep hillside creased by undulating, parallel gullies. The beds of the gullies are a bowling alley of loose stones, and the spines that separate one trough from another are of crumbling dirt. While sidling across a steep traverse, Caldwell tumbles, tucking and rolling in a cloud of grit and rocks. He comes up hugging his knee and groaning, but the pain is gone in a moment, numbed by endorphins, and he continues. Gradually, as they run, he begins "to feel a shield around them," as if someone or something is protecting them. Coincidentally, perhaps, right then Smith reverently invokes the names of Alex Lowe and Dan Osman; he tells his companions that they are in good hands, as those two men—both had climbed in these mountains, both are now dead—are looking over them. Lowe was killed a year earlier in Tibet in an avalanche on the eight-thousand-meter mountain Shishapangma; "Dano" had died in 1998 in Yosemite when a rope broke during a rope-jumping stunt and he fell a thousand feet. Both men had cut a daring swath through the climbing scene and had left their mark on Smith.

As Rodden paces along she talks nervously to Dickey, her protector during these many days. She asks over and over if he thinks Su is really dead, if he thinks Abdul heard the fall, if he thinks Tommy will be all right. Then, from out of the gully somewhere behind him, Dickey hears the clatter of shifting rocks. The resonance, the origin, and the echo of the falling rocks seem suspiciously wrong. Is someone following them? He peers into the night. Shadows and light morph every rock into an angry Abdul or a bleeding and vengeful Su. Smith, trailing the group, catches up. He's running.

"Did you hear that?" Dickey asks.

"Yes, I fucking did hear that," Smith says, and they begin sprinting forward.

The fear propelling them is infectious. When they catch up to Rodden and Caldwell they too begin running recklessly across the slope. When Dickey and Rodden come to a dirt cliff close to ten feet high that the others skirt around, they hop down the drop without a thought, sprawling in the soil at the bottom. They have no idea if a person or an animal set the rocks sliding or if the stones just moved as part of the normal creep of a scree slope. They continue running downhill in "ankle-breaker mode" until they reach the river. It is about one-fifteen, now the morning of August 18.

"Now what?" Dickey asks his companions as they catch their breath amid a cluster of junipers and pines. "Wait till light, or blaze on through the night?" They are on the west side of the Kara Su, a few hundred feet south of its confluence with the Ak Su.

Traveling by day will mean that the rebels will be hidden and the soldiers will be patrolling. At night, though, they run the risk of encountering ambushes or marauding rebels. Damned if they do, damned if they don't. In the end, the thought of Abdul drives them forward.

The gentle downhill grade beside the river is ideal for rapid travel. The trail is straight and the earth is soft underfoot. With every mile farther from the mountains, the storm clouds grow thinner and the moon brightens. After half a mile they cross a bridge consisting of three logs tied together, then they are on the east side of the Karavshin. The trail, the huts, and the bends in the river are all familiar to Dickey and Smith from their walk to Kurbaka eighteen days earlier. They keep to the shadows. A herd of cows, moonlit and barring their path, scares the wits out of them; for one brief moment they mistake them for rebels. This is like running through a haunted house, Dickey thinks.

By the time they cross a second bridge over the Karavshin and pass an apricot grove three and a half miles north of the river junction, they are nearly hallucinating from the tension. They turn northwest where the

Kundik River flows into the Karavshin, then travel another mile to a three-way intersection of rivers—the Ortochashma, the Karavshin, and the Kundik. They cross a footbridge, then at about 3:45 A.M. they see the shrine of Mazar ahead of them. Rodden and Caldwell have never been to this place, but they have heard about it; it is the spot Smith and Dickey had dubbed the Head Chopper's Place. Ibex skulls mounted on stilts, glowing in moonlight, make for an eerie sight. The shrine was a killing field a week ago. They crouch among bushes, regaining their composure and their breath. Close to seven hours have passed since they left their bivouac. They have covered ten miles.

"Listen up," Dickey whispers as they sit under the canopy of scrub. "That's the Head Chopper's Place in front of us. The army camp is less than a mile away. This is the home stretch, but it still could be dangerous. We don't know if anyone is in that hut, but we have to go right past it. We are gonna stand up one at a time and walk down that trail quietly and quickly. Got it?"

Dickey stands first, then Rodden, then Caldwell. Keeping intervals of ten feet between them, they move forward. Smith is last in line. When Dickey is about thirty feet out, Smith thinks, So far, so good, then he stands up too.

He hasn't taken more than a couple of steps when he notices a quick movement out of the corner of his eye. Three figures holding weapons stand up to his left. They are so close that they must have heard their whispered conversation a minute before. One of the figures shouts, then bullets start flying.

TO THE KYRGYZ SOLDIERS dug in around Mazar and scanning the valley with their night-vision binoculars, the four climbers appear as silhouettes on a yellow-green background. The soldiers have been tracking their movement along the trail, watching them hide behind rocks and trees. They move like the men who murdered their friends a week earlier, and the soldiers have them in their gun sights. Major Oktyabr Ryskulov, stationed in the block post at Mazar that night, said of that moment, "I called the soldiers by alarm, and everybody took his fire position. We were sure that these were the fighters, and we were ready to fire any minute. But there was something wrong. First of all, [these] strange people didn't have weapons. Second, [the] clothes on them were not appropriate for the season of the year. I clearly saw their light shirts."

But before Ryskulov could do anything, the situation changes: "Suddenly," he'd report, "there was machine-gun shooting from that side."

The climbers cannot tell whether the shooting behind them is from Kyrgyz guns or from rebels, but they react by sprinting forward. The automatic fire comes in three bursts of four to six rounds apiece. The bullets hit the dirt and the rocks around them, sending sparks dancing into the air. Dickey and Rodden dive behind a flimsy bush, while Caldwell takes cover behind a pile of rocks. The shooting stops. Dickey raises his head to look for Smith. He is suddenly wrenched by the thought that the gunmen were right beside his friend—Smith must have taken a bullet from point-blank range. But Smith appears, running on through, hurdling over them all. The guns behind them open up again. Dickey sees the amber tail of a bullet whiz past him, snapping at the air. I'm dead here, he thinks, and he gets in line behind Smith.

Smith, now a few paces ahead of them all, doesn't register that his friends are right behind him. The idea that he is alone makes him feel naked. He runs back a few steps to look for them, then he sees three people. He knows there are four in the group, and he panics. Where is number four? Is someone down? He realizes then that he is the fourth man and that he's somewhere outside of sanity. The four collide with one another, scattering across the ground, then they pick themselves up and run again. Rodden stumbles. Dickey picks her up by the scruff of her shirt and throws her forward onto her feet.

The shrine is surrounded by a stone wall breached by a single opening. Paces beyond the opening is the shrine itself. They see the outline of a figure crouching in the darkened doorway. It seems to beckon them forward. They hurtle toward the compound, with no idea whether the figure is friend or foe.

Three warning shots then fly over the Americans' heads, coming from the soldiers dug in to their front.

Shots in front, shots behind—they are in no-man's-land. They cringe, then they get up and run into the courtyard of the shrine. In a heartbeat shadowy figures are leaning over the walls of the compound, aiming rifles down at them and yelling in Russian.

"*Amerikanski, Amerikanski!* Don't shoot! We're fucking Americans!"

The soldiers run them into the hut at gunpoint. Smith is inside first. The others see him sprawled facedown on the dirt floor. A man stands over him, aiming a rifle at his head. Then strong hands push them from behind, onto the floor too, and they spread their legs and arms wide.

"I was taken aback," Ryskulov told a Kyrgyz journalist named Alexander Kim. "Where had these Americans come from? They had run to [the] fortification and were standing right in front of us. We could see they were hungry and worn-out."

One soldier kneels down and roughly frisks them. All the Americans see in the dim light are the black eyes of gun barrels and the cocked heads of nervous men fingering triggers. Rodden is certain that they are back in the hands of the rebels. Any moment, she's thinking, Abdul will step through the doorway. They are all as good as dead.

But second by second the others see a different picture: the men around them are beardless; the language is Russian; in the hut is a large, high-tech radio that seems more army than rebel. Caldwell, Dickey, and Smith realize they have escaped.

When the soldier frisks "the smallest guy," hc pulls up Rodden's shirt and uncovers her bra. "Oh, madame!" he exclaims, stepping back apologetically.

"Major, this is a woman!" he shouts to Ryskulov in Russian.

Rodden is waiting to die like Turat Osmanov. She catches Smith's eye across the dirt floor.

"Singer, we almost made it."

"We did make it, Beth," Smith says.

18.

FREEDOM

KURBAKA AND BEYOND

AUGUST 18–19

The soldiers help the Americans up off the ground. They pass them canteens of water and give them cans of sardines, which they devour ravenously. The climbers are shaking, yet the soldiers need answers fast.

"How many of you are there? Four? More?" They ask the question over and over, and in many languages, as the Kyrgyz in the hut speak virtually no English and the Americans know no Russian. The soldiers fear that rebels disguised as foreigners could launch a suicide raid on their position. A babble of Spanish, English, and Russian mixed with excited hand signs fills the room. When Rodden gets it across that she speaks a smattering of German, a captain named Kanat Tazabekov steps forward. In German, Rodden makes it clear that they are four—*vier*—and no more, and she tells them they are running from the rebels.

"Down there," Smith says urgently, pointing to the bushes where the shooters lurked. "Three men." He shapes a Taliban-style beard on his face, holds up three fingers, and shoulders an imaginary rifle. Smith dreads the possibility that they might have arrived at the outpost just in time for a rebel attack. The soldiers reply with a complex series of gestures—shaking knees, hands up in the air. Smith deciphers their meaning as being one of two things: the soldiers have flushed the rebels out of their hiding spot and they have retreated, or the rebels have been killed. In the madness of the moment, Smith doesn't know what to think. Caldwell, however, will assume the shooters were Kyrgyz soldiers they had spooked. Whatever the case, Smith starts to believe they are safe. Out of relief, he breaks into tears. Tazabekov offers them his cigarettes. Dickey and Smith each light up. They inhale the cheap, coarse, soldier's-wages tobacco. Smith, who doesn't smoke, coughs heartily.

"I can't believe we made it!" he says. "I just can't believe we made it!" Smith astounds them all by sobbing out an apology for running ahead during the final round of shooting. "I left you guys. I should have stayed with you." Through the whole ordeal he'd thought of the group as a single entity, but at the last minute he broke the rule he had set himself from the outset: stay together.

They settle him down.

Tazabekov points to the dawn hour on his watch and says "Batken" and "helicopter." It's still dark, but daylight isn't more than a couple of hours away. The Americans are struck by a sudden wave of shivering. The soldiers lay their battle jackets over them and tell them to rest. The men return to their posts. A few other soldiers lie on the floor, sleeping. But sleep is the furthest thing from the Americans' minds. They are wired.

Rodden extends her legs and arms to their fullest reach and smiles her first smile in days. "Hey, guys, look how stretched-out I am!"

Dickey stretches out too, and lets out a hoot of joy: "No more cramped bivouacs!" Then he realizes that he is lying between Caldwell and Rodden. "I'm done cuddling with Beth," he tells Caldwell. "You two need to do that." They trade places, and in a second Rodden and Caldwell are nested together, her head resting on his chest.

"I was lying there thinking about everything we'd been through and how it had created a bond between us that would last all our lives," Caldwell would later say. "Then Jason said some amazing things to us all."

Smith's emotions are close to the surface. "I need to talk to you guys," he says, sitting upright and fixing his companions with an intense glare. "This is an experience we will never forget," he begins, and then he turns to Caldwell. "Tommy, I've been thinking about you, and if you want, I'll take the rap for pushing Su. Or we can say the three of us did it. It's up to you."

Before anyone can respond, he continues. "There's something else I gotta say." He speaks now of Rodden, and of the need he felt these six days on the run to protect her, then he tells them of his admiration for the love that he sees between Caldwell and Rodden. He tells them both they are "a gift" in his life.

In a world of opposites, Smith and Caldwell could not be further apart. Their days cooped up together inside their bivouacs had produced a man-on-man tension that at times was palpable. Now Smith is telling Caldwell that he loves him like a brother. The four climbers lie close together, hip-to-hip, arm-to-arm, leg-to-leg. Rodden suggests that when they get home they should all go to the happiest place in the world.

"Where's that?" Dickey asks.

"Disneyland."

They laugh at the thought of it, though compared with the dark and terrible land they have inhabited the past six days and nights, it sounds good. In a moment when only the river and the snoring of soldiers can be heard, Dickey breaks the silence with a familiar bit of mockery: "Abdullah, Abdullah, Abdullah," he says in the most baritone voice his dry throat can muster. They all laugh, even though the thought of Abdul and the rebels terrifies them.

"I wonder where that fucker is now?" Dickey asks.

AT DAYBREAK—it is still August 18—Tazabekov and two young soldiers escort them to Kurbaka. They leave with souvenirs from the soldiers. "Here are the bullets they kill us with," one soldier communicates to them, handing them each an AK-47 round. "And these are the bullets we kill the rebels with," he adds, producing a handful of AK-74 rounds. Seeing the worn-out footwear of the soldiers, the Americans swap shoes with them. On the trail, the climbers look behind them one last time as the V-shaped walls of the Karavshin recede into the distance. They are not out of harm's way yet, however. The soldiers hurry them from one piece of cover to another. Rebel snipers are still in the hills, the men warn.

They are only a few hundred yards past Mazar when the soldiers order them to hunker down behind a rock, just a few steps from a footbridge over the Karavshin. One man goes ahead and carefully disengages a thin trip-wire that is strung across the bridge at foot level. It's a booby trap. If they had skirted around the soldiers at Mazar or run pell-mell through the warning shots and made it to this bridge, they would have been blown to bits by the explosives taped under the logs.

Not far beyond the footbridge they come to the narrow canyon that Dickey and Smith passed on their way to Kit Kim Saray. Where Dickey and Smith paused to touch the rocks and ponder ways to climb the polished walls sixteen days earlier there are now red-brown spatters of blood. Brass cartridges fill the gaps between the river stones. Rodden sees a bloodied camouflage jacket heaped beside the river. The soldiers tell them with hand signs about the slaughter of the Kyrgyz soldiers on August 10 and 11. Dickey and Smith learn that Ruslan Samsakov and his men are dead.

They reach Kurbaka at 8 A.M. The camp is filled with soldiers—at least sixty of them. The men welcome them with a meal of canned beef and bread. Even here they warn of snipers. Under the tarp, a medic dresses the angry wound that has been festering on Rodden's hand since the first morning, when she caught a chunk of flesh between thumb and forefinger in her rappel device while descending the Yellow Wall.

Later that morning an officer shows them a yellow five-mile-range Motorola.

"That's ours," Smith says. "That's the radio Abdullah was using. Switch it to channel seven and you might find his buddies."

"Dude, I don't think so," Dickey observes. "If this radio is sitting here, those guys are dusted."

An Mi8 flies in and another officer steps out. He speaks good English and introduces himself simply as Ruslan. He's spent time in the United States, he tells them, and he'll escort them to Batken. Ruslan produces a folder filled with mug shots of *"terroristas."* The Americans flip through pages of poor-quality photocopies looking for their captors.

"Isn't that the guy who was supposed to bring up our duffel bag?" Dickey says, pointing to one face in the book. They all moan at what now seems like an old, stale joke.

"There were probably one hundred faces in that book," Smith said a few days after his return to California. "Some of the pictures were badly drawn sketches. They were really funny. We were laughing at the forty-seven-chromosome terrorist and the Down's syndrome rebel. There was a sketch of a character that didn't have a face at all. He looked like Blank out of *Dick Tracy.* Some photos were crossed out—killed, I guess. But other photos were clear. We didn't see Abdul. But I could spot that guy's eyes from a hundred yards away."

AT KURBAKA they form their pact: to all comers, bar parents and their closest friends, they will say that the three males surrounded Su on the cliff and pushed him as one. It is a lie, but it is for Caldwell's benefit, as his sense of despair at taking Su's life is mounting. The pact makes Caldwell no happier, though, as it alters nothing. His mood alternates between moments of troubled introspection and feelings of bliss that he and his friends are alive. If Caldwell could reverse these weeks and edit out the entire journey to Kyrgyzstan, he would. Not so Smith. While hashing over the events at Kurbaka, he tells them this: "If there was a week in my life I would want to relive, then this would be it. To experience every human emotion in such a short time, under those intense, life-threatening circumstances, I would gladly go back."

So when the soldiers ask how the Americans escaped from the rebels, Smith doesn't hesitate to tell them: "We push *terrorista* off cliff," he says in broken English and with dramatic hand movements. At first the soldiers don't understand what Smith is saying, but when they grasp his meaning they slap him on the back and joke about giving the Americans a medal. Smith revels in the camaraderie, but Caldwell shrinks from it.

"Maybe we should be low-key about this," Caldwell suggests to him.

"I would stand beside myself with pride if I had pushed that guy," Smith replies.

"I don't see it like that," Caldwell says.

"Jason, cool it!" Rodden says sharply.

On the morality of pushing their captor, they will never see eye to eye.

IF THEIR ORDEAL took place in a mountainous black hole, Caldwell, Dickey, Rodden, and Smith now step into a whirlwind of attention when at noon on August 18 an Mi8 delivers them to the mobile anti-terrorism base outside of Batken. The base is the command center for the fight against the IMU, and it consists of a cluster of trucks and trailers housing communications gear, ringed by tanks and soldiers.

"Hey, can I take that tank for a drive?" Smith asks an officer while they walk across the helipad.

The officer politely declines the request and ushers them to quarters where they wash up and are issued clean military uniforms to replace their stinking rags. Then they are taken to the office of General Esen Topoev, the Kyrgyz minister of defense. Ruslan stands stiffly at attention while he introduces them to Topoev. The general has sharply chiseled Asiatic features and a stern manner, though his handshake is warm enough. Dickey detects a strong smell of alcohol on the general's breath and sees that he's swaying slightly on his feet.

Topoev says through Ruslan, "Tell your president in America that he should be careful who he sells arms to. This happened to you because America gave weapons to Afghanistan and Pakistan to fight the Soviets. That is where the terrorists who kidnapped you got their weapons. You should say this at your press conference." The Americans stare ahead, as confused as deer caught in the headlights of an oncoming truck.

After stuffing themselves with a meal of bread and condensed milk, they spend the night in an army trailer hut. Ruslan hands them paper and pens and asks them to write down everything that happened to them since their arrival in Kyrgyzstan. In the reports Caldwell, Dickey, and Smith share responsibility for pushing Su. The reports are filed at the Ministry of Defense in Bishkek.

———

THE PRESENCE of the Americans at the mobile base coincides with the arrival by helicopter the next morning of the president of Kyrgyzstan, Askar Akayev. He has come to award medals and promotions to a few officers for their roles in defeating the rebels, though fighting along the border will continue into September. The Americans are ushered into a marquis tent after the ceremony and stand in front of a battery of journalists and officers for a photo opportunity. The president enters to applause, and he greets the Americans. His press secretary and English-speaking interpreter, Ilyas Bekbolotov, translates the proceedings.

Akayev strikes Rodden as being not so presidential as "like somebody's grandfather, a jolly old fellow." Balding and slightly rotund, Akayev is, however, a political pit bull who has kept a firm grip on power since becoming president in 1991. Deregistering the candidacy of his political competitors shortly before national elections, tossing the political opposition leader in jail, and silencing journalists who criticize him in print by jailing them and suspending their licenses to work are among the criticisms of the Akayev regime that have irked the U.S. Department of State and Amnesty International in their reports on human rights in Kyrgyzstan. U.S. officials have also criticized him for using the conflict in Batken to oppress and imprison Muslims he suspects of being antigovernment.

Akayev starts a speech that praises the Kyrgyz army, then he turns to the Americans. "We like our U.S. allies," he says. "As you may know, our army has been fortifying its borders against these terrorists for the past eighteen months. That is why our army could release you from your captors. Tell your president we are very happy our army could rescue you."

The Americans stare back and stammer a few words of thanks. They are both shell-shocked and grateful. The press conference ends, and Akayev leaves. The Americans remain in the tent for fifteen minutes longer. Journalists gather around them and ask questions. Bekbolotov translates. The journalists ask for their names, their occupations, and whether the terrorists beat them. The Americans say they were treated well enough but say little else about their six-day ordeal. They mention nothing about pushing a rebel off a cliff. It is too hot a topic to mention to this gathering of army brass, politicians, and journalists. The presidential press entourage file their stories accordingly.

The Americans and several journalists hitch a ride on the Mi8 to the main airport at Batken, then they board the presidential jet for the flight to Bishkek. From the air they look down on a long valley stretching into the hazy distance; somewhere out there is Kit Kim Saray. "I wonder what Beidel Dar is doing?" Dickey asks, not expecting an answer.

Sitting in the back of the plane with the president's security guards, the Americans watch an attendant deliver several rounds of vodka into the sealed-off presidential cabin. When they disembark in Bishkek, they see Topoev leaving the plane in extremely high spirits.

In the VIP lounge of Manas International Airport in Bishkek the Kyrgyz hand them over to two men from the U.S. embassy, Ed Kulakowski and Greg Gardner. The men appear nervous. The four Americans are skinny, haggard, and dressed in ill-fitting army-issue camouflage uniforms. Their faces are so thin that their eyes appear to bulge out of their heads. Kulakowski and Gardner have no idea what kind of diplomatically sensitive baggage they've been handed.

"You just popped up on our radar screen," Kulakowski says, breaking the ice. He's the embassy's public affairs officer.

"Must have been a pretty rough time, huh?" Gardner asks.

They grunt a collective yes. Kulakowski tells them that he's going to take them to the embassy, where they can take a hot shower, get a good meal, see a doctor, phone home, and contact their travel agents to get themselves back to the States. Rodden sees that Kulakowski is wearing a sweatshirt that says TEXAS A&M DAD. Outside the VIP lounge she sees two Toyota Land Cruisers, one of them flying an American flag on the bumper. The men have the safe look of midwesterners. She realizes that she is one step closer to home.

Only Smith holds up their departure. He's talking to a pair of ethnic-Russian journalists from TASS and Interfax. Smith talks to them for five minutes. Bekbolotov translates, as neither reporter speaks English. Smith says little about their captivity. When somebody says, "Let's get out of here," Kulakowski cuts the meeting short, and they head out of the VIP lounge and into the cars for the drive to the U.S. embassy.

19.

A. K. A. ABDUL

———

One by one the rebel invaders escape the Kyrgyz army's encirclement by filtering back into Tajikistan, or they die. A photo of Obid's slack-jawed corpse will appear in the Bishkek newspaper *Delo Noma*. The rebels' bloody odyssey will be recorded by them on video, and Kyrgyz soldiers will capture the camcorder. Abdul, Su, Hamsa, the Artist, and others in this story will appear on the tape. Security officials in Bishkek will say that the video was shot to impress their sponsor of terrorism, Osama bin Laden.

Abdul will live for thirty-six more hours after he leaves the Americans. I'll learn about Abdul's fate from Lieutenant Colonel Akyl Dononbaev. His men detected Abdul at the head of the Ak Su valley on August 19 as he was heading for the Boz Toz Pass. Dononbaev will also be the one who confirms to me that Abdul's real name is Sabir. Like most of the rebels, he operated under a false name.

The weary rebel is moving slowly along the glacier that day when two Skorpions dug in below the pass spot him through binoculars. Abdul a.k.a. Sabir's progress toward their ambush is so slow, in fact, that one of the Skorpions takes the opportunity to leave his post and relieve his bowels. With one soldier glassing the glacial wasteland and the other squatting with his pants around his ankles forty feet away, Sabir slips out of the first soldier's field of vision just long enough to outflank him. When the rebel reappears, he is right in front of the Skorpion on lookout, aiming his weapon point-blank at the soldier.

He orders him to stand and move away from his weapon, which lies on the ground, then he pulls the trigger on his RPK. Rebel and soldier are stunned to hear a loud metallic *bing,* as the firing mechanism jams. The Skorpion lunges toward his own weapon as Sabir drops the machine gun and draws his pistol. The Skorpion is a step away from his own gun, but he sees that Sabir will be ready to fire before he will. The Skorpion lashes out with a kick that knocks Sabir backward and makes him misfire. The men fall on each other, wrestling and writhing on the ground. The Skorpion grips Sabir's wrist, trying to squeeze the pistol out of his hand. Three more rounds fire from the pistol; all miss their mark. The second soldier rushes onto the scene now, pulling at his trousers and aiming his submachine gun at the two on the ground.

"Give me his head, give me his head!" the Skorpion who is standing shouts at the writhing ball of legs and arms.

Sabir is forced onto his back long enough for the Skorpion with the rifle to aim and fire. A single shot hits him in the neck. He dies instantly.

In Sabir's pocket is a note. "If you are reading this letter you have killed me," it reads. It requests an Islamic burial. The soldiers leave his body for the birds.

THE REBELS CONTINUE FIGHTING along the border till late September. They launch raids near mountain villages with names like Dinay, Tilbe, Yangidavan, Jili Su, and Syrt, and the Abramov Glacier. In Uzbekistan there are raids near suburban Tashkent, shocking the local population. The rebels hit their targets with as many as eighty and as few as ten fighters.

They are driven back by Kyrgyz or Uzbek troops, by helicopters firing rockets, and by artillery. With their ranks in disarray, the "disposable rebels" limp back to their strongholds in Tajikistan.

Like the first Batken conflict, the cost to a poor nation is enormous. By its end, thirty-four Kyrgyz soldiers are listed as dead or missing, and forty are wounded. Thousands of border-dwelling Kyrgyz shepherds are forced to relocate, to protect them from being taken hostage and to clear the ground for bombardments. In the coming months, shepherds and livestock will be killed when they step on land mines left in the high country. The Kyrgyz Ministry of Defense will list a body count of sixty-two rebels. Kyrgyz soldiers will report bloodstains and body parts on mountain passes after bombardments, and they'll smell death rising from caves in the rugged valleys where wounded rebels crawled off to die.

No one will really understand why the IMU launched such a brutal attack, or why the rebels threw away their lives, seemingly for no gain at all. During the turmoil of Batken II, Namangami's second in command, Takhir Yuldashev, will fax and phone news agencies like Kabar and be monitored on Iranian radio and on *Voice of America*. In one interview in October 2000, he'll say, "The goals of IMU activities are firstly fighting against oppression within our country, against bribery, against the inequities and also the freeing of our Muslim brothers from prison. We are therefore now shedding blood, and the creation of an Islamic state will be the next problem. We declared a jihad in order to create a religious system, a religious government."

Kyrgyz, Uzbek, and Russian government officials will brush aside such lofty goals and say that drug smuggling is behind it all. Ever since the Soviet-Afghan war, Afghan-made heroin and opium have been funneled to Russia and Europe through southern Kyrgyzstan. But if drugs or hard currency were found on the vanquished rebels, there was no report of it from the Kyrgyz military. Speaking about the raids in southern Kyrgyzstan, a Bishkek journalist who didn't want to be named said, "If the IMU and the people said to be behind them—the Taliban, bin Laden, the Russian mafia, rich Arabs—really were trying to get their drugs through Kyrgyzstan and Uzbekistan, then they would smuggle them in secret. Fighting with the armies of Kyrgyzstan and Uzbekistan is not going to let them get their drugs to their buyers."

Nor did he believe that a few hundred men could fight their way to Tashkent, through the forty-thousand-strong Uzbek army, and overthrow Karimov, or that the arrival of the IMU would persuade Kyrgyz Muslims to rise up in revolt. The journalist believed that the reason behind the IMU attack was more primal: terror for the sake of terror.

In a rare public broadcast made in the months following the fighting in Batken, Namangani is reported to have said on Iran's *Voice of Shari'a* radio, "2001 will be a decisive year for the holy war on Uzbek President Karimov."

It would indeed be a decisive year in the holy war of terror, and not just in Uzbekistan.

20.

PARTING WAYS

———

BISHKEK

AUGUST 19–21

Short of being surrounded by fortress walls, most everything about the U.S. embassy in Bishkek suggests a building designed to weather any shit that might hit the Central Asian fan. Low-profile to the point of looking as if it is sinking into the ground, its sturdy horizon looks able to deflect rocket attacks. The building stands apart from suburban Bishkek, on a grassy acreage that affords a good view of approaching foes. An airstrip big enough to handle transport jets sits beside the embassy for rapid evacuation. To enter the compound, one drives along a winding road dotted with concrete berms to thwart suicide bombers from speeding headlong at the gates beyond. At the final turn in the road an SUV with the engine perpetually running bars the opening through this obstacle course. If you pass muster and get a nod from the driver, he reverses the SUV and you enter the outer sanctum. At two security posts documents are checked, bags and bodies x-rayed, and questions asked. The inner sanctum lies behind auto-locking doors, bulletproof glass, armed immigration police, and U.S. Marines. Inside this building, at around 5 P.M. on Saturday, August 19, Caldwell, Dickey, Rodden, and Smith call home. On the other side of the globe it is fifteen hours earlier, two o'clock Saturday morning in California, when the phone rings on Robb and Linda Rodden's bedside table.

"There's Beth," Linda says at the first ring.

She and her husband are wide awake. They know in their gut that something bad has happened to their daughter, though exactly what, they are not sure. Ever since the team left America, Robb has been surfing the Internet for news about Kyrgyzstan, and he's gotten into the habit of reading the news bulletins on Kabar. On August 14 he became "seriously ill at ease" after reading reports about Kyrgyz soldiers being killed in a raid by a terrorist group called the Islamic Movement of Uzbekistan. But the places where the fighting had occurred—Garm, Batken, Piramidalny Peak, Lyalyak—were meaningless names to him. He knew only that his daughter's team had gone to a valley called the Kara Su. In the Kyrgyz countryside Kara Su is nearly as common a place name as Main Street in America; there are many Kara Sus on the Kyrgyz map. On August 15 he e-mailed Elena Kalashnikova at Ak Sai Travel and to ask if the fighting was anywhere near his daughter. Kalashnikova replied promptly, saying that the "trouble" is far away from the Americans and that someone from her company would fly by the area to check on the expedition if the opportunity arose. He has heard nothing more from Kalashnikova. But when he checks the Internet on the night of August 16 the news is alarming: German and Russian climbers have been kidnapped in the mountains and have been rescued by Kyrgyz soldiers. By the morning of August 17 Kabar reports widespread fighting along the Kyrgyz border. Rodden called the Kyrgyzstan desk of the U.S. State Department to ask if they had any information about Americans in the area of fighting. They know nothing. On Friday, August 18, when Robb and Linda returned home from dinner with friends, he sat on the couch and opened the local newspaper, the *Davis Enterprise.* "It's a small paper that barely covers international news, but buried in it was a short filler article that stated that four American climbers who had been kidnapped by terrorist rebels had been rescued by the Kyrgyz army. I folded the paper so that the article was prominent, handed it to Linda, and said, 'I think this is about Beth.' "

Up till then he'd kept quiet about the Internet reports because in the absence of hard news he didn't want to worry his wife. Now he explained everything he had learned. "It was eerie that such a small newspaper would carry this particular bit of news," he would later say. "The newspaper knew nothing about Beth being in Kyrgyzstan. And still, it was not clear to us that this was about her team. There would have been several teams. The locations were imprecise, and Elena had not contacted me again with any expression of concern. But intuition told me this was Beth."

"Hi, Dad," his daughter says over the background buzz of satellite relay.

"Hi, Beth," he replies.

"How are you doing, Dad?"

"Where are you?" he asks, calm yet urgent.

"At the U.S. embassy in Bishkek."

"What happened?"

It's a tone of voice Beth knows from her childhood. Her father is a straightforward man, and he's telling her to cut to the chase. He can tell that she is trying hard to hold back tears.

"We were taken hostage."

"By who?"

"Islamic militants, I think. I don't know what they wanted us for. Ransom, I guess."

"Are you sure you are all right? Really all right?"

"Yes. They didn't hurt me."

She tells him they had been held for six days until their escape.

"How did you escape?"

"One of the guys got pushed."

"Who pushed him, honey?"

The question hangs over her in the heaviest way. She is sitting in a cubicle in the U.S. embassy. She doesn't know if the line is being monitored or who she can trust with the story of what happened on the cliff. Her voice is a whisper. She wants to tell her parents the truth, but she is bound by the pact with her friends.

"The boys did."

She assures her father that embassy staff are taking care of them, but she has to hang up because the building is closing down for the night. "One other thing, Dad," she asks. "When we get home, can we get a home security system at our house?"

"Beth, do whatever it takes to get home as soon as you can."

"I'm sorry I woke you up," she says.

"We love you, honey."

Robb Rodden is struck by the trauma in his daughter's voice. "She was making every effort not to make us worry about her. It didn't really work. We know her real well and could tell from the sound of her voice that she had been through something that had shaken her to the core."

TOMMY CALDWELL'S CALL to Estes Park wakes his parents, Mike and Terry, from a deep sleep. "I think it put them into shock," he recalled later of their reaction to his tale. "My dad rambled something about us going climbing together in Colorado, then we hung up. They didn't know that there was trouble in Kyrgyzstan. After the conversation they realized what I had told them, but they couldn't call back because the embassy was closed. They called Beth's parents and got a better understanding of everything. For the next twenty-four hours they paced the house till I called them again."

"How did you escape?" Mike Caldwell asks his son then.

"We pushed one of our guards and ran."

Something instinctual makes Mike Caldwell ask, "Were you the one who pushed him?"

"Yes."

IN TEXAS, Dickey's parents, Ed and Jackie, are also unaware of events in Kyrgyzstan. His mother doesn't immediately grasp his meaning when he tells her he had been taken hostage. Only after the call, when they phone his girlfriend, Rita Di Lorenzo, and learn more, does the seriousness of his words sink in. Dickey catches Di Lorenzo at the Attic, the watering hole around the corner from their apartment in San Francisco where she is working as a bartender. The Friday-night crowd is staggering out the door, and she has an armful of empty glasses and bottles when her boss tells her that her boyfriend is on the line.

"I'm just calling to let you know we're okay, in case you hear anything on the news."

"What happened? Are you all right?"

"Yeah. Everyone is okay. War broke out in Kyrgyzstan. We were held hostage by some pretty rough people. We'd probably still be there except we threw one of our guards over a cliff."

"Are you serious?"

After the call Di Lorenzo recalls something odd. A few days earlier she'd been struck with hunger pains so severe she had to stop in her tracks and sit down. With the pains came a thought: is John okay? "Maybe it was coincidence, but I chalk it up to emotional connection," she later said.

SMITH'S MOTHER, Lorene Wayman, is asleep when her son calls. She's in the process of packing her belongings for a move from Utah to Texas and she has no idea what her son has gone through, but the moment she hears his voice she senses that something has gone wrong. He would not call from Kyrgyzstan otherwise. Smith says hello, then they start spontaneously sobbing. His description of running for his life so moves his mother that after the call she fires off an e-mail to a large address list that includes many of Jason's climbing friends. The e-mail circulates like wildfire, forwarded from one address to another, till by the end of the weekend it sits in the in-boxes of hundreds of Jason Smith's friends and family, as well as reporters and others who have never met the climbers but who become connected to the e-mail tree. Wayman's account describes the events with the high-flying relief of a mother who feels that her son has returned from the brink of oblivion. In retelling the story she innocently introduces a few minor errors that will become widely reported.

My information is sketchy, but this is the best I can remember. . . . Jason called collect at around 4 A.M. today. He was at the US embassy in Kyrgyzstan, safe and okay, but the past 6 days had been a nightmare. [Jason], John, Beth, Tommy were approximately

1,000 feet off the ground on their portaledges, climbing a wall in Kyrgyzstan. Terrorists started shooting at them from the ground to get them to come down. They were taken as hostages, along with another man (unknown where he came from). They communicated by "charades" and it was made known that if they didn't do as they were told, they would be shot in the head. At one point, the terrorists took this other hostage behind a rock and executed him! Jason was forced to sit on a dead body for 40 minutes. They knew they must find a way to get free. After several days of being kept hostage, they were walking with a terrorist on a ridge. The guys overcame him and pushed him off the ridge, killing the terrorist. Jason said he "ran like Forrest Gump!" They ran 18 hours. I think they were nearing the border when once again terrorists started shooting at them. Bullets were whizzing by their heads! John, Tommy and Beth hit the ground but Jason continued running. He was suddenly surrounded by Kyrgyz troops, where Jason yelled that they were Americans. The president of Kyrgyzstan picked them up in his private jet, returning them to the capital. The crew of the plane called them "heroes" for killing a terrorist! They were taken to the US embassy where they were debriefed. . . . They did not eat for 6 days! When I think about the ordeal they must have gone through, I cry my eyes out! The only thing they have left is the clothes on their backs . . . everything else is gone. Thank God they have their lives!

News about the former hostages streams into America via satellite and wire even as they speak on the phone. The story hits U.S. television screens a few hours later, at midmorning on Saturday, August 19, when CNN broadcasts the footage shot by Kyrgyz TV reporters at the Batken mobile anti-terrorist base. Like many climbers, I received a phone call from a friend who'd just seen the clip of Caldwell, Dickey, Rodden, and Smith in army uniforms boarding a helicopter. "Hey, you won't believe what I just saw on TV," a friend in Moab told me by phone. "Those guys in Kyrgyzstan got taken hostage by terrorists."

The Salt Lake Tribune tracks Wayman to her home in nearby Sandy,

Utah, and on Sunday, August 20, the paper runs a front-page story on the kidnapping by a staff writer. An Associated Press photo shows Smith and Rodden (incorrectly identified as Beth Radley; the misspelled name would delay reporters from finding her family) at the mobile anti-terrorist base. Smith looks angry and animated as he talks into a reporter's microphone. Rodden appears gaunt and bewildered. The story runs much like Wayman's e-mail: "'My son and the other hostages knew if they didn't get a plan together they were going to die,' Wayman said tearfully. 'So they pushed the terrorist off the edge and ran.' " The story states that the terrorist had been killed.

Smith had grown up in the Salt Lake area, so the *Tribune* approached the story like local news. A photo shows a beaming Wayman and Smith's sister, Angela, holding a graduation portrait of Smith between them. He's wearing a tuxedo. " 'Can you tell I love my son?' Wayman said. 'He's a crazy kid. I live through his adventures.' " The story concludes with a picaresque and fictional description of his lifestyle: "After graduating from high school Smith went to Yosemite to climb. Without a job he lived in a cave and a tree and begged for food."

Reporters descend on the homes of the Roddens and the Caldwells too. They pound on their doors and phone them, and they camp on the street in TV vans. With no news yet as to when the former hostages will make it home, TV crews leave baskets of fruit, food, and flowers on their doorsteps, hoping to get lucky and film their return. The *Rocky Mountain News, The Denver Post,* and the *San Francisco Examiner* run stories about the hostage drama on Sunday and Monday. Mindful of their children's concern over reprisals and their discomfort about pushing their captor off a cliff, the parents report only that the climbers had escaped, or had been freed by the Kyrgyz army. Again, errors are introduced into the story. Mike Caldwell's statement that the team had searched the State Department Web site and had found no warnings for southern Kyrgyzstan raises the ire of State Department staffers, who point to several warnings regarding rebel activity in Kyrgyzstan that were active at the time the climbers were planning their trip.

The U.S. embassy in Bishkek contributes to some confusion in the media too, by making no comment to the media. When presented by embassy staff with the option of waiving their right to privacy and permitting the embassy to give out information about their kidnapping and their identities, or requesting that the embassy make no comment, the climbers choose privacy. Interfax journalist Igor Shestakov will later say that the policy of nondisclosure was so tight that embassy staff even denied to him that there were any U.S. tourists in Kyrgyzstan at all. Shestakov was the reporter Smith met for five minutes at the Bishkek airport. The silence will strike the Russian as odd, and it will fuel later speculation that the Americans were keeping something quiet.

The Americans are a pitiable sight in their ill-fitting army uniforms. Over the next couple of days embassy staff go out of their way to make the climbers comfortable. They drive them around Bishkek on errands, they loan some of them clothing until they buy clean shirts and pants, they get them checked over by a doctor. Some staff even let them watch TV and videos in their apartments. All that the climbers have left from their expedition is a bundle of stinking clothes that they carry in Caldwell and Dickey's rucksacks. The army has recovered the two rucksacks from the site of Osmanov's murder and returned them in Batken. Dickey's sports a bullet hole. It becomes a conversation piece as they socialize with embassy people. To Smith's regret, his trophy—Abdul/Sabir's camo cap—is lost. He had left it as a marker for Kyrgyz soldiers, hanging on a bush that final night, high on the cliffy hillside above the Kara Su.

Getting home as fast as possible is priority number one for the Americans, but they learn from their airline that leaving earlier than their scheduled departure of August 29 will be expensive. They can buy new tickets for twelve hundred dollars apiece and fly in two days from Almaty in Kazakhstan, which is a four-hour drive from Bishkek, or they can pay eight hundred dollars to change their tickets and fly from Bishkek in five days. It's money they can ill afford. The value of the gear they have lost on the wall and in base camp, and the cost of Dickey's cameras, totals nearly thirty thousand dollars. Most of the gear is uninsured, and those with insurance policies will learn that losses incurred in "acts of war" are not covered. In Bishkek they depend on Caldwell and Smith's credit cards and the crumpled wad of cash—two hundred dollars—that Caldwell kept in his socks since their abduction. Bishkek moneychangers laugh at the sweat-stained, fetid banknotes and push them back through the bars of their booths when he tries to convert them to Kyrgyz som. The U.S. embassy comes to their aid here too by exchanging the money for new bills.

An attempt to get a refund from Ak Sai Travel for the unused return portion of their helicopter flight—an amount in the order of four thousand dollars—falls flat when Elena Kalashnikova tells them that the money was spent when she and Svetlana Fedina chartered a helicopter to go to Batken to search for them. Ak Sai Travel offers them no receipt for the helicopter ride, and the Americans wonder why their travel agents flew by expensive helicopter rather than the cheap commercial jet service. But money matters seem inconsequential to Rodden. She walks away from their losses without concern. To her, being alive is all that is important. Relations between the Americans and Ak Sai Travel sink a notch lower, though, after Ed Kulakowski gives a stern lecture to Kalashnikova and Fedina at the embassy. He berates them for not registering the climbers at OVIR despite charging them for the service, for failing to notify the embassy that they were delivering U.S. clients to a dangerous area, and for waiting so long before faxing the embassy that Americans were in trouble in a war zone. Kalashnikova will claim that none of the above were her responsibility.

Caldwell and Rodden are desperate to leave Kyrgyzstan, but they are stuck in Bishkek for at least a few days, so they all book into the Hotel Eldorado. Those first days of freedom come with a need to cling to one another. They sit arm in arm in taxis and around the pool of the hotel, and they are seldom out of one another's sight. As they check in to their digs, Smith declares, "We're not going to separate for a week." He explains that the worst thing for their mental states would be to uproot themselves from Kyrgyzstan and fly home. To his way of thinking, they need time to decompress and segue out of one another's lives, and to try to make sense of the experience. Besides, it's midsummer in Bishkek, the cafés are lively, the people are friendly, and the elegant and long-limbed Eurasian women of the city are second to none in beauty.

They are not in agreement when it comes to handling the media. When Rodden and Caldwell see the *Salt Lake Tribune* story the next day on the Internet on an embassy computer, they are upset that the story is out that they had pushed Su, and they're alarmed that the report states that he's dead. They assume Su is dead too, but they don't know for sure. Caldwell keeps it well hidden, but he is deeply affected by the thought of what he did to Su, and he worries that people in America will react negatively to him. Thinking of the jihad's eye-for-an-eye justice, Rodden too has begun to be plagued by visions of the terrorists tracking them down at their hotel or in America to avenge Su's death. Embassy staff also advise them against publicizing that they have killed a terrorist. The *Salt Lake Tribune* story makes Caldwell and Rodden storm into Smith's hotel room to vent their displeasure.

Smith hasn't seen the newspaper, and it was his mother, not him, who talked to the reporter, yet he sees no harm in her retelling their story. It happened. How could they avoid talking about it? They argue, and Smith apologizes. While Rodden and Caldwell feel compelled to keep the story out of the media, Smith appears comfortable wearing the mantle of terrorist slayer. During the argument he scoffs at their concern that rebels might "pull a drive-by." He tells them they're being "paranoid."

That night at the restaurant in the Hotel Eldorado they gorge on hamburgers, platters of barbecued meat, and pasta. Dickey, the thinnest of them all, starts their feast with a shrimp salad. By midnight he is puking from food poisoning. It marks the beginning of their physical breakdowns. "I felt as if every tendon in my body had been stretched or broken," Dickey said. Rodden will wake aching every morning for the next two weeks, a side effect of their cramped, cold bivouacs. They'll be assailed by fatigue, deep sleeps interspersed with insomnia, insatiable appetites, and painful heartburn. Rodden will be struck by thirteen days of constipation.

They spend the morning of August 20 sitting around the hotel pool, discussing the night on the cliff and the morality of pushing Su. By now their pact is set in stone. They have stated in writing to the Kyrgyz military that the three males threw him to his death, and they have said the same to soldiers and reporters at Kurbaka and Batken. They've told the truth, however, to Greg Gardner, Ed Kulakowski, and other embassy officials during a taped interview at the embassy. They agree to stick to the three-who-pushed-Su story when talking with reporters in the United States, until such a time as Caldwell wants to let the truth come out. The pact helps Caldwell cope with his angst. He is grateful to his companions, but the "white lie" changes nothing: he pushed Su, the others didn't. He sits staring at the shimmering water of the pool, withdrawn and sad.

"You have nothing to be ashamed of, Tommy," Smith tells him. "Su was at war, and whether we like it or not, he dragged us into his war. We were forced to play a role in it, just as if we were enlisted soldiers. In the end we had to step up and save our own arses, simple as that. And we probably saved the lives of a lot more Kyrgyz soldiers too, by dusting that fucker."

Caldwell says nothing.

"It's a good thing that you did it, Tommy," Dickey adds. "Because when you come right down to it, most people wouldn't have had the balls. Most people would have just sat back and died."

"I just don't see anything good in this at all," Caldwell says quietly.

ON THE AFTERNOON of August 21, while Dickey is sleeping off his food poisoning, Caldwell, Rodden, and Smith walk to the Beta Store, the chic new shopping complex of Bishkek. They shop around for a while, then at dusk they walk back to the Eldorado.

On the way they encounter an old drunkard who staggers after the Americans, raving in Russian. Caldwell and Rodden ignore him and walk on, but Smith lingers, having a bit of fun with the old-timer. Rodden wants no part of it. She calls to Smith to hurry along.

"Wait, maybe this guy has our duffel bag!" he calls back.

No one is laughing at this joke anymore.

"Singer, let's go," Rodden says.

Smith turns to the drunk. "Askar Akayev, he's our buddy. We flew in his plane. We kill *terrorista*. Maybe you saw us in the newspaper?"

Rodden shouts at Smith. He bids the drunk adieu. A few paces on, two men block their path. Embassy staff have warned the climbers about thieves masquerading as plainclothes police. They demand to see your passport, then your wallet, then they divest you of both. It's a popular scam with local hoodlums.

"Passporty!" one of the men says with authority. He opens his wallet and flashes some sort of ID card, but he pockets it before anyone can examine it. The men are unkempt. They don't even remotely resemble cops.

"This is the scam we were told about!" Caldwell says.

The men hem them in. On the advice of embassy staff, the Americans have left their passports at the hotel, and they show the men photocopies of the documents. When the men begin frisking them, Rodden backs away. Smith lingers, though, bantering with the hoods. After the events of the past week these small-time crooks are a joke. The Americans break free of the men and head off.

"Scaredy-cats," Smith mutters to Caldwell and Rodden.

"I just don't want anything else to go wrong," she says.

THE PASSPORT SCAM is the last straw for Rodden. The next morning an embassy staffer helps her arrange tickets for Caldwell and her from Kazakhstan to the United States. Back at the hotel, Rodden tells Dickey and Smith that there is room on the plane if they want to go.

"We don't have the money," Smith says. "Besides, Bishkek is a bitchin' hang."

"I'll pay for you guys to go home," she replies.

They decline.

That night they eat their last meal together in an Indian restaurant. Whenever the conversation turned to food in Caldwell and Smith's bivouacs, Smith talked about curries. The air at the table is tense. The four climbers and a couple of embassy staff fraternize awkwardly. Smith's ebullience about their actions, the way he tells their story to all who listen, grates on Caldwell. It is Smith's nature to be the raconteur, Caldwell's to be reticent. The two are like oil and water. Dickey's relaxed, take-it-as-it-comes attitude has remained the counterpoint to them both, but now he seems distant as well. The need to stay together to survive has passed. They can drift apart now.

A month earlier at San Francisco International Airport, Robb Rodden looked the group over before they left and thought, What a mix of totally different personalities. He guessed this would be the group's first and last expedition together.

Rodden and Caldwell leave the restaurant early in the evening to get some sleep before their dawn departure to Almaty. They thank the embassy people and say good-bye to their teammates, telling them that they'll meet them at the San Francisco airport when they return. Caldwell doesn't say much; fever, headache, hot flashes, and cold sweats are setting in as his immune system falls apart.

"Be careful," Rodden says to Dickey and Smith as she leaves.

"Careful is our middle name," Smith replies.

Greg Gardner and a Kyrgyz driver escort Caldwell and Rodden to Almaty in an embassy SUV. It is still dark, predawn, when they leave Bishkek. Caldwell sleeps in the back, while Rodden and Gardner make small talk. Along the way Gardner asks what souvenirs she is taking home from Kyrgyzstan. Rodden tells Gardner about the memorabilia she has squirreled away in her pockets: yogurt balls, a small rock she pocketed moments before the firefight of August 12, tiny wildflowers she picked at bivouacs and pressed between the pages of her passport. And bullets.

"You mean you have live ammunition?"

"Yeah, the Kyrgyz soldiers gave us a bunch of different bullets when we traded our shoes with them."

"Pull the car over right now," Gardner orders the driver. "I need to get rid of these before we hit the border."

The car stops. Rodden and Caldwell search through their belongings, then they drop a half-dozen bullets into Gardner's hand. He rolls the window down and pitches the rounds.

"It never ends with you guys, does it?" he says, shaking his head, and they continue driving. He's a kind yet nervous man, the climbers have noted. He'll be a lot calmer after they have left.

21.

GETTING HOME

I enter this story on August 21, when an editor named Mike Benge at *Climbing* magazine calls to ask me to write about the Kyrgyzstan drama. I haven't seen any newspaper or TV coverage of the kidnapping, though the climbing grapevine is abuzz with the word that Islamic militants took a group of well-known climbers hostage. What little information I have heard tells me that this is a hot story and that big-name journalists will mob the climbers when they return home. I am reluctant to try to elbow my way through the throng of magazines who'll be jockeying for interviews, but I agree to look into the story, as I am a regular contributor to *Climbing.* Benge gives me the phone number of the Roddens and forwards me Wayman's e-mail. The beats of that e-mail—American climbers forced off cliff at gunpoint, held hostage by fanatical rebels, shoot-outs with Kyrgyz soldiers, fellow hostage executed, climbers kill terrorists to save their lives—confirm to me that a journalistic feeding frenzy is about to happen. It is the first time I have ever heard of hostages turning the tables on their captors.

I don't think I stand a chance at getting a minute of the climbers' time, but I call Robb Rodden anyway. He is polite but reluctant to talk. His daughter and Caldwell are still flying from Almaty, he tells me, and he doesn't want to say anything that could jeopardize the safety of Dickey and Smith, who are still in Bishkek. He agrees to pass to Beth my request for an interview when she gets home the following day, but he mentions that TV and newspaper people are camped out in front of his house and that she'll be busy.

Next, I call The North Face to see what they know. I have been a member of the company's climbing team since the early 1990s, and I am in their employ as a professional climber in addition to working as a writer. Although the Kyrgyzstan expedition was sponsored by The North Face, I know nothing about the trip and barely know the climbers involved. Some of them are half my age, and although we share the same sport, we occupy very different generations within it. I have never met Caldwell or Dickey and have only been briefly introduced to Rodden, who struck me as shy. I knew Smith in passing from visits to The North Face and from a few friendly encounters at climbing areas. He impressed me as a witty and capable big-wall climber.

A harried PR man takes my call at The North Face. He's been deluged with calls from the media and gives no comment. No one knows what happened over there, and The North Face has never dealt with an international hostage crisis, so they're keeping quiet. I am feeling doubtful about getting anyone to talk when I call the desk of Topher Gaylord, an executive in the company and a personal friend.

"Can you believe what happened to Singer and those guys?" Gaylord says excitedly. "You should write a story about it."

"I'm checking it out, but I'm getting nowhere. I can't get any information."

"Phone Singer in Kyrgyzstan. I've got his hotel phone number right here."

It hasn't occurred to me that Gaylord would have spoken to Smith, but it turns out that he is helping Smith and Dickey get out of Bishkek by rearranging their flights. In addition to being a company executive, Gaylord himself is a climber, a skier, and a cross-country distance runner, as well as a friend of just about everyone on the company's climbing team. I jot down the number of the Hotel Eldorado, and within a few hours I am talking to Smith. Ever the wiseacre, he calls me Uncle Greg. He sounds glad to hear my voice and tells me his story. I am riveted. When he hedges around the death of the rebel, I decide that Smith did the pushing but they are covering their tracks for fear of reprisal.

To line up every element of a hot story and have everything point in a direction that favors the writer is as rare as finding all the right conditions for getting to the summit of K2. I tell Smith right away that I smell a book in this and that my literary agent in New York, Susan Golomb, might be able to sell the rights. I suggest we collaborate. He agrees. Within a few days of all four climbers returning to America, Caldwell, Dickey, and Rodden, and the latter pair's families, decide that they need representation too, for the telling of their story and to manage the media that are hounding them. So, the collaboration agreement expands to include the whole team, with Golomb representing everyone.

Golomb approaches the sale of the story with the aplomb of a savvy New York agent. She reminds me that several successful books in the true-life adventure genre started out as articles in *Outside* magazine. Among these are *The Perfect Storm* and *Into Thin Air.* I have just completed an assignment for *Outside*, so I pitch the story to the editors there. *Outside* (circulation 600,000) snaps up the story, offering a substantial contract for the personal experience of the climbers. *Climbing* magazine (circulation about 50,000) has offered me a fraction of *Outside*'s fee. I take the money. My friends at *Climbing* are not happy when I back out of the story four days after verbally agreeing to write it for them, but when they reassign the article, I make amends by providing the new author with information from my interviews with the climbers.

The deadline for *Outside* is demanding. The issue is about to close and go to the printer. I interview the former hostages and research and write the story in two weeks for *Outside*'s November issue, which will hit newsstands two months after the Americans' escape. By early fall the story has gained momentum as the climbers appear on the *Today* show. Golomb auctions book rights, and Universal Studios options film rights.

I feel privileged that the four climbers choose me above all the others who vie for their story. A dozen writers and a host of magazines pitched offers at them, including the former girlfriend of a famous rock star who, over the phone, bid six figures for Smith's life story. I'm a climber; I have been writing about climbing for over twenty years, and I have been to Kyrgyzstan. The four climbers trust that.

THIS STORY HOOKS ME for many reasons besides the need to pay the bills. I feel an affinity for it; I walked over the same ground in Kyrgyzstan in 1995. I have also made seven mountaineering expeditions to Pakistan, making for over a year spent in the Islamic world.

Even though Pakistan ranks high on the State Department list of danger spots for terrorism and drug trafficking, I have always felt safe there, though I did learn to feel uneasy during jeep and bus rides in the far north when, on a couple of occasions, gun-toting men flagged down the buses I was in and hitched rides. The men had the look of Afghan mujaheddin, and they were, I assumed, heading to or from their wars across the border.

The question of what to do if you are on a plane or a bus that is hijacked by Islamic militants is a topic I have discussed with fellow travelers. During the long flights to and from Islamabad I went through mental exercises to prepare myself should the plane be hijacked. These exercises were usually analytical: should I try to overpower the hijacker, join a rebellion among passengers, or wait to be rescued? My daydreaming occasionally devolved into Walter Mitty fantasies in which I wrestled the Uzi away from the hijacker and filled him full of lead.

Call me paranoid, but I know a passenger from Pan Am flight 073, which was hijacked on September 5, 1986, while on the ground at the Islamabad airport. Michael Thexton, an Englishman, is the brother of Peter Thexton, whom I climbed with on an expedition to Pakistan's Karakoram Range in 1983. Peter died on our climb of an eight-thousand-meter mountain called Broad Peak, and in 1986 Michael was in Pakistan to visit his brother's last resting place. Flight 073 was supposed to take Michael home after his pilgrimage.

I first met Michael in 1983 when I flew to London from Islamabad to bring the news of Pete's death to his family. Pete had been a careful man who climbed hard but did not seek out undue risks. He was a doctor, and as we hiked through the Braldu River Gorge toward the mountains that spring, passing through the villages of the Balti, Pete tended to the ills of people who had never known medical care. Pete and I had been strangers before that expedition, but we became good friends. Early in the expedition we made three new climbs on the granite spires of the lower Baltoro Glacier, then we headed deeper into the mountains to our next objective, the triple-summited massif of Broad Peak, the twelfth-highest mountain on earth. By mid-June we figured that our bodies were adapted to the altitude and we set off up Broad Peak's snowy west flank. We climbed quickly, and within a day and a half we were camped at twenty-five thousand feet. The next morning we woke with aching heads—not unusual, due to oxygen deprivation and dehydration—but after a couple of cups of tea and some aspirin we felt ready to climb the long ridge to Broad Peak's 26,400-foot summit.

When climbing big peaks, the eight-thousand-meter point marks the passage into the most painful physical territory. Those who can push through the reeling disorientation and fatigue caused by high altitude learn that the key to surviving low atmospheric pressure and oxygen starvation is to spend as little time as possible above eight thousand meters. But no matter how fit one may be, or how fast one climbs, getting to such a summit is a slow grind, and there is ample time for high altitude to short-circuit all kinds of mental and physical body chemistry. In my case, eighteen vertical feet below the summit, my mind began to behave like a television on the fritz. Pete nursed me through a half-hour spell of incoherence during which I sat semiconscious in the snow, then my senses returned. By then we knew well enough to let the summit alone, though it lay less than half an hour away. As we headed down, the mountain K2 loomed in front of us, five miles distant and shining pink with alpenglow.

At twenty-six thousand feet I recovered and was damning my altitude-induced blackout for cheating us out of the summit, when Pete stopped in his tracks. "Are my lips blue?" he asked. His beard was frosted, but I could see a bluish, oxygen-drained pallor to his face. Then he told me that his breathing was in trouble. We knew what this meant. Pulmonary edema was filling his lungs with fluid. Every minute we lingered allowed the fluid to build up and drown the tiny lobes of alveoli that extract oxygen. Rapid descent to a thicker atmosphere was the only option, so we set off down the mountain, bounding through the snow. But Pete's pace weakened to a crawl, night fell, and a bitter wind whipped up a blinding ground blizzard. Pete dragged himself through my tracks; then, when he couldn't crawl anymore, I dragged him. At midnight he told me he had lost his sight, a sign of worsening altitude symptoms. At 2 A.M. we found our camp. Two of our companions there, the Briton Don Whillans and the Pakistani climber Gohar Shah, pulled Pete into a tent. We lay in there, aching with fatigue, drinking stove-melted snow, and planning to head farther down at the first hint of dawn. Pete asked me how I was feeling just before I dropped off for a snatch of sleep. His voice had enough life in it to make me believe he was going to make it, but when I woke he was dead. Losing him was as sharp a pain as I have ever known.

Three years later I returned to climb the mountain next to Broad Peak, Gasherbrum IV. While on G4 I often looked over to Broad Peak, where Pete's body still lay, and thought of him. After my companions and I got to the top of G4, I ran into Michael Thexton in the frontier town of Skardu. He was about to begin his pilgrimage to Broad Peak and we stood on the grounds of the K2 Hotel, with the Indus River sprawling before us, talking about his brother and about days in the mountains both great and terrible.

Three weeks later I was back in the United States watching the evening news when I saw that a Pan Am flight had been hijacked at the Islamabad airport. A fleeting thought went through my mind: could this be Michael's plane? I dismissed the idea, having just read some throwaway statistic claiming that the odds of an air traveler suffering a disaster on a plane were so remote that one would have to board a flight at random every day for twenty-six thousand years before your turn to crash or be hijacked came up. That statistic, today, is no doubt inaccurate. Michael was on flight 073, and in London his parents prepared for the possibility that a second son would not return from Pakistan.

The terrorists were members of the Abu Nidal organization, a Palestinian group notorious for hijacking the *Achille Lauro* cruise ship in the Mediterranean and for murdering an elderly American passenger who was confined to a wheelchair. To hijack flight 073, four terrorists had infiltrated the airport, probably with inside help, and rushed up the steps of the Boeing 747 shortly before it was due to take off. Armed with automatic weapons and hand grenades, the gunmen demanded the release of three fellow terrorists who were in jail for blowing up an Israeli yacht in Cyprus. They threatened to kill all 350 passengers if their demands went unmet.

Soon after taking control of the plane the gunmen shot a passenger and dumped his body out of the forward door, to show that they were serious. Michael was selected as victim number two. Brought to the front of the plane where the first hostage had been murdered, Michael stood with a pistol pressed to his head. The terrorist made peculiar small talk: "Do you like Margaret Thatcher?" Michael replied that he did not. While Michael contemplated his fate, the pilots bailed out of the cockpit. Knowing they would never take off, the hijackers became edgy. Michael sensed he was about to be shot when the cabin was plunged into darkness. Pakistani commandos had crawled into the baggage hold of the plane through hatches under the fuselage and disabled the cabin lights. The next thing Michael saw was the muzzle flash of weapons as commandos stormed the main cabin. The gunmen returned fire and threw hand grenades at random. Michael's guard left him to join the fight, and Michael joined a stream of passengers clambering through an open exit that led onto the wing. Tracer bullets whizzed over his head through the night, and explosions rocked the fully fueled 747. Knowing that the fuel tanks were located in the wing, Michael jumped onto the tarmac and ran into the dark, until Pakistani soldiers tackled him. He escaped with nothing more than a scratched elbow, but twenty-one passengers and all four terrorists died. One hundred others were wounded.

A few weeks later Michael appeared on an American morning TV show. "Why didn't you try to overpower your guard?" the host asked. Michael looked at the TV personality quizzically, wondering if the question was serious. Then he said slowly, as if speaking to a child, "Because he had a gun."

————

RODDEN'S NIGHTMARES BEGIN soon after she returns to California, on August 22. In the dreams she is running through a battle scene. Sometimes she's dodging bullets and explosions with Caldwell; sometimes she's running through the battle with friends who were not even with her in Kyrgyzstan. In other dreams reporters and people with TV cameras are chasing her. In nearly every dream she sees Abdul's face. It will be months before any of us learn that Abdul/Sabir is dead. The fear of meeting him in her dreams makes Rodden dread sleep.

Her unease is evident to her parents. After she goes hiking with her father in the Sierra Nevada along a section of the Pacific Crest Trail in September, she reveals that during the walk she felt barely able to contain her anxiety, as the terrain reminded her of the Kara Su valley. She also begins to identify the act of climbing with her abduction, and in the weeks following her return she shows little enthusiasm for the sport. Fear of retribution by the men who held her captive permeates all her actions during those first weeks. While I'm writing the story for *Outside,* she even asks me not to label the rebels as terrorists, in case it angers them.

U.S. embassy staff spotted her trauma. Greg Gardner's escorting of her and Caldwell to the airport of another country was above and beyond the assistance typically extended by an embassy toward Americans in trouble. He arranged special treatment for them on the airline too, by getting their tickets stamped "Emotionally Distressed Passenger." Rodden was deeply nervous on the journey home. While changing planes in Amsterdam she and Caldwell found themselves surrounded by passengers from an Islamic country. The sight of men with bushy beards triggered a sense of panic she found hard to suppress. Back in California, she visits therapists to talk through the fear that had burrowed under her skin.

"The first therapist I went to handed me a multiple-choice questionnaire," Rodden said. "It asked, *Why are you here?* You had to tick the right box from a long list. The choices were things like *broke up with boyfriend,* or *pet died.* At the bottom was a category called *Other,* so I wrote *kidnapped in Kyrgyzstan.* Then the therapist sat me in a big soft chair. He said, 'Close your eyes, take a deep breath, count to ten. Go to a place where there are only happy times. Capture that feeling. When you're completely content, open your eyes.' He compared what I'd been through to the experience of a rape victim. He kept talking about getting back to this happy place. I couldn't take it seriously. I never went back."

But Rodden does go back, to a different therapist, after more weeks of sleeplessness wear her down. Thinking of specific moments like Su falling through the air or Caldwell's visceral scream when he pushed the rebel was enough to make her physically ill, while speaking about her experience was nearly impossible. Her tongue would just stop. Guided by a therapist who understands post-traumatic stress syndrome, she learns to process and re-lease the emotional experiences that have become trapped inside her and that she is unable to speak about, through a form of therapy called EMDR (Eye Movement Desensitization and Reprocessing). It will take a year before she can face her memories, and she will never see the world in the same light as before her trip to Kyrgyzstan.

THEIR SIX DAYS in captivity have left a mark on Caldwell too. In media interviews held following his return he appears calm and controlled. "I don't want to go into that right now," he coolly tells reporters who ask about the pushed terrorist. But guilt is tearing him apart. His pact with Dickey and Smith to share the deed deflects the media interest from him, but lying about it weighs on him heavily.

Caldwell tries to get on with his life, but everywhere he looks something pricks his conscience. Television and movies trigger reminders, and in the days he spends at the Rodden household after their return, he and Beth spend a lot of time watching TV.

"I would react to things in films," he'd tell me, "like a certain line, that would take me totally by surprise. One night we were watching some movie and out of the blue, one of the characters said, 'Killing is something good people don't do, no matter what.' I felt terrible for hours after that. I found that I couldn't stomach violence at all. We went to see the movie *Hannibal*, about the insane murderer. What was I thinking? I was horrified by all the killing. Even now I don't like to watch violent films."

Caldwell's inability to shake himself out of his funk surprises even him.

"I'm pretty level-headed," he said, "and I've always known where I've been going with my life. But this was a time I could look at myself and not know what I wanted." He and Rodden find it hard to walk down the street without someone who has read about their ordeal wanting to talk about it. It becomes easier to stay at home.

Their parents feel at a loss as to how to help. Climbing defined Tommy Caldwell, but when his father tries to steer him back toward being the athlete he was before Kyrgyzstan, by declaring like a coach one morning, "It's about time these kids stopped feeling sorry for themselves and got back into training," Caldwell withdraws further—even away from his best friend, his father. Taking long runs alone through the streets of Davis, he tries to reason himself out of his darkness. Gradually he understands that someday he will have to admit the truth.

One day when Rodden sees he is having a hard time she hands him a gift she's had made by a local jeweler. It's a silver disc, like a soldier's dog tag. The inscription reads:

TC

MY LIFESAVER

MY HERO MY LOVE

B

He hasn't taken it off since the day she placed it around his neck.

22.

CONFESSION

AMERICA

AUGUST 2000

ickey and Smith hit the tarmac at San Francisco International Airport at midnight on August 25. They are met by Dickey's girlfriend, Rita Di Lorenzo, a Yosemite climber named Chris McNamara, and Jason Oelkers and John Garippa, both from The North Face, supporter of the expedition. The media are unaware of their return. McNamara is one of Smith's closest climbing partners, and he slaps his friend a welcoming high-five handshake. Dickey and Di Lorenzo collide in a tight embrace. As she wraps her arms around him she feels ribs and hipbones protruding from his frame. He's thirty pounds lighter since she saw him off thirty days ago. Dickey and Smith strike Oelkers as contemplative and subdued. "You could tell they had been through a lot," he said.

Caldwell and Rodden don't make it to the airport. Caldwell is in bed with a high fever, and Rodden is anchored to the toilet. After two weeks of constipation caused by dehydration—she's even had an X ray to try to figure out what is jamming up her innards—her doctor has prescribed a laxative he calls "dynamite in a bottle." The treatment is living up to its name. Oelkers conveys their apologies, but Dickey and Smith are disappointed by their absence, especially Smith, who was hoping they'd bring his van—his home—to the airport. It is parked in Davis, in the Roddens' driveway.

Oelkers puts Smith up in his apartment in Berkeley, and McNamara takes Dickey and Di Lorenzo to their apartment in the city. Di Lorenzo curls up with her man on the couch and listens to him talk nonstop till 4 A.M.; Smith talks fast and furious to Oelkers too. Anger, confusion, and terror tinge their stories. They have left Kyrgyzstan haunted by a multitude of unknowns. From the moment they reached Mazar their departure from the mountains was so fast that they've had little time to digest the information coming their way. In the calm of Bishkek and on the long flight home, Dickey and Smith took the experience and broke it down point by point. The knowledge that practically all the soldiers they met at Kurbaka are dead troubles them deeply. They can't recall all their names, but they shared friendly moments, smiles, and sometimes a cigarette together. The instantaneous leap from peace to war, from paradise to hell, blindsided everyone in the Karavshin—climbers, shepherds, even soldiers.

Di Lorenzo likens Dickey's first days home to a binge. He turns up at the Attic a couple of nights after his return, when Di Lorenzo is working at the bar, and he drinks enough gin-and-tonics to render himself legless. "He needed that," said Di Lorenzo. A week later he's in the Nevada desert partying his brains out amid thirty thousand people at Burning Man, a multiday festival of hedonism and New Age rock music.

"We'd had this huge experience," Dickey told me. "I felt full of life. I wanted to be everywhere, go out, visit friends, see bands, have fun." When fireworks start going off at Burning Man, Di Lorenzo sees him jump in fright. In San Francisco he is lethargic, restless, and ill. His stomach is in turmoil. The stress of captivity has left him feeling as if he has an ulcer. So he heads to Yosemite for a few days, where he knows he'll find Smith. Smith needs him and he needs Smith.

—————

SMITH MOVES BACK into his van, renegotiates his job at The North Face to a part-time position then to no position at all, and breaks up with his girl-friend, all within a few weeks of getting home. He then makes a beeline for Yosemite. There he makes leisurely solos of moderate climbs that he has done many times before, and on which he knows every move.

When I travel to California to interview him for *Outside*, on August 28, I find that he has a photographic recollection of events and a desire to in-terpret every nuance of his experience. I also see anger. Sometimes the anger is directed at the men who threatened his life and his freedom; some-times it's directed at his fellow hostages.

A day before Smith and Dickey returned to California, Caldwell and Rodden held a press conference attended by some two dozen newspaper and TV reporters at a local climbing gym called the Rocknasium, in Davis, California. It had been organized by their parents and with the help of the University of California at Davis. The young couple stood side by side while Rodden read a short prepared statement about their experience, and she thanked the Kyrgyz military for their assistance and sacrifice. Then the two of them, followed by their fathers, answered questions from report-ers. The Roddens and Caldwells had felt forced to hold the press confer-ence without waiting for Dickey and Smith to return, because reporters had been badgering their children since their arrival home on the after-noon of August 22. Reporters' vans had filled their streets. Most were pushy and insistent, phoning and knocking on the door day and night, gushing with fake concern. Some of the reporters had to be physi-cally removed from the doorway. Caldwell and Rodden shrink from the attention.

Dickey and Smith are infuriated when they learn of the press confer-ence. They thought they were all in this together. To Smith, it's an unforgiv-able breach of trust. Caldwell and Rodden hadn't meant any harm, and they apologize to Dickey and Smith. The damage to their relationship will be done, though, and by the time I begin writing their story the two parties will barely be on speaking terms. The loss of friendship will wear hardest on

Rodden and Smith, as they had held each other in high esteem ever since they met in Yosemite a year earlier.

IN THIS TENSE CLIMATE the four of them are awkward celebrities, hedging around one another and around discussion of pushing Su, in media interviews. We all pushed him, they insist. That's the pact they made; they will stick together regardless of their feelings toward one another. Only those closest to them know the truth. Also in the know are the FBI agents who visit their homes to interview them and who cruise the parking lot of The North Face, searching for Smith's van. To federal agents, however, Caldwell confides that he alone pushed Su.

In their interviews with me for the *Outside* article, the four climbers repeat the same scenario: the three men surrounded Su, and they pushed as one. Though they saw no body, they agree that no one could have survived such a fall. Only Smith hints that Caldwell applied more force than the others. Then, one night in mid-September, Caldwell calls me from Davis just as I am finishing the story for *Outside.* He has been reticent all along, reluctant to talk to me. This time, though, he sounds sure of himself as he tells me he has something that I need to know.

"This is the deal," he says. "I was the one who pushed Su. It was something I wasn't prepared to do, so when I did it I was pretty shaken up. Jason and John said that we would say we all did it. That helped me a lot. I'm still coming to terms with it. But I've changed my mind about keeping the story a secret. It's not something I want to hide anymore."

"You did the right thing," I reply. "Don't feel bad about it. It's right to fight for your survival."

He talks for a half hour. He is forthright, as if he has come to terms with what he did and is now ready to move on. "I've had all kinds of thoughts going through my head since that night," he says. "I've been trying to figure out what kind of person I am, to be able to do a thing like that. What is evil inside me that I could do that? But now I have come to think that I really wanted to live. I really wanted us all to live."

Truth is, hardly anyone believes they all pushed Su together. It's too pat. Many people suspect one of them did it alone and they are protecting that person from being singled out for retribution. "Come on, give me the scoop," I would hear from people who knew I was writing the story. "Singer pushed the guy, right?" Smith's more "aggro" nature made him the most likely candidate to most people.

Caldwell's decision to accept the burden, and the kudos, of his actions strike Dickey and Smith in a variety of ways, but the overriding feeling is relief that the truth is out.

"Have you ever seen the movie *The Man Who Shot Liberty Valance?*" Smith asks me when I speak to him the day after Caldwell's confession. It's an old Western about a softhearted sheriff who agonizes over the truth when he becomes a hero for shooting a villainous gunslinger in a showdown and freeing his community of the outlaw who's been terrorizing the town. His glory is false, though, because the actual shooter is another man, one who stood on the sidelines and fired anonymously. I tell Smith I know the movie.

"Well," explained Smith, "I didn't want to be the man who shot Liberty Valance."

BY NOW speculation over who really pushed Su has fueled more than one spurious story. The weirdest of these is a piece in the *Sunday Times* of Britain, titled "So, Beth, Did You Push Him Over the Cliff?" The story opens: "Beth Rodden has vowed to take a dreadful secret to her grave. What neither she nor her three climbing companions will admit is which of them pushed an Islamic terrorist holding them hostage . . ."

In asking the question "Who did it?" the author describes Rodden as America's favorite fantasy figure since Rambo and calls her the "most levelheaded of the traumatized quartet," suggesting that she is most likely "the person who shouted 'Now!' prompting either Smith or Dickey to propel the armed terrorist off the cliff."

"Ironically," the article continues, "one of Rodden's favorite books is Donna Tartt's 1992 best selling novel, *The Secret History,* in which a group of middle-class American students cover up a killing in the woods of Vermont. Later, their relationships and personalities crumble under the strain. How long can Rodden, her boyfriend Tommy Caldwell, 22, photographer John Dickey, 25, and Smith protect the identity of the killer in their midst?"

"I never spoke to this guy and I've never heard of that book," Rodden tells me. The *Sunday Times* story was based on the reporter's five-minute talk with her father. Robb Rodden didn't discuss the pushing of Su with this reporter at all. Although a laughable piece of Fleet Street tabloid journalism, it shocks the young climbers to see the way lies so easily make it into print, and it makes them distrust the media.

23.

BACK FROM THE DEAD

AMERICA

OCTOBER 2000

It's the beginning of October 2000. The story for *Outside* is written, the magazine is printed, and advance copies are circulating. When it hits the newsstands the strange and tragic tale of misadventure and war, along with Tommy Caldwell's confession, will be public. Magazine-industry reviews are giving "Fear of Falling"—the article's title—good marks as a fast-paced adventure tale. *Variety* magazine reports the book- and film-rights sale and calls the story the next *Into Thin Air.* There is a bittersweet taste to all this success, given the blood and strife that underpin the story, but there is also a feeling of relief for the climbers that, with the story told, it will finally be over.

The story is, however, far from over.

I'm sitting at my desk, starting work on the book, when the phone rings. The caller is Nancy Prichard, a climber and writer known for her equipment reviews in the outdoor press. She also holds a part-time marketing position with Five Ten, the rock-shoe manufacturer that is Caldwell's main sponsor. The two have never met, however. Prichard has been interested in the story since it broke, covering it, she says, for *Playboy.*

"The guy they pushed off the cliff," she tells me, "he's alive."

After an I-don't-believe-what-I'm-hearing pause, I reply, "I . . . guess . . . the plot just thickened."

She tells me that someone in Kyrgyzstan has told her by phone that a Russian-language Bishkek newspaper has reported that the rebel the climbers knew as Su has turned up in a Bishkek jail, after being captured by the army. The newspaper report, I will learn, is two and a half weeks old, but neither the U.S. embassy in Bishkek nor the FBI has informed the former hostages of the report.

While the news settles in, I hit the mental playback button to recall my interviews with Dickey and Smith. Their words ring out. Dickey: "He went all the way to the river, fifteen hundred feet below." Smith: "I watched him arc through the moon from my view . . . he was bicycling, pedaling the air . . . he hit the ledge flat, then rolled off."

"Could this be a mix-up?" I ask Prichard. "Maybe the guy in jail is another rebel?" Scenarios play through my mind. Maybe a captured rebel leader had tried to slip into Su's skin to save himself from more serious crimes?

She is adamant that her source is good. But as yet, she says, she doesn't have a copy of the newspaper article or a photograph of the jailbird.

As a writer covering this story for a different publication, Prichard has been competing with me for the same information from the outset. By telling me that Su is alive, she's getting a reaction to revive her own story, which was hit hard when the climbers stopped giving in-depth interviews to all but the book's author—me. Their decision to keep a lid on the story followed an agreement with the publisher to save the core of the tale and the buzz of any new publicity for the book. With access to the climbers limited, several magazines have canceled features. It's a simple matter of business, common in publishing. Good money was offered for the story, and with that came an embargo to protect its exclusivity. The arrangement is not unlike a professional-athlete contract: Nike doesn't pay its sponsored athletes to wear Reebok shoes. *Outside* is exempt from any embargo because it was contacted before the book sale. More to the point, the climbers are content to quit talking to reporters and get on with their lives. They've had a gutful of the media, and they are still in the thick of it. *Dateline NBC* is interviewing them, and stories about them have also appeared in *People* and *Climbing.* Rodden can't bear to read any of them. They dredge up too many bad memories.

After an hour and a half of phone interviews, the climbers politely told Prichard they couldn't say much more to her either. Ultimately, and unfortunately, *Playboy* would not publish her story. Despite this, and despite the embargo, the climbers would later remember that Prichard continued to pressure them for interviews. Each time they declined, the climbers noted, she became more disgruntled. Even before Su surfaced, the animus of her reporting looked critical. Journalists who communicated with Prichard, and friends of the climbers whom she interviewed, relayed back impressions of a reporter with a negative take on the hostage story.

Over the phone Prichard tells me that she's unearthed contradictions between official Kyrgyz-government reports and the accounts of the former hostages, citing, for example, the government's statement that the army freed the climbers, as well as discrepancies over the distance the climbers said they ran that last night. Then she asks a question that's unsettling but, given the new twist to events, fair: does the information I've just heard alter my belief in the story?

I'm staggered by the suggestion that the climbers may not have told me the truth. My story recounted what the climbers saw and experienced. They felt sure that Su must have died as a result of his fall, and that is what I reported.

"Why would they lie?" I ask Prichard. She cites the money that's riding on the story, and the kids' sudden unwillingness to speak with her any longer. She finds their silence "very strange," she tells me in a tone belying suspicion and doubt.

The climbing world has had its share of hoaxes and controversies, but I do not believe that Caldwell, Dickey, Rodden, and Smith conjured up their kidnapping or embellished their tale to profit from a book and a film, as it seemed Prichard is suggesting. In Oakland, California, a day after Smith's return, I looked him in the eyes during an all-day interview, and I interviewed the other climbers by phone. Their accounts meshed seamlessly. There was no confusion of details, no averted glances. Caldwell with his anguish about pushing Su, Rodden with her trauma, Smith and Dickey with their crystal-clear recollections of sights imprinted in their minds—they all struck me as being utterly genuine. If they had invented this complex story, they deserved to win Oscars.

Still, for anyone looking for holes in the story, Su turning up alive is a potential Grand Canyon. Instead of leaping to the conclusion that the story is false, I try to imagine, with the phone to my ear, what actually happened on the cliff above the Kara Su on August 17. The simplest explanation seems the most likely: the climbers did push their captor; they thought he fell hundreds of feet and died—but they were wrong. In their panic and fatigue, maybe the cliff did seem taller and steeper than it really was and Su had tumbled only a few dozen feet and was able to walk away. In the frenzy of the moment, rather than check to see if their armed guard was alive or dead—and risk being shot—they ran for their lives. I would soon learn from Russian maps that the eighteen miles the climbers estimated they ran after pushing Su was more like ten. Panic and fatigue, again, had affected their reckoning of distance. The mistake did not affect my trust in them, but it would soon be cited by critics as proof of a deception.

"I see where you're going with this," I say to Prichard, "but no, I don't think they're lying. Though if they are telling a lie, I assure you, that's the story I'll write."

After I hang up, I lean back in my chair and gaze out the window. If Su is alive, I think to myself, this story is far from over. If Su is alive, this story is about to become controversial.

At *Outside* the editors are as shell-shocked as I am when I tell them the as-yet-unconfirmed report of Su's survival. The magazine is printed; it's impossible to update the story—if indeed the rumor is true.

After I contact *Outside* I phone the climbers. Some of them have already heard the news from Prichard. Caldwell and Rodden are in a parking lot in Rocky Mountain National Park, about to take a run up the trail to Hallet's Peak, when their cell phone rings and Susan Golomb, having heard the unconfirmed report from me, tells them that Su may be alive. The news is Rodden's worst nightmare, a matter of life and death. They get back in their car and drive home. Inside their house, they lock all the windows and doors.

"Panic ran over me," Rodden said. "I thought the rebels would come after us. I thought they'd want revenge."

She phones Prichard, but Prichard won't divulge any information about Su; to do so wouldn't be fair to *Playboy*, Rodden recalls Prichard telling her. Rodden hangs up and calls Ed Kulakowski at the U.S. embassy in Bishkek. He's seen the story about Su, and he's surprised she hasn't heard about it already. He tells her he'll fax it to her, and he tries to calm her down, jokingly asking her to return the sweater he loaned her boyfriend in Bishkek, and reassuring her that the likelihood of IMU bandits getting into the United States to avenge Su is zero.

Kulakowski faxes the newspaper story to her and Caldwell at midnight. The article that rolls out is in Russian, and the photo of the rebel accompanying the story is murky, but Caldwell needs only a moment to make his decision. The mole on the corner of the man's lip is unmistakable.

"Yeah, that's definitely him," he says. Rodden takes his word for it. She cannot bring herself to look at the photos of her former captor.

Neither of them sleep much that night. Caldwell lies in bed reliving the moment of pushing Su, trying to figure out how the rebel survived. They all saw him fall into a gaping void. The bands of rock they were scrambling over had stacked up into a steep, tall precipice. Su's survival defies his understanding. But by morning Caldwell's anxiety has turned to relief: he hasn't killed anyone after all.

At about the same time that Caldwell is looking at the fax of Su, I find an image of the resilient rebel on a Kyrgyz Web site. To find the photo I called the press officer at the Kyrgyz embassy in Washington, D.C. He gave me the Web addresses of a few Kyrgyz government–sanctioned publications, then told me to call back after 5 P.M. Only after office hours was he allowed to talk about "opposition newspapers." The press officer explains that in Kyrgyzstan's press there is a distinction between government information (censored and official) and opposition information (free-press and unofficial), and he coaches me on navigating through the Russian-language Internet portal leading to Bishkek's on-line newspapers. In the archives of *Vechernii Bishkek*, I see Su's face in the September 14 issue; the printed report was published a day or two earlier. Su looks bedraggled and frightened as he stares at the camera. His nose is swollen, perhaps broken. There are abrasions on his face, along with the telltale mole on the corner of his mouth that the climbers had described to me. The walls behind him have the drab look of a prison cell. I get the story translated the next day, and I e-mail the picture to Dickey and Smith. After some initial hesitation, they both confirm that it's Su.

Dickey is flabbergasted that the man is alive. "I don't see how anyone could survive that fall," he says. Smith prints the Web site photo, and for a while it sits on the dashboard of his van. He's stunned too, but he's also glad.

A couple of days later I obtain more proof of life when I get my hands on a videotape shot by Kyrgyz state television showing clips from interviews and interrogations of the captured rebel by Kyrgyz military authorities. When the tape is translated to English, it provides the basis for an update that I write for *Outside*'s Web site, Outside Online; it appears, along with a photo of Su, on October 9. The story is the first article in America to break the news about Su's survival, and it also appears in a later issue of *Outside*. Su is alive, the update reveals; Tommy Caldwell killed no one. Still, far from clarifying matters, the news and its timing will play into the hands of a host of individuals who will pursue a theory that the four climbers are not being straight with the truth.

SU'S REAL NAME, the new information reveals, is Ravshan Sharipov, and he is one of two rebels captured in the Karavshin. The other is Hamsa, whose real name turns out to be Ruslan Abdullin. Su a.k.a. Sharipov is twenty years old and a native of Tajikistan. The newpaper article is titled "Captivity Is Better Than Death," and the author is a Bishkek journalist named Alexander Kim. Kim, a retired lieutenant colonel with six years in the Kyrgyz army, was present at an army camp outside Batken on August 27 when "a terrorist, beaten to bleeding," was dragged in. Kim was at Sharipov's initial interrogation by the regular army, and he was privy to information from Sharipov's next interrogation, by agents of the Ministry of

National Security. Kim also interviewed the prisoner separately for his newspaper.

On the subject of the Americans, Kim wrote:

> The captive also told how in the mountains they took hostage several alpinists. To guard the four Americans fell to Sharipov's lot; there was a young woman among them. The bandits robbed them blind; the foreigners were dying from cold and hunger. Truly, they were lucky. Taking advantage of the moment, when Sharipov lost his vigilance, one of the mountain climbers pushed him down from the cliff, after they were taking to their heels.
>
> Fortunately, in several hours the military reconnaissance encountered them and brought them to the headquarters of the Southern Military Group. The soldiers gave them their coats and fed them. These unlucky mountain climbers were hardly standing on their feet as a result of the nightmares they had experienced. They will have much to recall in far away America!

About Sharipov's fall and survival, Kim wrote:

> Falling on the stones, Sharipov, as it turned out, did not die but joined his band. For almost ten days the fighters were dashing around the mountains, not seeing a way out from the situation. There was no need to talk about Vorukh—that operation was doomed to fail. They could not return either—all of the passes were blocked with soldiers.

"It is not known," Kim mused about the fates of Sharipov and Abdullin, "which was worse—to be taken prisoner or rot under the stones on Batken's mountains with dozens of their companions."

Kim's encounter with Sharipov within hours of his capture confirmed what the Americans had said all along: they pushed Sharipov. A subtler element of Kim's story was also revealing: the story reported Sharipov saying that one of the Americans—and only one—had pushed him. In each of their written statements to the Kyrgyz army, the Americans had claimed that the three males had pushed their captor. Only Sharipov, and the Americans, knew that a single hand had sent him flying.

I would meet Kim in Bishkek in spring 2001, and he would confirm his reporting to me. As for Ravshan Sharipov, whom I would also meet, he was in prison awaiting trial on charges of terrorism.

OF ALL THE CHARACTERS in this story, Ravshan Sharipov is perhaps the most enigmatic and intriguing, not because he was a poster boy for international terrorism but because he appears to be a morally shallow, easily led, and hapless bumpkin—a disposable terrorist. Those attributes would strike me as being as much the face of international terrorism as the images of Juma Namangani or Osama bin Laden.

Sharipov hails from Isfara, a Tajik city of forty-five thousand located twenty miles northwest of Batken. He was barely twenty years old early in the year 2000, aimless and unemployed in Tajikistan, trying to get work in the service of the Tajik government as a military border guard when he fell under the spell of an IMU recruiter from Tashkent. Ironically, border guards are charged with keeping out bandits and terrorists like the IMU. The recruiter told Sharipov that he'd be a fool to work for the military and earn almost nothing. He recommended to Sharipov a military-style training camp where the money and the equipment were good. If he was a "true Muslim" and a real man, he told Sharipov, he'd enlist.

After his capture, Sharipov would strike his jailers and interviewers as being more an opportunist than a religious fanatic. Tajikistan, where the typical worker earns ten dollars a month, is among the poorest of the former Soviet countries. The salary that Sharipov claimed he'd been offered by the IMU recruiter—five hundred dollars per month—was, if true, an irresistible amount. Indeed, the money would prove to be much too good to be true; he would tell interrogators that he never received a penny of it.

In May 2000 Sharipov headed west into rural Uzbekistan near the Tajik border to a training camp he called Japay. As one of a hundred recruits, he undertook several weeks of guerrilla-warfare training there as well as in the mountains around Garm, closer to Tavildara in Tajikistan. Recruits were

grouped into five-man cells and kept apart from other men. The base commander, he said, was an Afghan. Sharipov characterized his duties in the
camp as a cook, though he admitted to training with automatic weapons
and grenade launchers. Prayer, he said, was an integral part of their instruction.

Sharipov never expected the Americans to turn against him. He saw the
prisoners pass over many chances to escape. The night that Sabir departed—
August 17—he had ordered Sharipov to march the hostages over the ridge
to the Ortochashma valley. Sabir would join them later, he informed Sharipov, and they would then connect with what was left of Abdurahman's men
and fight their way back into Tajikistan.

However, it's unlikely that Sabir had any intention of climbing up the
side of the Kara Su valley and rejoining Sharipov and the Americans that
night. The mission was a rout, most of the mujaheddin were dead, and
Sabir knew it. A radio call from the rebel base in Tajikistan that Sabir received on the black radio he was always so secretive about had ordered him
to get out of Kyrgyzstan and save himself. To escape he would have to move
with speed and stealth. The hostages would slow him down, so he had to get
rid of them. If he let them go free, they could lead the army to him, but
killing them would create problems too. Gunshots, or screams if he knifed
them, might be heard by soldiers. Perhaps conscience even played a role in
his decision to spare the Americans. Perhaps the thought of killing the
young woman and her friends was something even he could not do. So, on
the night of August 17, Sabir sent the unwitting Sharipov up the cliffy hillside with "the goods," while he went alone to the Boz Toz Pass, to an ap-
pointment with destiny.

AROUND MIDNIGHT ON AUGUST 17, at the base of the thirty-foot cliff
he had just tumbled down, Sharipov gathered his senses and tried to figure
out what happened. One moment he'd been clawing his way up a rock face,
the next he was airborne. He stretched his limbs. Nothing broken, just
bruises and scratches. The impact of his fall onto the rocky ledge had
smacked the senses out of him, and when he'd regained consciousness it
was still dark. He sat tight till daybreak, lying on the sloping ledge with his

feet jammed against the fir tree he'd collided with and his assault rifle still slung around his torso, not daring to move for fear of sliding over the cliff in front of him. One of the Americans had pushed him, he guessed, or he had slipped. At any rate, his prisoners were gone, so was his commander, and the time had come for him to escape too.

At daybreak he scrambled back down rocks and slopes to the river and hid out for the rest of the day. For the next seven days he wandered hungry, eluding army patrols and the helicopters that shuttled men and supplies between outposts near the passes, where Kyrgyz sappers were laying mines. In some of his accounts Sharipov says he briefly rejoined the retreating rebels; in others he claims he was alone. As always, he traveled by night and hid by day. Somewhere along the way he found civilian clothes and sneakers, probably cached earlier in his foray into the Karavshin, and he cast off his camouflage fatigues, Smith's shoes, and anything else that would link him to the rebels or the Americans. But he kept his AK-47. A couple of days after his fall, he crossed a gap between a row of rocky towers that took him out of the Kara Su valley and into the Ak Su, and he headed south to the Boz Toz Pass. He didn't know that Sabir lay dead on the path to that very pass, or that sappers were mining the trails leading to it.

On August 25 he stopped at a shepherd's hut far up the Ak Su valley, near the rubble-covered snout of the glacier. Inside the hut was a sack of flour. He was desperately hungry, thinking only of bread and a full stomach as he mixed up the flour and water and kneaded the dough with his hands. But his luck was about to run out. Skorpions had spotted Sharipov at the hut through binoculars, and sappers led by a colonel named Isbazaroff had found his footprints along the trails. The two groups called for helicopter support and converged on the hut from north and south.

Sharipov shut himself inside the hut when he heard the helicopter. While the Mi8 circled low, Isbazaroff and his men used the cover of the engine noise to surround the hut. The soldiers kicked down the door and stormed inside, surprising Sharipov. His hands covered in dough, he ran for his weapon, which stood upright in a corner of the hut. The sappers knocked him to the floor before he could grab it. Sharipov kicked and bit at the men while they overpowered him and dragged him outside. The soldiers inspected his Chinese-made AK-47. It was standard rebel issue. Judging by its sooty barrel, it had been fired recently and heavily. With the weapon were three magazines. Two were empty; the third was fully loaded. The soldiers gathered around Sharipov, pummeled him to the ground, and put their boots to him. By the time the colonel called the men off, Sharipov was bleeding from the lips and his nose was broken.

"Who are you?" Isbazaroff demanded.

"I'm a shepherd."

"Don't lie. Who are you?"

He tried another story: he had been taken hostage in Tajikistan, and the rebels had forced him to come to this place; when the soldiers barged in he'd been cooking bread for three rebels who were in the mountains. Sharipov spoke in Tajik, claiming he didn't understand Russian.

By now the helicopter landed and the pilots joined the men surrounding Sharipov. One of the pilots was Colonel Sydykov, who'd flown the Americans into the Kara Su.

"Let's just blindfold him now and kill him," one soldier suggested in Russian over the whine of the Mi8's winding-down turbos. "We can say he was shot during a fight."

"But then we'll have to bury him," another soldier said wearily, also in Russian. "I'm not digging his grave."

"Let him dig his own grave."

A shovel was tossed at Sharipov and he was ordered to dig, but another soldier took the shovel out of his hands, complaining that no, digging a grave would take too long; he wanted to kill him now. He volunteered to bury the prisoner under stones, and he leveled his gun at Sharipov's head. The men were laughing, soldiers' black humor. It was too much for Sharipov. He fell to his knees. Tears streamed from his eyes, and a wet stain appeared on the front of his trousers. He pleaded for his life, loudly and in Russian. He told them his name and where he was from, and he confessed that he was one of the rebels, but he begged them to believe he had killed no one. The soldiers cuffed his hands behind his back, bundled him into the Mi8, and took to the air.

As the chopper came in to land at the military base outside Batken, it paused a few feet above the ground and the soldiers on board threw Sharipov out the door. He landed hard on the tarmac, at the feet of a score of soldiers. Word was out that another rebel had been captured, but the beardless, weeping, and scrawny individual on the ground looked nothing like one of the feared mujaheddin. When the men in the helicopter tossed Sharipov's well-used AK-47 out behind him, though, the mood of the soldiers changed abruptly and he got another beating.

Alexander Kim, being an ex-soldier and a war correspondent, was at the base that day, and he inveigled himself into the room for Sharipov's first interrogation, by regular army officers. Again, whenever an incriminating question was asked, Sharipov claimed not to understand Russian. When asked what he was doing in Kyrgyzstan, he said, "I was going home."

"Sharipov portrayed himself as a victim," Kim told me months later when recalling that meeting. "He said he was wounded and did not participate in the killing of the Kyrgyz soldiers captured by the rebels. He was very, very scared. In spite of the fact that Sharipov was not educated, not intelligent, he understood that his participation among the rebels could lead him to the worst thing in his life. Just a few days before, our soldiers had been captured and murdered. It was the first time our army had the experience of finding our men shot down in such a cruel way. Sharipov knew about the murders—he probably had some part in them—and he knew that death had now come to him."

Sharipov's interrogation that day of Kim's presence ended with no mention of the foreign hostages. Agents from the Ministry of National Security arrived next. They asked Kim to leave the room and they interrogated Sharipov through a Tajik-speaking soldier. The questioning lasted all afternoon. The interrogators also gave Sharipov a medical exam. Scratches on his elbows, calluses on his hands, and bruises on his right shoulder caused by the recoil of his "automat" all indicated that he'd fired dozens of rounds. The interrogation—one of many Sharipov would be subjected to—is videotaped. Although Kim wasn't permitted to sit in on this second interrogation, an officer who had been in the room told him that Sharipov had let it slip out that he had guarded the Americans, and that an American had pushed him from a cliff. It is the first link between Sharipov and the hostages. According to Kim, the officers there were not aware that the Americans had escaped by pushing their guard off a cliff.

Kim realized that he had a story, and late in the evening, after the interrogation ended, he was granted an interview with the prisoner. When Kim asked about the Americans, Sharipov was circumspect. "I had the feeling that Sharipov was scared of having been with the Americans. He didn't want to take something more on his shoulders," Kim would tell me.

The next morning the Ministry of National Security officers put Sharipov on a helicopter and whisked him to the prison in the old KGB building in Bishkek. Sharipov's sudden removal seemed odd to Kim. By contrast, the rebel Abdullin, who, the media knew, had held the German and Ukrainian climbers, remained in Batken for two more days and was visited by many journalists. "Because of the Americans, Sharipov had a political color," said Kim. "He wasn't just a simple rebel. There was also talk that the rebels had treated the Americans badly. It was negative for Kyrgyzstan that these rebels got the American hostages. That is why they isolated Sharipov immediately."

Sharipov's days became a succession of interrogations. Layer by layer he revealed more of his story as he was questioned in Bishkek and in Tashkent, where he was loaned briefly to assist security forces in a cooperative antiterrorism campaign. He abandoned his attempts to portray himself as an innocent wanderer or a cook for the IMU after the videotape captured from the terrorists showed a gun-toting Sharipov marching over the mountains with Sabir, Abdurahman, and a host of rebels killed by Kyrgyz soldiers.

IN AMERICA THE STORY TAKES new turns as well. In mid-September 2000 the State Department adds the Islamic Movement of Uzbekistan to its list of international terrorist organizations. The list at this time contains twenty-eight organizations determined by the Congressional Research Service to be sponsors of terrorism. An organization's inclusion on the list makes it illegal for U.S. citizens or residents to provide it funding or material, and the U.S. Treasury can block assets it may have in America. U.S. embassies and immigration officials can deny visas and deport suspected members of such organizations too. In notifying Congress of the newly listed organization, State Department spokesman Richard Boucher calls the IMU a movement that "has threatened the lives of civilians and regional security and undermined the rule of law," and he identifies the movement as a part of Osama bin Laden's global Al Qaeda network. Boucher also mentions that the organization kidnapped four American mountain climbers in August. A little later, an FBI agent from the Washington Field Office, who has requested anonymity, tells Tommy Caldwell that the agency is considering interviewing, extraditing, and prosecuting Sharipov for his participation in kidnapping American citizens.

Yet no twist is more bizarre than one thrown up by Sharipov himself and the Kyrgyz Ministry of National Security. The Kyrgyz state TV videotape, which I obtain in the fall of 2000, shows clips of questioning sessions with Sharipov at the army base in Batken and in a cell at the former KGB prison in Bishkek. The prisoner is a forlorn man dodging questions that implicate him in the IMU invasion, yet he ultimately admits to being in the command of Sabir, and he makes a tangential mention of the Americans. Cut to the face of a military prosecutor, who summarizes the deposition: ". . . we realize it is difficult to assume that the people participating in these illegal groups will provide a complete and true picture. We can reason that by the following: they are specially trained people, and they have been warned by their people and threatened with death for the divulgence of any data. . . . Prisoner Sharipov was part of that group who captured the hostages, the American tourists. In his deposition he did not deny that. . . . He was entrusted to stand guard over them. The rest of the group were accomplishing other assignments following their field commander. . . . According to his testimony, according to his version, it seemed to him that the American tourists he was guarding treated him with food from their food supply and put him to sleep. . . . When he awoke he noticed that the Americans had disappeared. He was by himself, and in a few days he was taken prisoner."

I play the tape over and over, reading the transcript of the translation, watching the faces of Sharipov and the prosecutor. Why is the prosecutor saying Sharipov was drugged? Why is he not saying that Tommy Caldwell pushed him? The tape doesn't show Sharipov speaking about the Americans himself; the military prosecutor speaks on Sharipov's behalf. Is Sharipov lying, or is the prosecutor? Did Sharipov hit his head and lose his memory that night on the cliff? Could the climbers be lying?

24.

DOUBTS

AMERICA

FALL 2000–SPRING 2001

By spring 2001 a small but determined coterie of people have taken up the story of the Kyrgyzstan kidnapping and pronounced it a hoax. It began with a campaign of whispers and rumors that made the rounds of the climbing scene. It grew into a barrage of e-mails, sometimes of anonymous attribution, sent to magazine editors. It culminated in debunking articles and hostile letters published in magazines and on Web sites. The doubters propose that the episode, in whole or in part, never happened but that the tale was crafted by the climbers to create a product to sell to New York publishers and to Hollywood. The accusations are false, but rather than lash out and defend themselves and thus dignify the assaults on their integrity, the climbers remain quiet, watching in bewilderment as a tide of ugly press laps around them.

Allegations that the climbers are liars hit them at a time when they are regaining their footing in the world after a disorienting, dehumanizing, and humiliating experience, and they hit where it really hurts: at the heart of their integrity. Reflecting on the yearlong campaign in which nearly every detail of the climbers' experience was held up to doubt, *Outside* magazine's editor in chief, Hal Espen, noted, "There seems to be something about [this story] that has driven a number of otherwise sane people to impatient fits of spurious deconstruction."

EXHIBIT A in the argument spurring on the disbelievers is Sharipov, alive in prison and, according to the Kyrgyz official on that videotaped interrogation, not saying that an American pushed him from a cliff. Sharipov's survival certainly makes me take a step back and ask myself, and the climbers, if they could be lying. Climbing has always depended on the honor system. If a climber says he stood on the summit of a mountain, then other climbers have traditionally taken that climber's word for it. Lacking marshals or judges on the summits, there is really no other way. Given the deeply personal nature of climbing, to lie about a climb is only to cheat oneself. Nevertheless, the history of climbing is dotted with spectacular acts of deception.

In 1906 American Frederick Cook received sponsorship from *Harper's* magazine to try the first ascent of Mount McKinley (now called Denali), the highest peak in Alaska. Cook returned claiming victory, but his partners later confessed that they reached only 10,000 feet on the 20,320-foot mountain, and that to bolster his claim Cook had faked a series of summit photos on another Alaskan peak. Later he attempted to reach the North Pole and made a fraudulent claim that he had done so. Had his claim been true, he'd have been the first to reach the earth's most northerly point. Later still he was jailed in Texas for mail fraud.

Another controversy, this one in Argentine Patagonia, on the fanglike, ice-spattered spire of Cerro Torre, concerned the great Italian climber Cesare Maestri, who claimed the peak's first ascent in 1959. His claimed route was a bold and futuristic climb of ice and rock harder than anything done before, and he set off on it with an experienced climber named Toni Egger. But at the bottom of the mountain days after they began their climb Maestri was found wandering around alone, exhausted, and emotionally devastated over his partner's death in an avalanche that had swept Cerro Torre during their descent from the summit. Yet a subsequent climb of that wall revealed that all signs of Maestri's ascent—pitons hammered into cracks, caches of gear, and ropes fixed to the cliff—ended only a short way up the mountain. Suspicions were raised, but nearly half a century later Maestri stands by his claim even though numerous tries by expert climbers have failed to retrace his route or to find a single piece of his gear on the upper mountain to support his ascent.

In Nepal in 1990 a Slovene named Tomo Cesen claimed a superhuman feat: the first solo ascent of the south face of Lhotse, a twelve-thousand-foot alpine wall on the world's third-tallest peak, adjacent to Everest. Several of the world's top climbers had died trying to master this hazardous eight-thousand-meter peak's southern flank, and when Cesen came down from his witnessless climb he was honored with awards and sponsorships. But suspicions arose when it was discovered that the photos he had used as proof of his ascent, published with his magazine story, were in fact borrowed from a friend who had tried to climb Lhotse years earlier. Cesen, it turned out, had no photos of his climb, despite having claimed to have taken pictures along the route. The closer Cesen's ascent was examined, the greater the inconsistencies in his story became. In the end, Reinhold Messner felt that Cesen's credibility was so eroded that he withdrew the Snow Leopard Award he had honored Cesen with and struck out the dedication to Cesen he'd made from future printings of one of his books. The climbing world is now divided equally between those who believe Cesen and those who feel he fabricated the story of his ascent.

Another controversy, on Everest, concerned a young New Zealand woman, Lydia Bradey, and the media. She set out alone up the south ridge of Everest in 1988, along the way passing several Spanish and Nepalese climbers. According to Bradey, she reached the top, becoming the first woman to do so alone and without oxygen. But Bradey and her male companions in base camp (who hadn't succeeded on the mountain) had fallen into acrimony earlier, and by the time she got back down to base camp she found they had left for home. Back in New Zealand they told the media that Bradey had not climbed Everest and any claim by her that she had was fraudulent. Newspapers rallied against her without ever really hearing her side of the story. Two years later the Spanish team she climbed along-side and journalists in the UK, New Zealand, and U.S. media examined and largely verified her claims, and the tide of belief swung against her detractors. She's now credited with the first female oxygenless ascent of Everest, but the media scandal she endured led her to drop out of active climbing.

Yet another controversy concerned a climber who claimed the first ascent of what could have been the world's hardest sport climb, a steep and nearly blank stretch of cliff in California that several of the best American climbers had dismissed at the time as impossible. The climber who claimed its ascent had no history of climbing such cutting-edge routes, and when asked to produce proof that he had done the route, he could not name a witness or even the partner who had held his rope to belay him. As criticism surrounding his claim intensified, he took a hammer to the route and smashed all the holds off it, rendering any ascent impossible.

Yes, climbers have lied, been lied about, have argued with and sued each other over claims made about them, all in the effort of fortifying their egos, settling scores, or making a buck from fame and sponsorship. But in the case of Caldwell, Dickey, Rodden, and Smith, I have looked long and hard at their story and at the individuals themselves. After spending hundreds of hours with each of them, and after being admitted into the most personal corners of their lives, I have no doubt they are telling the truth.

SHARIPOV'S CREDIBILITY is another matter. Potentially facing the firing squad for his role in the terrorist attack by a wing of the Al Qaeda network and the slaughter of Kyrgyz troops, he would say anything to save himself. Watering down or altering the story of his time with the Americans and denying anything resembling a scuffle between him and his prisoners might, in his mind, lessen his punishment.

NEVERTHELESS, Sharipov's survival inspired wild and very public speculation about the climbers' honesty. The speculation—in the form of letters and articles in magazines—was tinged with malice and disinformation. Virtually none of those who questioned the climbers' honesty had met them or interviewed them about their experience.

Much was made of the e-mail from a Russian-studies professor from Washington who claimed to have led commercial treks to the Karavshin, who, in a forum in *National Geographic Adventure Magazine*'s Web site, wrote: "I have become very familiar with the terrain [of the Karavshin], thus reading Rodden et al's account of their ordeal led me to smell a rat. I could think of no 1500 ft. cliffs in the specified region where they claimed to have 'offed' their captor."

The claim began making the rounds that an "expert" on the region had pronounced that no cliffs of any kind existed in the northern end of the Kara Su valley, near the junction of the Kara Su and Ak Su Rivers. Yet photos depicting the cliffs in that section of the valley were posted on a University of Washington Web site, and I had seen those cliffs with my own eyes. Back in 1995, while photographing Kyrgyz farms near the intersection of the two rivers, I had snapped a photo that showed the west flank of the Kara Su. When I showed Caldwell and Rodden the photograph, they recognized the cliff from which Sharipov had taken his tumble. The cliff is a loose-looking layer cake of rock and rubble—hardly a proud wall of glacier-carved granite like the Yellow Wall but a cliff from which one could fall far.

Then there was the weapons enthusiast who presented a screed about ballistics to *Outside,* in which he likened the rebels shooting at the climbers on the Yellow Wall to the lone-gunman controversy in the assassination of President Kennedy in Dealey Plaza. "The rebel shooter made two or three shots worthy of Lee Harvey Oswald. I don't buy either story for a minute," he declared in his letter, claiming that neither an AK-47 nor an AK-74 had the range or accuracy to place a shot one thousand feet up the wall. The weapon actually fired at the Americans turned out to be an RPK light machine gun with an effective range of twenty-four hundred feet; Kyrgyz officers told me that Sabir's men had captured the weapon from a Kyrgyz patrol. The writer was also under the mistaken impression that all three shots fired at the wall had formed a neat bull's-eye pattern between the portaledges. No such claim was made by the climbers, nor was that suggested in *Outside.* The climbers had always stated that the shots were scattered around the wall, with one shot hitting twenty feet away.

British tabloids entered the fray too. The *London Observer* was about to publish the fallacy that the Hollywood deal had fallen apart when the intended director, Francis Ford Coppola, discovered that the story was a hoax. The editors pulled this article before publication when they were reminded that Coppola was not involved in the film and that the deal still had the green light.

Most vocal of all was a former president of the U.S. branch of the Russian international news agency Interfax who also chimed in with a score of caustic letters to *National Geographic Adventure, Brill's Content, Climbing,* and *Outside,* as well as to a wide-reaching mailing list of like-minded critics. The "Man from Interfax" even phoned executives at Universal Studios in Hollywood, who had optioned film rights, to heap doubt on the story. This man had never been to Kyrgyzstan, had never met any of the climbers, and had not researched the story. His regular correspondence, however, publicly eviscerated every claim the climbers made.

The Man from Interfax got involved when those researching this story queried him about an Interfax news bulletin dated August 19, by Kyrgyz Interfax journalist Igor Shestakov, who spent five minutes at the Bishkek airport that day with Jason Smith, who was misnamed John Smith in the story. The English-language version of that two-hundred-word bulletin stated in part: "After the fighting with government troops began the guerrillas left the base and abandoned the Americans." The key word was *abandoned,* and the Man from Interfax, along with those who disbelieved the climbers' story, claimed that this proved that the story of pushing Sharipov off a cliff was an invention, and that the cliff did not exist at all. In a hostile letter published in *Climbing* in September 2001 he called the cliff "the money-making focal point of book and movie deals."

Smith denies he ever told anyone they were abandoned, but the Man from Interfax wouldn't concede that the Interfax report could be inaccurate. When I met the Kyrgyz journalist in question in Bishkek in March 2001, he was bemused by the attention his report had attracted, and he distanced himself from it as a whole, saying, "The word *abandoned* can be interpreted in Russian [with] many other words with the same meaning. . . . I am responsible for the last version [of the report] which was in my handwriting. What happens to the information when it goes through e-mail or through fax I cannot say. It may be changed by some extra people. And there is one more thing that is very important: [Smith and I] were talking not directly, but through an interpreter."

Shestakov's honest recollection of what he'd been told on August 19 by the Kyrgyz president's interpreter, who was translating for Smith, was that the Americans had run away from the rebels. Shestakov had heard no talk from Smith about pushing, because Smith did not tell him about it.

"We don't care how you got away; for you to be alive is enough," Shestakov added, speaking to Dickey and Smith, who were with me at the meeting in a Bishkek café. He also reminded us that the official government version at the time, handed down from the minister of National Security and conveyed by the president's interpreter Ilyas Bekbolotov (who doubled as his press secretary), was that the army had rescued the climbers.

Brill's Content, a now-defunct New York magazine whose banner touted SKEPTICISM IS A VIRTUE, latched on to the Interfax report in a snarky story called "A Killing in Question," in March 2001. Using Sharipov's survival and the word *abandoned* as the centerpiece for its theme of doubt, the story jabbed at the honesty of the Americans, wondering aloud if financial interests lay behind the omission of Sharipov's survival in the original *Outside* story—ignoring completely the actual reason that news of Sharipov's survival did not appear, which was that the magazine had been printed by the time the information was discovered. The head of the Central Asia division of Interfax, Andrew Zharov, a resident of Moscow with no direct connection to the story, was quoted in *Brill's Content* saying, "When these Americans were in Kyrgyzstan they didn't say anything about pushing their guard off a cliff. . . . I communicated with people in Kyrgyzstan: they don't believe the pushing story."

The Man from Interfax continued his letter-writing jihad well into 2001. He was so determined to debunk the story that he resorted to false accusations, telling the editors of *Climbing* that at the Bishkek meeting I had handed Shestakov a "legal document" demanding that Interfax recant the August 19 story. The Man from Interfax claimed that I asked Shestakov to sign the document, that he refused, and that the document went all the way to Moscow, where it outraged directors. *Climbing* published the letter with its claim that I had tried to persuade Interfax to withdraw its story. The claim was fantasy, but had it been true, I would have been guilty of a serious breach of journalistic ethics. After I complained that they'd done me a disservice by printing a false accusation about me and the former hostages, and that they'd done so without giving any of us the chance to view the claim before publication, *Climbing*'s editors contacted the CEO of Interfax USA, the director of Interfax's International Operations in Moscow, and the reporter Shestakov. All three of them said that no such legal document existed, and Shestakov could not recall any discussion of a recantation of his story at our meeting. By then the Man from Interfax was no longer in their employ, and Interfax's directors were keen to distance their company from the Stalin-era–style smear campaign he was waging. After publishing the Man from Interfax's accusations, *Climbing*'s editor in chief, Duane Raleigh, printed a note in the magazine's letter section saying that the accusations were false, and he e-mailed me an apologetic letter that called the accusations of the Man from Interfax "unfounded and untrue."

One observer of the long campaign to discredit the story of the former hostages suggested to me, jokingly, that a demon was at work, tempting these total strangers to join in these attacks.

"I FELT HUNTED," John Dickey said, describing the experience of seeing his honesty doubted so frequently during the months after his return from Kyrgyzstan. "It seemed so ridiculous at first. I felt detached from it, as I was still getting used to being back at home. But then all kinds of people were calling my home, and calling my friends, asking for their opinion of my integrity, trying to squeeze some detail out of them that would give fuel to their idea that we were lying. That's when I started getting angry. These slimy reporters like that girl from *Brill's Content* with their childish, loaded questions, talking to me as if I'd crack under pressure and confess to some crime. It was so obvious they were going to twist everything I would say into something they could use against us. They had their stories all planned out. They would bring up the question of money, like we made the whole thing up for money. But then I realized: all these people writing these stories, they were trying to make a buck from this story too, right? People get pissed-off when others are making money and they're not."

The idea that the climbers had walked out of misfortune and landed book and movie deals seemed to fuel much of the criticism. One letter writer to a magazine Web site all but demanded that the climbers give over their money to the families of the soldiers who'd died fighting the rebels. The Rodden family has, since then, worked with Kyrgyz military authorities to establish an account to distribute funds to the families of fallen soldiers.

None of the accusers seemed to care that the four climbers had been deeply traumatized by their ordeal, or that their false accusations were unkind at the least and libelous at the worst. The academic resource center REECAS, which covers Central Asian issues, published a long and withering judgment on the former hostages penned by the Russian-studies professor from Washington: "My sarcasm stems from bitterness," he wrote; "bitterness that these young climbers might very well have been responsible for the deaths of several Kirghiz soldiers; bitterness that they didn't seem to know, or care, about the culture of the land that they were visiting; bitterness that they have clearly exaggerated much for their personal gain without considering the harm that their false bravado might cause others; and bitterness that my Shangri-la [the Karavshin region] is forever marred."

BUT ALL THESE ATTEMPTS to discredit this story pale against the efforts of one man who disbelieved the climbers so strongly that he traveled to Kyrgyzstan four months before my own visit, helicoptered in to the Yellow Wall, and had a colleague head up the ropes toward the portaledges of Caldwell, Dickey, Rodden, and Smith. His name is John Bouchard, and I had run into him once or twice at cliffs or climbers' parties in disparate parts of America, though we had never really spoken. Notwithstanding, there was a tenuous connection between us: in the mid-1990s, he had made the second ascent of the East Pillar of Shivling, a route on a 21,500-foot peak in India that I had pioneered with three friends in 1981. The climb had been one of the best and hardest of my career, and for fourteen years all comers failed to repeat it. That is, until Bouchard, and his partner, came along. I admired him for that.

Bouchard had been one of the best and boldest alpinists to come out of New Hampshire in the 1980s. One of his friends, a climber from Boston named Barry Rugo, tried to help me understand Bouchard and the reasons he worked so relentlessly to debunk the story of four climbers he has never met. Rugo described him like this: "Quick-witted, well-read, a fearless climber, and delightfully mad. A New England classic is John. He's dropped off our map, though. Neatly cleaved his old self off and has never looked back."

He had, in fact, left New Hampshire in 1998 to settle in Oregon with his second wife, the writer and climber who had been looking into the Kyrgyzstan story for *Playboy*, Nancy Prichard.

25.

ACCUSERS

THE YELLOW WALL

NOVEMBER 2000

John Bouchard's rented Mi8 ambles noisily up the canyon of the Karavshin. It veers right where the Ak Su and the Kara Su fork, then it lands by the river, below the Yellow Wall. It's a cloudless, cold winter day in November 2000. Three months earlier gunfire resounded through these canyons and blood soaked the soil. Now snow covers the meadows and laps at the feet of the tawny granite monoliths. The huts of the shepherds who lived in these parts that summer are deserted. As they do every winter, the shepherds have taken their animals to the lowlands, but this time they are uncertain if they'll return in the spring. The risk of more fighting and land mines planted in the highlands near the border make the Kara Su and Ak Su region a dangerous paradise.

First off the helicopter are two Skorpions. Armed with automatic weapons, they've been sent with the American visitors to protect them from

IMU scouts who might be lurking in the mountains. They declare the spot safe, and the others step onto the snow. Bouchard, traveling with his friend Michael Dmitri, has chartered the Kyrgyz army helicopter to fly to the Kara Su as part of his investigation into the kidnapping story.

They are joined by Garth Willis, an American who lives in Bishkek, where he runs a State Department–funded project to introduce Kyrgyz youth to the mountains. Willis knows little about the kidnapping story, but he's a climber, he speaks some Russian, and he's familiar with the lay of the land in the Karavshin. He's even climbed the Ramp Route on the Yellow Wall. Bouchard contacted Willis to help him with logistics in Kyrgyzstan.

Two Kyrgyz are among the party. Turat Akimov, a journalist for the Kyrgyz news agency Kabar, is helping Bouchard wade through Bishkek's media and political maze; Saed Sultan is the group's interpreter.

The men slog uphill through snow that's knee-deep in places, and they reach the base of the Yellow Wall by midafternoon. Two portaledges are visible one thousand feet up the cliff. The four-by-six-foot platforms hang side by side, with a large tan haul bag slung between them. Nothing has changed since the day the Americans were ordered off the wall by the rebels; the gear and Dickey's cameras and film are still up there. A chain of ropes hangs down from the portaledges. The ropes sway gently, flanked on the right by a sunlit buttress of rock that Caldwell, Dickey, Rodden, and Smith had hoped to break out onto back in August, before their climb turned into a nightmare. To the left of the ropes is a shadowy wall festooned with thick and gleaming icicles that cling to the underside of granite ceilings. The rope line trickles down the cliff to ground level, where it disappears into the snow. Standing a few feet below the Americans, Willis and the others watch them confer briefly, then Dmitri takes from his pack a pair of rope ascenders connected to foot slings. He clamps the ascenders to the nylon line and starts climbing up.

To those on the ground, and to anyone else in Kyrgyzstan, Bouchard has made no bones about the fact that he doesn't believe the story of the four young Americans. Now the appearance of the portaledges on the cliff, exactly as the four climbers described them, seems to be a fly in the ointment of his theory. "So that means that John is proven wrong, yes?" the interpreter Sultan says in puzzlement to Willis once they've all seen the portaledges from the airborne helicopter. Willis shrugs, unsure what to believe, as the scenarios that he remembers Bouchard outlining to him are no less fantastic than the story of the kidnapping itself.

Scenario one, as Willis recalled to me, is that the kidnapping never happened; it was all made up. Scenario two held that the climbers were kidnapped, but the circumstances were far less dramatic. Being shot off the wall, pushing Sharipov off a cliff, and running through a gauntlet of fire were all dramatic embellishments they added later. Scenario three, Willis recalls being told, is that the embellished story took on a life of its own with the media, becoming a big-money deal that trapped the climbers in a lie. Some members of the team wanted out of the charade—which explained reports of a falling-out between Caldwell and Rodden on one side and Dickey and Smith on the other—but their story became impossible to recant once it was reported in America.

Sultan would be circumspect about Bouchard's theory when I met him in March 2001, at his workplace in the VIP lounge of Manas International Airport in Bishkek, but he would tell me this: "John said the *Outside* article was too much heroic. He said he and his friend were champion climbers and they did not believe this story could be true."

UP ON THE CLIFF, Dmitri heads up the rope for about fifty feet till he can see that it is clipped to a single bolt drilled into the ramp—just as Dickey told me he'd left it—and that the ropes above the ramp hang down from the portaledges in a single chain, all knotted together. He calls the information down, and Willis now understands the point of the exercise: if the ropes had been clipped to multiple anchors on the way down, that would contradict the climbers' story, suggesting something more leisurely than the hasty, forced descent ordered by the rebels.

Dmitri returns to the ground. It is late in the afternoon, the winter days are short, and there isn't time to go higher on the ropes before the helicopter is due to depart. Before they leave the wall, the Skorpion lets Willis fire a couple of rounds from his automatic rifle. Willis has never fired a gun in his life, and the power of the discharge packs a punch that slams the stock into his shoulder. Willis hears Bouchard, who is a gun enthusiast, ask the Skorpion if he thinks it would be possible to fire with any accuracy at the portaledges. The Skorpion looks up, then Willis hears him say in Russian, "Yes, if you're a good shot, you could do it."

John Bouchard is convinced that something is not right with this story. "He felt it was his big chance to make it as a writer," Willis later recalled of his encounters with him in Bishkek that winter. It was the first of two self-funded trips Bouchard would make to Kyrgyzstan, and he'd interview most of the people who had crossed paths with the Americans in the mountains. During the helicopter flight out from the Karavshin that November day, when the Mi8 touched down at the Batken airport Willis saw a German TV crew on the tarmac, filming a helicopter taking off. When Willis wondered aloud at what kind of program the Germans might be shooting, he noticed Bouchard become "agitated."

"It's obvious, isn't it?" Willis recalled Bouchard saying. "They're after the same story as me."

THE CLIMBING WORLD is like a small town. It's hard to keep secrets, and everyone knows what everyone else is doing. By April 2001 the climbing scene is abuzz with the news that Bouchard has been to Kyrgyzstan and that he and his wife are convinced that the story is some kind of hoax. They make little secret of this, telling as much to climbers and journalists across America. Hal Espen recalls a meeting with Prichard in which she told him that she could prove that the climbers were liars.

Another journalist who heard their theories but who did not succumb to the temptation to scandalize the story was Vince Sturla, from *Dateline NBC*. Prichard and Bouchard contacted him frequently while he was gathering material for a documentary on the kidnapping. "Nancy said that almost everything the kids said was made up," Sturla told me. "But by the end of the year, she'd backed off each point. I wasn't sure if John and Nancy were engaged in a news-gathering process. It seemed like an agenda to prove the kids guilty." When a neighbor and climbing friend, Jay Smith, tells me that Bouchard phoned him and referred to the story as a hoax, I phone Prichard to ask exactly what she and her husband believe. She denies they ever characterized the story as a hoax. Nevertheless, Bouchard would publish reports about the story in which he would write that his research could not confirm the claims made by the former hostages.

When news that Bouchard has been to Kyrgyzstan reaches the ears of Caldwell, Dickey, Rodden, and Smith, they are perplexed and outraged, especially Dickey. As far as he is concerned, the act of heading up the ropes toward the portaledges, even though everything in them was abandoned, is the ultimate violation. Dickey phones Bouchard at his home and asks if he retrieved his cameras and film. Bouchard says no, then asks if Dickey will comment on or confirm the portrayal of events in the *Outside* article. Dickey tells him that what was in the story is the truth, then hangs up.

This is the only contact between the climbers and John Bouchard. A line has been drawn in the sand. After this, events take on a warlike tone.

In my own reporting, I did not contact Bouchard, nor did he contact me. I decided to let him draw his own conclusions about this story.

Mark Richey, Bouchard's climbing partner on a score of hard alpine routes as wild and committing as the Eiger in the Alps, Latok I in the Karakoram Range, and Shivling in India, explained Bouchard's viewpoint to me like this: "John has always been obsessed with seeking and knowing the absolute truth of things. It's one of the reasons he studies history so much. He's also been scrupulously honest about his own accomplishments. I think the idea of others lying or even exaggerating about their experiences in the mountains, or wherever, really gets him going because it tends to discredit the climbing community (and him) as a whole. My understanding is that John approached the kids to try to get the story and they refused to divulge any information. That probably pissed him off, so he assumed they were lying. I think he figured that certain facts just didn't stack up right, hence their tight lips. Also, I think John just likes to play the devil's advocate or at least be controversial."

What did Bouchard believe happened in Kyrgyzstan?

During Bouchard's second visit to that country in April 2001 (a month after my own visit), reporter Alexander Kim interviewed him for *Vechernii Bishkek.* Kim's story, titled "Above the Precipice of Lies," described the motive behind Bouchard's mission in Kyrgyzstan like this: "Millions of Americans were sincerely interested whether the mountaineers were heroes or liars."

Kim reported that while Bouchard had come to believe that the climbers had been kidnapped, he was sure they had embellished their tale. He offered a reason: the loss of their gear, reported to be worth thirty thousand dollars. "I can assume that [the] guys had a good chance to solve their financial problems with the help of the story about their adventures," Kim quoted him saying. "Maybe more sophisticated advisors told them to add 'colors' to their story." Kim recounted the points that aroused Bouchard's suspicions: the speed with which the climbers gained an author and an agent, the large sums their story had sold for, and their refusal to give interviews. Apparently, to Bouchard, it all seemed too neatly and quickly sewn up by big business.

Bouchard also claimed to Kim that parts of the story were contradicted by the Kyrgyz army. He'd found an army officer who, he said, denied the mêlée of gunfire the Americans had described when they had run into the block post at Mazar in the early hours of August 18. The soldier had told him that except for a single warning shot fired over the heads of the Americans, there'd been no shooting at all. Bouchard's source was Major Kanat Tazabekov, the man who spoke to Rodden in German that night at Mazar; he'd been promoted from captain since he'd met the Americans.

Bouchard said Tazabekov had heard a single shot from the guard at the Mazar bridge around the same time that he received a radio message warning of approaching intruders. Tazabekov had already spotted the Americans through night-vision binoculars and was about to give the order to fire when he identified them as civilians. He said he had jumped into their path with his weapon ready and hustled them into the hut—a version at odds with the Americans' story. Kim's article quoted Tazabekov's surprise over Bouchard's interest in the story, and surprise too when Bouchard had told him that the mountaineers he'd rescued "had caused a huge scandal in America. A lot of people wouldn't believe that they had managed to push their guard into a precipice and run away. This journalist decided to come to Kyrgyzstan to find out what was true and lies."

However, the Americans' account of their last night on the run was backed by an earlier report of another soldier at Mazar. This report appeared in *Vechernii Bishkek* in March 2000, and it too was written by Alexander Kim. Major Oktyabr Ryskulov described events much as Tazabekov did but with the added detail that sudden "machine-gun shooting," rather than a single shot, had prompted the Americans to run into the block post.

Bouchard also reportedly unearthed a captain named Baktiar Shergeliev, who claimed he had met Dickey and Smith when they passed through Kurbaka on August 3, and that he and the late Captain Ruslan Samsakov had told the Americans that "war is coming and you should leave immediately." According to Bouchard, Shergeliev claimed the Americans had ignored the warning. Dickey and Smith deny meeting Shergeliev at Kurbaka and they recall no such warning. Shergeliev was, however, with Samsakov when he went to the Australian women's camp to order them to leave. Unlike Samsakov, Shergeliev survived the bloodbath at Mazar and Kurbaka. Bouchard also reported that on August 9 Shergeliev sent an urgent message via shepherds to the American base camp, telling them to get out of the area. This was the same day that Turat Osmanov's patrol was ambushed. The Americans are adamant that no shepherd visited them with any warning message.

Following my own visit to Kyrgyzstan, I wondered if the Kyrgyz military and the soldiers on the ground were simply covering their arses by distancing themselves from the out-of-control shooting the Americans had described when they'd run to Mazar, and by claiming they'd issued warnings for foreigners to leave. The men in the bushes who'd leapt up and sprayed bullets at the Americans were very possibly Kyrgyz troops, not rebels. If the American hostages the Kyrgyz troops had been searching for had been slaughtered by friendly fire, it would have been acutely embarrassing.

As for warnings, the military was inconsistent at best. Samsakov's stated reason to the Australians for evicting them was over a permit irregularity. The Germans, camped near the Australians, say they received no warning. The Ukrainians were stopped and warned of trouble by border soldiers near Vorukh, but Kyrgyz helicopter pilots were willing to circumvent this authority and fly them in for a bribe.

Heightening the intrigue surrounding this story was Bouchard's own prison interview with Sharipov, which he secured in April 2001 after Sharipov had been transferred to Osh. Said Bouchard to Kim, "He [Sharipov] just denies the version that he had been pushed into the precipice. From his words, the Americans made him fall asleep with some powder mixed into the drinking water, and then ran away." Kim also cited Sharipov's words from the interview: "I wanted to drink water; therefore one American man gave me his flask. After an hour I started to see bad, and lose my consciousness. I thought that I was poisoned. In the morning I woke up, I found myself lying. My feet were stretching against [a] fir [tree]. The Americans were not there, so I understood they had run away." In an article by Bouchard in the September 2001 issue of *Climbing*, editors would interpret Sharipov's account, as quoted above, to mean something rather different. They would print ". . . he had very little to eat for the past two weeks and simply passed out." With this new twist there existed to confuse those following this story five versions of how the Americans got away from the rebels:

- They pushed Sharipov off a cliff, as they claimed.
- They had been "abandoned" by the rebels and had wandered lost till soldiers met them, as per Interfax.
- They had run away after drugging Sharipov, according to the rebel's own version.
- Sharipov had fallen asleep due to weakness and lack of food, as printed in *Climbing*.
- They had been freed by a military action, according to the Kyrgyz army.

How reliable was testimony from a young, uneducated man facing trial and perhaps execution for terrorism and murder? Yet what would he gain from lying? Was he embarrassed that his captives had overpowered him? Was his story of being drugged a warped attempt to save face? Was it too wild to imagine that the Kyrgyz military were ordering Sharipov to deny that the Americans had pushed him, in order to bolster the official claim that the army had rescued the climbers? Perhaps four young Americans overpowering a terrorist when nearly two hundred soldiers couldn't pin him down just wasn't palatable to the high command.

WHEN BOUCHARD MAKES his second visit to Kyrgyzstan in April 2001 Garth Willis runs into him at a public press conference that Bouchard holds at the offices of Kabar. There he sticks to his guns, affirming to Kyrgyz reporters that he has evidence disproving the climbers' story. The reluctance of the Americans to speak with him is high on his list of reasons for suspicion, but most of his evidence is the testimony of Sharipov, who by now is denying that the rebels shot at the Americans in their portaledges, or that they made a log bridge over the Jopaiya River.

Bouchard seems sure that the story is a grand embellishment, and in the brief conversation he has with Willis at the press conference he says that his greatest fear is that I will find out that the "kids" are lying and I will scoop him.

I find this encouraging. It hints that his determination to prove this story false is rooted in conviction. I suppose I respect him for that.

26.

RETURN TO BISHKEK

BISHKEK

MARCH 2001

When Dickey, Smith, and I learn that the departure of our Aeroflot flight from Los Angeles to Moscow will be twelve hours late, we leave the airport to get a meal and take in a movie. It's the beginning of March 2001. I'm just getting to know them, and we have decided to travel together to Bishkek.

We drive across L.A. in Smith's Ford van to loud, thumping rock music. The van is crowded with our bags as well as a contingent of Smith's friends who've come to see us off. I'm feeling my age around these guys, feeling a little like the chaperone of a teen punk-rock band. Smith is dressed like the kids I see in skateboard magazines—baggy denim pants, T-shirt, and woolen beanie pulled down to eyebrow level. The hat will stay glued to his head for the whole trip, as will the headphones to his mini-disc player. The cheap rubber thongs he's wearing will remain his footwear of choice even when we get to Moscow, where it'll be a numbing −11 degrees Celsius. Dickey wears army pants and for reasons I can't guess has painted his fingernails a glittering metallic green. I imagine the fingernails will cause a stir among the staid government ministers and generals we plan to meet in Bishkek.

We pull into a mall and find one of Dickey's favorite eateries: In-n-Out Burger. He dreamed about the hamburgers from this fast-food chain during his hungry days with the rebels. We order, and sit at a Formica table. As I drink a shake I see a notation for a Bible verse printed on the wax paper cup: John 3:16. Dickey sees me looking at it.

"For God so loved the world that He gave His only begotten son, that whosoever believeth in Him shall not perish but have everlasting life," he says rapidly. "The management here are Christian."

"You know this verse by heart?" I ask.

"I can recite verse and Scripture all night. I grew up in a religious family. I entered preaching competitions when I was a kid."

It's the first I've heard of this side of John Dickey. We finish our burgers and find a theater. We buy tickets for *Traffic*, a film about drug smuggling between Mexico and the United States. It's a long film, realistic and documentarylike, bleak and violent. Midway through the movie two Mexican cops run afoul of a corrupt Mexican army colonel who commands a narco-empire. The colonel's hit men hijack the cops, and they're taken to a lonely, cactus-covered stretch of desert. At gunpoint they dig their own graves. When a hit man points his pistol at the head of one of the cops, my travel companions tense up and appear ready to flee. When the pistol fires and the cop buckles at the knees, Dickey and Smith arch their backs and squirm. The scene has jolted their memories of the murder of Turat Osmanov.

After the film we walk back into the warm L.A. night. "Did you see us twitching in there?" Smith asks me. The past few weeks, whenever we've talked about being under fire or about the murderous men and deadly weaponry that surrounded him, he's spoken like a war veteran, using gun-savvy lingo; Su was "running an AK-47"; Abdul's pistol was "some sort of Russian nine-mil job." But it's just talk. Smith and Dickey are uneasy about returning to Kyrgyzstan.

It is, in fact, the strangest of times for the former hostages. Allegations that their story is fishy have risen from a whisper to a dull roar with the publication just before our departure of an article called "A Killing in Question" in the now-defunct *Brill's Content*. It's the first of several speculative stories that will suggest that the climbers stretched the truth in the name of money. In this climate of scandalmongering, it's hard to guess what sort of reception we'll get in Bishkek, but my contacts there have warned me that the Kyrgyz army has somehow gotten the idea that the "kids" are ungrateful for the efforts by the soldiers to stop the rebels from taking them to Tajikistan, and that the word on the street among Kyrgyz journalists is that the story stinks. It doesn't require much forethought to figure that the idea of the Americans' making money out of the tragedy of the Batken crisis is enough to raise the hackles of the poor and embattled Kyrgyz.

THE MECHANICAL PROBLEMS that delay our flight from LAX to Moscow cause us to miss our connection to Bishkek. Even though it's two and a half days before the next flight, Aeroflot's surly customer-service staff refuses to transfer us to another airline. Nor can we go into Moscow, because we don't have transit visas. Instead, Aeroflot puts us up at the airport hotel. We wait for five hours until enough passengers from missed flights have accumulated to fill a bus, then we drive five hundred yards to the hotel. It's directly across the road from the airport. We've been staring at it the whole time.

The busload of passengers gathers in the hotel lobby while a no-nonsense middle-aged woman shouts out a list of rules. She tells us that we cannot leave the third floor of the hotel, that we are permitted one brief phone call at Aeroflot's expense, and that security guards will escort us to and from meals, which are downstairs at precisely at 8 A.M., 2 P.M., and 7 P.M. A guard unlocks an elevator and shuttles us up to the third floor. The elevator opens into a holding room. We step into it, he locks the elevator behind us, then he unlocks the door to the hall. Once all the passengers are out of the holding room, he locks that door behind us too.

The hall is crowded with Europeans, Indians, Japanese, and a group of Iranian women who have made a pilgrimage to Mecca. All are Aeroflot passengers whose flights have been delayed or canceled. Most of them stand around a pay phone, taking turns explaining to whoever was supposed to meet them at their final destinations that they'll be a few days late. A Turk yells angrily in English at the supervisor, demanding to see Russian president Vladimir Putin so he can complain about the lousy service he's getting from Russia's national airline. The supervisor, who is another gray nononsense woman with her hair tied up in a bun, ignores him as he follows her down the hall yelling obscenities about everything Russian. He's obviously been stuck here too long.

"If this is how they treat guests, I'd hate to go to jail in this country," Dickey says as he opens the door to his room.

Aeroflot's hospitality has a prisonlike quality to it, so we dub the hotel the Aeroflot Lubyanka, after the KGB prison in Moscow made infamous in Cold-War literature. I pass the next two days interviewing Dickey and Smith, piecing together a moment-to-moment portrait of their trip. When we're not talking about Kyrgyzstan, I sit back and watch their antics as our forced confinement sends them stir-crazy. They amuse themselves by jumping up and down on their beds, doing press-ups, and tampering with the surveillance cameras lining the hallway. Smith discovers that if he aims his own video camera at the hotel's cameras, he can create a dizzying kaleidoscopic effect on the monitor that sends the security guard seated at the end of the hall into a fit of annoyance. Smith has a bent for mischief and sarcasm. After all, he's the guy who told me that if he could ask Sharipov just one question, it'd be, "Where did you hide my Metallica CDs?"

At mealtimes security men escort us to a dining room where meager portions are served that leave everyone hungry. Coffee at breakfast is so carefully measured that those last in line get nothing from the pots. No amount of begging brings more. People who've been trapped in the hotel for several days shamelessly pick over the plates of other guests at the end of meals and return to their rooms clutching rounds of cold toast. Back on the third floor, when a Japanese traveler politely asks the supervisor for enough hot water to fill a teacup-sized container of instant noodles, he's met by a yell of "No!" delivered with such vehemence that he steps back in shock. The woman's response is emblematic of everything about Aeroflot's attitude toward its customers, but it's entertainment to the bored guests milling around the hall. They start laughing and hooting. The mockery softens the woman a little. She points to a small bottle of mineral water for sale on a shelf and yells to the Japanese guest that for five dollars she'll boil it.

Nights we spend in a small and insanely overpriced bar on the third floor. There we befriend a thirtyish Iranian-born Californian who was on the same flight from LAX as we were. He's a smooth dresser, in a black silk shirt and with a heavy gold chain around his neck. He tells us his story over shots of vodka that he pays for with money he peels from a tightly wound cylinder of cash worth five thousand dollars. He's being deported back to Iran, he reveals, for selling automatic weapons from the trunk of his car in the L.A. suburbs. He's done time on weapons charges before, and this conviction is his third strike. At his trial the judge gave him a choice: leave the United States and forfeit his green card, or do ten years in prison. Though he'd lived in America since childhood, ever since his parents fled Iran following the fall of the shah and the rise of the fundamentalists, he'd never taken U.S. citizenship. As a resident alien the court could permanently deport him. All the stories we've ever heard about what happens to a guy in prison are true, he assures us, and he wasn't going back inside. So he sold everything he owned and bought a one-way ticket to Tehran. The cash he's blowing on rotgut vodka is his entire life savings.

The big news on CNN in our rooms, and in the English-language Russian newspapers that make it upstairs, is the destruction by the Taliban of two 174-foot tall, two-thousand-year-old Buddhas carved into a cliff in the Afghan province of Bamiyan. The Taliban had ruled to destroy the statues because they regard all human likenesses of divinity to be un-Islamic and offensive. Despite an international outcry, the information and culture minister for the Taliban had declared, "The statues are not our pride . . . whatever means of destruction are needed to demolish the statues will be used." As we pack to leave the hotel on March 4, CNN reports that rocket launchers and explosives are turning the relics to dust. At our final breakfast at the hotel we sit across from two new arrivals. Smith asks the men where they are from. They glance from side to side to see who is listening, then one of them says softly through a thick black beard, "Afghanistan."

WE HIT BISHKEK on March 4. It's that time of year when the weather cannot decide whether to unleash snowstorms or to give up the sky to the spring sun, so it does both, on alternating days. When the sun doesn't shine, though, the city is as gray as Moscow and nearly as cold. It doesn't help that Uzbekistan has cut off the natural gas it pipes to Kyrgyzstan, due to an unpaid bill and a political argument or two. We take a room in a crumbling apartment block located within walking distance from downtown Bishkek, and we meet the men I've hired to help me with my research. Both are jet-haired, proud-faced ethnic Kyrgyz. Turat Akimov is a journalist from the Kabar information agency, and Erkin Atabekov is an interpreter who had previously been assigned to the Kyrgyz ambassador in Washington, D.C.

It's no secret to Bishkek's journalists that intrigue and skepticism surround the young Americans I'm traveling with. For Akimov and Atabekov, however, the story is a cash cow. Akimov worked for Bouchard in November, while Atabekov would hire on as Bouchard's interpreter the following month when he returns for his second trip. It's a comical and perverse twist to an already surreal state of affairs, yet somehow it's consistent in a post-Communist society where nepotism and bribe-taking are institutionalized. Regarding bribery, I would shortly find in my dealings with the Kyrgyz military that the documents I applied for could only be procured by paying the bribes requested by a certain high-ranking officer, who prefers anonymity. It wasn't corruption; it was business.

I grow to like Akimov and Atabekov for their frankness. They assure me that no one in Kyrgyzstan cares a som for this story, and chasing after people in Kyrgyzstan to prove whether the Americans are liars or heroes seems like a typically American waste of money and time. It's the IMU and the Taliban, Russian and Uzbek meddling in Kyrgyzstan, narcotics smuggling and addiction, unemployment, and the submerging economy that concern the Kyrgyz.

Nevertheless, the hostage story and all the money being thrown at it titillate the Kyrgyz. The director of Kabar, Kuban Taabaldiev, tells me that he's heard on good authority from the governor of Batken that a photograph of the four climbers posing with the rebels recently sold to someone in the United States for one million dollars. He seems disappointed when I tell him the story is bogus.

While some of the people looking into this story sought to expose a lie, I am interested in exposing the truth, whatever that might be. Having Dickey and Smith with me in Kyrgyzstan is sometimes a double-edged sword, suggesting bias to the skeptics. But their presence could also bring out truths that might otherwise remain hidden. I want to see how people react to Dickey and Smith, and how the Americans react to others. Trying to remain objective is like walking a tightrope. Sometimes Smith wonders whose side I'm on. At least once he accuses me of not believing him. I keep thinking of a scene from the movie *Almost Famous*, about the 1970s rock-and-roll scene, where the character based on the budding rock reporter Cameron Crowe is told by his mentor, the gonzo journalist Lester Bangs of *Creem* magazine, that there's only one way to keep an eye on the truth when writing about the glitzy bands and stars who are their subjects: "Don't become their friend."

Bishkek's government buildings are grandiose Parthenons of Soviet architecture, separated by parks and paved squares that are decorated with statues of proletarian heroism and Kyrgyz legend. Despite ten years of Kyrgyz independence and the collapse of the Soviet system, occasional busts of Lenin peek down at us as we go about the city. These suggest to me the relaxed nature of Bishkek's residents and contrasts with my recollections of Tashkent, where in 1995 locals pointed to a concrete pedestal in the city's central square where a tall bronze Lenin had been unceremoniously pulled down when communism crumbled. The statue had been shipped off to a buyer in Seattle, where I was living. For months Lenin could be seen strapped facedown on a flatbed trailer in an alley in the trendy suburb of Fremont. No one seemed to want him there either, though he's since become a sentinel outside a Mexican restaurant. Also relaxed in Bishkek is the Kyrgyz approach to Islam. Though the harsh religious dictatorship of the Taliban ruled just 350 miles to the south, the Kyrgyz wear their Islam lightly. Vodka is sold in street stalls, women wear European fashions, and bare-chested models are not uncommon on newspaper front pages. None of this would fly in Kabul, where even lipstick is illegal.

A reminder of Bishkek's Soviet past is the old KGB building, now the homes of the Kyrgyz Ministries of Internal Affairs and National Security. Atabekov, Dickey, Smith, and I walk past it on a day when the sun is coaxing blossoms and buds from the trees lining the avenues. It's a plain structure, distinguished only by a perimeter of tall steel bars. One could walk past it a hundred times without noticing it.

"Inside is your friend Sharipov," Atabekov says wryly.

"This might be as close as we get to seeing him," I say.

It's midway through the trip, and though we have interviewed a host of people germane to the story, we have made no headway with our requests to see Sharipov. Yesterday I submitted a request to the prosecutor general of Kyrgyzstan, a snowy-haired elderly bear of a man named Chubak Abyshkaev. He accepted my application, translated into Russian, but he told me not to expect an audience with such a dangerous criminal. The government's investigation of Sharipov and the other captured rebel, Ruslan Abdullin, had recently closed. Their trial would begin in May. The charges they face under the Kyrgyz criminal code are grave: article 226, terrorism; article 227, taking hostages; article 231, participating in criminal groups; article 241, illegal possession of firearms; and article 346, illegal crossing of the state border. They'll also become the first men in Kyrgyz history to be charged with "participation in a military conflict and hostilities as a mercenary." The cumulative jail time of the charges exceeds seventy years, but the court also could impose the death penalty, although a moratorium on executions exists until December 5, 2001.

Sharipov and Abdullin are to the Kyrgyz what Oklahoma City bomber Timothy McVeigh is to Americans. I asked Akimov if he thought the rebels would be sentenced to death. Anything less, he said, would produce an outcry from the families of the soldiers who were slaughtered "like dogs" at Mazar and Kurbaka. Yet President Akayev could show his mercy and gain international kudos by commuting any death sentence to prison time.

Dickey walks to the corner of the old KGB building to shoot a few photos. I caution him to be discreet. He's two hundred yards away, snapping frames, when an unmarked car appears out of nowhere and grinds to a halt beside him. A serious-looking man steps out and orders Dickey to produce his ID.

"Oh, now John will experience being arrested by the KGB as well as being kidnapped by rebels," Atabekov says with a touch of mirth as he goes to Dickey's rescue.

Atabekov talks Dickey out of trouble and we are allowed to walk, but the official solemnly warns us that General Bolot Januzakov himself will be told that we tried to photograph a sensitive government installation.

"Maybe this is good," Atabekov says. "Maybe this will help you to get your meeting with Januzakov."

If anyone holds the key to our seeing Sharipov, it is Januzakov, the secretary of the Security Council and head of the Kyrgyz security forces. His office lies inside the building Dickey just tried to photograph. I have submitted a written request to Januzakov too, on the subject of interviewing Sharipov, but as yet I've received no response.

DESPITE AKIMOV'S CLAIM that everyone in Bishkek is indifferent to the Americans, I find that in this city opinions regarding the story fall into two camps: those who believe it and those who vociferously do not.

Alexander Kim, the journalist from *Vechernii Bishkek* who "broke" the news of Sharipov's capture in September, is as interested to meet the Americans as we are to meet him. We speak with Kim for two hours in our rented apartment one sleety night. He's of Korean descent, a little chubby in the midriff, and possessed of a natural calm. When he sits expansively on a couch in the living room I'm reminded of a statue of the Buddha. He talks about the Batken conflict and about Sharipov, and he confirms that the officers who interrogated Sharipov also told him that the Americans had pushed Sharipov and had run away. When I tell him that Sharipov's survival and his conflicting claims have led some people to doubt the word of the young Americans, Kim asks Dickey and Smith a rhetorical question: "If you did not take matters into your own hands, how could you have gotten away?"

Kim suggests that if conflicting stories have sprouted around their experience, it's due to the lack of information that was available about the kidnapping. Reporters had based their stories on the only information they had, which was the official government version. Lacking detail, they had innocently created different interpretations and versions of the story to fill the news gap.

Kim has a respectable résumé: former editor in chief and majority shareholder of *Vechernii Bishkek,* retired lieutenant colonel, war correspondent with a knack of getting closer to the fighting than other journalists. But like so many people we meet in Bishkek, there is more to Kim than meets the eye. Two years earlier he was hounded by tax authorities, police, and Ministry of Internal Affairs officials, who surrounded his office and attempted to arrest him for tax evasion. Human-rights watchers who covered the events characterized the government's charges as being trumped-up and in retaliation for a series of articles in Kim's independent newspaper about political candidates who hoped to run against President Askar Akayev in the 2000 elections. Kim eluded arrest by hiding for several days at friends' houses, until he was hospitalized for a heart condition that was said to have been brought on by the incident. An audit forced on the newspaper by tax authorities found no irregularities, but Kim stepped down as editor in chief.

The meeting with Kim is calm and businesslike, but things become explosive at another meeting the following night at the offices of Kyrgyz state television. Irena Balakina is a well-connected and feared reporter in Bishkek who had procured the videotape of Sharipov's interrogation that I got hold of four months earlier. She'd also been among the entourage of journalists traveling with Akayev when the former hostages had landed at the mobile anti-terrorism base at Batken.

She greets Dickey and Smith, though they barely recognize her, then she ushers us all into an empty room. We sit around a table, Atabekov on one side and Balakina's own interpreter, a young university student, on the other. She speaks passable English. My objective in meeting Balakina is simple: I want to ask her for her impressions of Sharipov, whom she has met, and whether she has other videotape that might aid my research. She gives me far more than I bargain for.

I ask Balakina if we can record the conversation on audiotape. She declines. I ask if she has met Sharipov. She tells me enigmatically, "You can trust Sharipov's words." I ask what she means. "I never believed he was pushed," she says. I ask her to tell me what she thinks really happened. "He says he was treated with food that made him sleep. When he awoke he saw that the hostages were gone. At the same moment he was arrested." I ask her if she has read the story by Alexander Kim, which mirrors the climbers' version. "Kim is prone to exaggerate," she says dismissively. She continues dismantling the Americans' story: there are no cliffs where the climbers escaped, she says; and anyway, she's a former mountain climber herself, and she knows that to travel over the mountains in that part of Kyrgyzstan one must be very strong. The implication of her statement seems to be that the two climbers sitting at the table don't look tough enough to have kept up with the rebels.

She then faces Smith, fixes him with a derisive smirk, and asks him bluntly, "Do you think you freed yourself, or was it the army?"

Smith and Dickey stare at her in amazement. "I don't have a thing to say to her," Smith says in disgust, standing to leave. "If she doesn't believe us, she can go to hell." He has warned me that he has a hot temper, and I see that Balakina has lit his fuse. But I motion for him to stay. We are in the belly of the disbelieving beast. Perhaps this irritable woman will lead us somewhere.

"What is your understanding of how they were rescued?" I ask Balakina.

"A special operation was formed. The army found the Americans. I myself saw them get off a helicopter with soldiers. They were wearing fresh army uniforms. They were rescued. I heard them thank the army at the press conference. Even the president called it a rescue operation. There was nothing said about pushing their guard off a cliff."

Her interpretation is skin-deep, but I understand how we have gotten to this place. She cannot see beyond the official government statement about the kidnapping. The army said they rescued the Americans, the president too, end of story. There was no news in Kyrgyzstan of what the Americans experienced because they told no reporters about it, and none sought them out. The picture in Balakina's mind is of soldiers plucking the Americans out of the clutches of the rebels. The American version sounds more like self-rescue and doesn't shine as brightly on the army.

Balakina turns the discussion to the journey Smith and Dickey made down the Karavshin looking for a telephone. It never happened, she says; the soldiers would not have let Dickey and Smith pass Kurbaka.

"Oh, really?" Smith says. "Well, explain to me how a guy who lives in California knows that if you go over the hill beyond the army base and walk west, you'll come to a village called Kit Kim Saray, and at the last house on the trail through the village you'll find a man named Beidel Dar? He speaks English. Go there, find him, and he'll tell you he met us and took us down the trail to a teahouse by the road that goes to Batken. Maybe he'll be wearing the North Face socks I gave him."

She waves aside Smith's suggestion. Although I realize it is futile, I show her a photograph in a newspaper of Captain Ruslan Samsakov and tell her that, according to Dickey and Smith, he let them pass through the base and even drew them a map to help them get to Kit Kim Saray and Batken. The caption under Samsakov's photograph explains that he's in the medical corps. Casting me a superior smile, she pushes the newspaper back across the table. "He's a doctor," she declares. "He would never be in the front lines." Had she read further she'd have seen that Samsakov was killed in the fighting on August 11. When I mention this she springs to her feet.

"You are calling me a liar," she says angrily in English. "I don't need anything from you." She storms out of the room and slams the door behind her.

"What is going on here?" Dickey asks, breaking the stunned silence at the table.

"It's the government, it's the government," her interpreter says under his breath. He's shaking, terrified, it seems. It's nuts, but I find myself wondering if the room is bugged.

I'm doubly dumbfounded when Balakina returns a minute later, just as we are about to leave. With her is a tall man who stalls our departure with vigorous handshakes. He says nothing, but Balakina's interpreter mutters nervously that the man is some sort of managerial heavyweight at the TV station, and that matters are getting serious. I'm expecting some sort of sneak attack from Balakina when she walks toward me, but she's all smiles. She thrusts her phone number into my hand like an insistent date and tells me to call her; she'd like to interview us on state TV. Yeah, sure thing. I step onto the elevator. On the street we spontaneously make a run for it, as if in fear that she might follow us. When we slow to a walk Atabekov passes around his cigarettes. Even those of us who don't smoke puff away.

"I have never had such a strange job," Atabekov says as we hail a taxi. He's enjoying this.

THE WEIRDNESS CONTINUES at the American embassy. From our first day in Bishkek we'd left messages asking for appointments or casual meetings with the staff who'd so kindly helped the climbers in August, but no one has time to receive us officially or unofficially, not even for five minutes.

The embassy's position on the hostage story has consistently been "no comment," though it seems strange to find the policy extended to the hostages themselves. Only at the end of our two-week stay in Bishkek when we announce we are leaving Kyrgyzstan do we get five minutes with Greg Gardner in the hermetically sealed waiting room of the visa department. Gardner escorted Caldwell and Rodden out of Kyrgyzstan to the airport at Almaty, and they have spoken fondly of him. By the time I meet him, though, he seems to have taken fright of the controversy surrounding this story. He's businesslike, dressed in a crisp shirt and tie, and he makes a few words of friendly small talk with Dickey and Smith before turning to tell me he cannot say anything. He hands me the card of the Public Affairs officer, Ed Kulakowski, who we've been trying to contact since our arrival. He's busy, again, and regrets that he cannot make it down to see us. Gardner recommends that I e-mail him. I do, repeatedly, from the States. I receive no reply.

It all looks like a royal brush-off, but several weeks later I'll learn the likely reason we were such pariahs at the embassy: prior to our arrival, the FBI had been in town, interviewing Sharipov. The reason for that interview, an agent at the Washington Field Office would confirm to me, was for Sharipov's possible extradition to the United States to face kidnapping charges. The agent also lets me know that Sharipov said in his interview that the Americans ran away while he was asleep.

THE VILLAGE OF TUZ lies an hour's drive southeast of Bishkek. Akimov has learned that Turat Osmanov's mother and sister live there, in the home he grew up in. But there's no phone in the Osmanov house, so we drive there unannounced. When I ask Akimov how he can be sure that she won't be away, he replies, "She is poor. She has nowhere to go but the village."

We drive a rutted road through hills where drifts of melting winter snow are interspersed with flocks of sheep tended by horsemen. We follow a clanking tractor past fallow fields, then turn onto a dirt road that transects a collection of hardscrabble houses. This is Tuz. At one end of town is a school, at the other end, a cemetery.

Locals direct us to the Osmanov home. It's a whitewashed cottage with a couple of sheds for farm animals. Akimov approaches the house and calls through the door. A tiny old woman emerges wearing traditional Kyrgyz dress—white scarf, floral housecoat, and snug black leather boots. A woman of about thirty follows her. They are Turat Osmanov's mother and sister. Visitors from the city are uncommon in these parts, and they have a tendency to bring bad news when they do come, so the women eye us apprehensively. Akimov hands the mother a basket of flowers we've brought. He introduces himself and the young Americans who were with her son in the Karavshin. Hearing Akimov's first name—Turat—reduces the mother to tears. Akimov holds her in his arms, as he would his own mother. She embraces Dickey and Smith, then we enter her house.

We sit cross-legged on rugs around a long, low table while she serves us tea. Pictures of Osmanov hang on the walls around us. The mother brings out an album containing snapshots of Osmanov through the years, and she shows us the medal for courage—the Erdik medal—that the army gave her on her son's behalf. Dickey and Smith describe their hours with her son. They paint a picture of a defiant man, who died without granting his killers a whimper. The mother is hungry to hear any detail the Americans can provide about her son, no matter how hard, but it's too much for the sister. She leaves the room weeping.

Osmanov's mother then tells us about her son. Before he left for Batken he'd tried to keep the news from her that he'd been assigned a tour of duty there, where fighting was feared, out of concern that she'd worry. When he'd been captured he was supposed to be on leave, at home, but he was doing double duty to cover for an injured friend, taking his place because he and the family needed the money. She'd known "in her heart" that something was wrong when he did not return home as expected on August 10, but the army rebuffed her inquiries day after day at the nearby base. Reports of fighting started circulating soon afterward, but details were scarce; no one knew where the fighting was, or if there were casualties. Yet the silence of the officers and the unusual activity around the base worried her.

She learned on August 16 that her son was dead. She was standing at a bus stop, returning from another visit to the base to ask about Turat, when a foreign car offered her a ride home. The driver said nothing and asked for no money. At her home she found more strangers and a zinc coffin. She wasn't allowed to open the coffin, she said, because her son's body was terribly decomposed and badly shot up. In addition to his head wound, she said, he had other bullet wounds, in the shoulder and knee; it's probable that the advancing border guards had laid down a field of protective fire as they approached the boulder where the rebels were shooting from and Osmanov's corpse had taken additional hits. The state of the body would be the subject of contrasting and baffling recollections. The Uzbek cook Mischa Volosovitch would recall that when the rebels brought Osmanov into camp on August 11 he was beaten badly, with a swollen eye and a bleeding ear, and that he had knife slashes on his legs and chest. Volosovitch's fellow hostage, the German Roland Laemmermann, would recall seeing no wounds on the soldier, nor would the Americans. Other reports would say that in addition to his head wound, he'd been found with a slit throat. The Americans did not see that either.

The authorities who brought her son's body to her then took him away again, for three days for a military ceremony in Bishkek. When the authorities returned the body to her for cremation, the mother said, it was with the promise that the government would provide financial assistance to the family and to the village of Tuz. Nothing came of the promise, though, she told us with resignation rather than bitterness.

The cemetery is a short walk from her house. We leave the table to visit the grave. She places the flowers we've brought at the foot of the granite tombstone, into which Turat Osmanov's likeness has been etched. We kneel on the soil, while Akimov recites an Islamic prayer.

Turat Osmanov was the youngest of her six children. He'd been born the day his father was lynched by a mob of Uighurs during an outbreak of ethnic unrest. While his siblings moved on to different parts of Kyrgyzstan, Osmanov's bond with his mother kept him in Tuz. She remembers that every evening after he finished work he walked her home from the pasture where she watched over a small flock of sheep. His pet name for her was Umka, after a children's cartoon character of a snowy white bear. He loved to play soccer with his friends on his days off. He married and divorced. He worked as a heating-systems engineer, and he was a graduate of a military-tank academy in Russia. He is gone now, she knows, but sometimes she imagines he's come back; sometimes things in the barn are moved around. She wishes she could talk to him, and she wonders where, exactly, he has gone in this universe.

When Osmanov's mother says farewell to Dickey and Smith she takes them in her arms and kisses their cheeks. "I'm glad you met my son," she says. "I'm glad he could help you in some way. I hope he can live on through you."

Dickey presses a hundred American dollars into her palm and tells her it's a gift from him and Smith for the family. She refuses the money, but he and Smith insist. Then we drive to Bishkek. Dickey and Smith sit silently the whole way.

A MONTH LATER an article appears in Kyrgyzstan on the Kabar Web site. Titled "American Climbers in Batken: A Re-examination of the August 2000 Hostage Rescue," it's another angry debunking by John Bouchard. "As far as the Americans' story?" he wrote. "I was unable to corroborate any of it." It's the same litany of distorted facts that the climbers have seen in the past, but there's one new bit of vituperation at the end, about the meeting between Osmanov's mother and Dickey and Smith: "And while they were here in Bishkek in March to 'prove' their story, they gave $100.00 to the mother of the soldier who was killed with them and then took her picture for their book."

27.
MEETING WITH A TERRORIST

BISHKEK

MARCH 2001

Two days before we are due to leave Bishkek we are summoned to meet General Bolot Januzakov, secretary of the Security Council. While we wait outside his office, I stare at a white plaster frieze in the ceiling of the lobby. Dagger, five-pointed star, hammer and sickle, laid over a shield—the insignia of the Soviet KGB, the building's former tenant.

Januzakov's office is the size of a small house. The general rises from a desk covered in telephones and strides toward us. Handsome, in his early forties, dapper in a business shirt and tie rather than a military uniform, he looks like a corporate CEO. His smile is welcoming. As he shakes hands with the former hostages I'm glad to see that Dickey has removed the green polish from his fingernails.

We sit at a long, hardwood conference table with his secretary and an ethnic Russian colonel, and Januzakov begins to deliver a lecture. He's one of the most powerful men in Kyrgyzstan. When he talks, you listen. Looking at the former hostages, he tells them he's glad they are well, and he thanks them for returning to Kyrgyzstan. It's a peaceful country, he assures them, with practically no history of warfare, so the attacks by the rebels came as a terrible and costly surprise. But now, thanks to help from friends like the American military, the Kyrgyz army has special equipment and training and will wipe out the rebels if they return.

"The men who kidnapped you," he tells Dickey and Smith, "are bandits, drug smugglers, and mercenaries who hide behind Islam. The Taliban and Osama bin Laden control them and fund them. They didn't come to Kyrgyzstan to kidnap you, but you were in their way, so they took you for ransom. Their purpose is to destabilize southern Kyrgyzstan so they can smuggle narcotics from Afghanistan into Russia and Europe." He adds that one of the rebels in prison, Abdullin, is a Russian citizen with a criminal charge awaiting him in his home republic, for rape.

We listen respectfully to Januzakov's lecture. It's information we are familiar with, but we are hearing it from one of Kyrgyzstan's top military players.

"The army knew where you were at all times," Januzakov tells his guests. "When our communications outposts intercepted a radio message to Tajikistan that said, 'We have goods in our hands,' we knew they had you." That's when Kyrgyz troops were airlifted to the passes to cut off the rebels' escape. The plan was to deprive the rebels of food, water, and ammunition. When they were weak, they would give up their prisoners, Januzakov explained.

"Is it possible for us to see Sharipov and Abdullin?" I slip the question in when the general pauses for a breath, but he carries on talking as if he hasn't heard my interpreter make the request. I nudge Smith to repeat the question.

"Certainly. Why not?" Januzakov says to him, as if the matter has never been in question.

Half an hour later we are standing in a dimly lit and narrow hall, listening to the clank of unlocking tumblers as a security man wearing a sports coat and tie opens a steel door with a medieval-looking key. When the door swings open on grinding hinges, we enter a cell painted a sickly buttery yellow, brightly lit with a bulb caged behind a wire grill. A cherub-faced yet pallid young man wearing a maroon sweater and jeans stands beside a table and chair. He seems to be shivering. It's the prisoner Abdullin, and he's nervous as hell.

Ruslan Abdullin, a.k.a. Hamsa, sucks in short, tense breaths as we take our seats an arm's length from him. His brown eyes sweep quickly over us as well as the hard-faced security man who positions himself in a corner of the room. Dickey and Smith did not encounter Abdullin in the Karavshin, but Januzakov has granted us ten minutes with him as well as with Sharipov.

The guard orders Abdullin to sit. He does so, obedient as a dog. Abdullin clasps his hands in his lap. His fingers twist and fidget as if he's trying to strip the skin off them. When I study those animated hands I see that his fingernails are chewed back to the quick. He's the first terrorist I have ever met, and the most scared human I have ever seen.

Abdullin came from Aznalino village in the Russian province of Kurgan. He felt the call of Islam and had been studying in a religious school in the city of Tyumen when two Tartar men recruited him to go to Tajikistan for training so he could fight in the jihad.

Abdullin came reasonably close to escaping back into Tajikistan after he abandoned his hostages on August 14, by sneaking down the Karavshin Valley, heading for the Ortochashma valley and the Turo Pass. But the region's churning rivers had foiled him. He knew he'd be most vulnerable when crossing the bridges spanning those foaming rivers, especially the one at Mazar, where soldiers were sure to be stationed, but the bridges were the only way he knew to get back to the Ortochashma. He thought he was in luck when on August 15 the German climbers who'd earlier eluded his capture and who'd been strafed by the Kyrgyz Mi8 hurried past his hiding spot beside the trail during their own escape bid down the Karavshin Valley. Abdullin shadowed them, hiding in brush and keeping his distance, figuring that soldiers hiding along the trail would challenge the climbers as they passed, revealing themselves and allowing Abdullin to skirt around their positions. His plan seemed to be working when Kyrgyz troops intercepted the Germans at the Mazar bridge and several troops left to escort the climbers to safety.

Abdullin waited a while till he thought the coast was clear. Figuring all the troops were gone, he made his move across the bridge. Soldiers still in hiding were stunned to spot the rebel out in broad daylight, and they opened fire. Abdullin ran under the bridge, firing back. Flushed out by a hand grenade hurled by a soldier, he scurried to a boulder and continued firing. While he was changing the magazine on his AK-47, one of the Kyrgyz rushed the boulder and clubbed Abdullin into surrender with the butt of his rifle. Soldiers handcuffed him and dragged him to Kurbaka. The man who captured Abdullin was Captain Kanat Tazabekov. He would meet the Americans three days later when they run into Mazar. Tazabekov would be promoted to major for his valor at the bridge.

One final bloody fight took place, that same evening, when Abdurahman and his surviving rebels ambushed a Kyrgyz patrol far up the Orto-chashma valley. Six soldiers died before the Kyrgyz gained the upper hand, wounding or killing most of the rebels. Abdurahman, wounded himself, finished off some of his own men rather than let them be taken prisoner, then he blew himself up with a hand grenade. The only rebel to escape this final skirmish ran off with a rocket-propelled grenade launcher, which he fired at an Mi8 flying toward the battleground. The rocket fell short of the chopper, and the rebel disappeared into Tajikistan.

IN THE PRISON CELL, Abdullin's nervous, shaky energy spreads to Dickey, Smith, and me. The meeting has come so unexpectedly. The ministry man videotaping our every move and reaction adds to the tension. I videotape the meeting too. Smith finally summons the pluck to start talking. We communicate through Atabekov. The prisoner gives short answers to simple questions. Smith asks Abdullin why he joined the rebels. "Islam," Abdullin replies. Abdullin tells us that before he took up arms he was a farm worker in the Kurgan region of Russia. He denies participating in the fighting or the killing around Mazar.

While shifting position to get a better shot with my video camera, I back into the guard. He's a barrel-chested, bouncer-sized figure, and he shoves me forward aggressively. When I turn around to apologize I notice that the folded-in-half newspaper he's been carrying so carefully is draped over a pistol.

Ten minutes pass and the guard declares our time is up. He opens the squeaking steel door and leads Abdullin away. "The big fellow who is the guard," Atabekov says, "he lives in the same apartment block as me. I see him going to work every morning. Now I know what is his job."

The door squeals open again. Ravshan Sharipov enters the room. The guard, holding his newspaper conspicuously aloft, returns to the corner. Sharipov recognizes Dickey and Smith immediately. His face breaks into a wide smile. Booted and interrogated from the Karavshin to Bishkek to Tashkent, then back again for nigh on six months, the Americans are the friendliest faces he's seen in a long time. The three men stand to shake hands, but the Americans aren't smiling. They don't know what to feel.

"Tell him he looks well," Smith tells Atabekov when they return to their seats.

Prison life does seem to agree with the former terrorist. His pie-shaped face and belly have rounded out since August, when videotape and press photos showed a starveling with a startled rodent face and caved-in cheeks. He seems relaxed, even good-humored.

Sharipov asks the Americans how they are.

"A lot better," Dickey says.

The room falls uncomfortably quiet for a few heartbeats while the hostages and the terrorist acclimatize to one another. Smith's lips twitch and curl as he stares at the man he slept next to and talked of killing for six days. Dickey just looks stunned. Sharipov raises his eyes up to the ceiling, sighs, and appears to laugh inwardly as if he's suddenly got the punch line of some great cosmic joke. In their mind's eyes the three men are remembering the days and nights when they were in the maw of it all: the firefight, the murder of Osmanov, the bivouacs, the wandering, the fear, the plotting, and the escape. I can only guess at Sharipov's thoughts, but it's fair to imagine he was ruing the day he picked up that AK-47 and fell in with Sabir. Or maybe he was thinking of Isfara, the sleepy town he'd so keenly wanted out of and which he'd likely never see again. Joining the IMU was supposed to have been his ticket to excitement and money; instead, he's in jail.

"Does he remember the last night we were together?" Smith asks.

Atabekov translates the question, then relays Sharipov's answer: "He remembers. After his falling he lost his mind for a while. When he was fall down it was very difficult for him to identify where he is, at night."

"Tell him I'm sorry for that," Smith says. "Ask him if he remembers how far he fell."

There's another exchange in Russian, then Atabekov says, "He doesn't remember exactly his falling. It was unexpected thing for him."

"I can imagine he hit pretty hard. Did he get hurt at all?"

"He lost his mind for a minute or so, then it was a dark night."

Smith, muttering to himself, staring into Sharipov's eyes: "He blacked out. For sure."

Dickey: Did he think we would try to escape?

Sharipov: No, I did not expect.

Smith: On the mountain, when you woke up, were soldiers there immediately?

Sharipov: I was eight days alone in the mountains. After that I ran into the soldiers.

Dickey: Did you ever see Sabir again?

Sharipov: No. I don't know what happened to him. He left me and I was alone.

Dickey: Does your mother and your family know you are here?

Sharipov: Yes, they know.

Smith: Have you got any letters from your family? Can we write you a letter?

Sharipov: No one has sent me a letter. You can write, if you want.

Too quickly our ten minutes end. The guard calls the prisoner to stand at attention. The door opens. We shake Sharipov's hand as we file out of the room.

"Good luck," says Smith, the former hostage, to Sharipov, the former terrorist.

SMITH SELDOM DRINKS, but he quaffs several screwdrivers that evening. Back in our apartment he sits on the edge of his bed, swaying and talking in a stream of consciousness about Sharipov, whom he reverts to calling Su. Smith calls the meeting in the cell "one of the most positive experiences in my life." I ask him why, and he says that seeing Su again, on different terms, has freed him of the aggression he felt toward the man. He's glad Su didn't die. "Su wasn't so bad to us, really," Smith says. "He let us sit in the sun outside our bivouacs. We smiled and joked around. But Abdul— that guy had a deep-seated vengeance." We know now, though, from the military, that Abdul/Sabir is dead. If there is a score to be settled with him, fate and a Kyrgyz soldier's bullet have taken care of it.

"I was surprised to hear you tell Su that you were sorry for pushing him," I tell Smith. The Kyrgyz authorities in the cell would, I'd later hear, also be flabbergasted by Smith's statement. "Su had you at the point of a gun," I say. "If Abdul had ordered him, he'd probably have shot you. And who's to say he didn't kill some of those soldiers, before he met you, or at the firefight when they executed Turat? Someone's bullet killed that soldier at the bridge."

"It's hard to explain. I guess I feel that if he gets the death penalty, I don't want him to go down thinking I hate him. His life is shit. Why make it worse?"

Smith's position: liberation through forgiveness. Dickey, sitting on the couch, expresses no such resolution. "I don't know how I feel," he says introspectively. "All I can tell you is that for a few moments back there I had to fight back an overwhelming urge to get up and punch the son of a bitch in the face."

But the urge passed. Behind bars, minus his AK-47, maybe facing death, grinning like a fool, dressed in a ridiculous harlequin-patterned sweater and beanie, Sharipov seemed anything but dangerous. He seemed like a dim-witted farm boy. A child.

I play the devil's advocate with Smith. "Sharipov certainly said he fell off a cliff, but he didn't exactly say you guys pushed him."

Smith is dragging his sleeping bag into the hallway. He's bedding down closer to the toilet, in case the head spins he's getting from the booze make him ill. He looks me squarely in the eye and says, "I know the truth. You know it. Sharipov knows it. Anyone who doesn't believe us—they can go to hell." He flops onto the floor.

I WAS DRAWN to write this story in the beginning because the climbers who were kidnapped in Kyrgyzstan had returned to the world with an insight into the minds of a tribe that I suspected would become increasingly threatening to the American way of life: the fanatical Islamic terrorist. In that way, the climbers seemed like explorers, bringing back tales and grim treasures from a place the majority of us would never know.

That is, until September 11, 2001, when hijacked jets destroyed the Twin Towers of the World Trade Center in New York and rammed into the Pentagon. On that day, everyone in America moved several steps closer to the terror and helplessness that befell the climbers and soldiers in this story. Thousands were murdered and maimed in the September attack, hundreds of thousands witnessed it, millions more watching television saw the global jihad arrive in America. It seems now that everyone knows someone, directly or indirectly, who perished in the World Trade Center or the Pentagon, or who was close enough to smell the smoke and dust of the destruction. Susan Golomb, the agent representing this book, who was by then a close friend and confidante to me as well as the four climbers, watched from the roof of her apartment in New York as a jet struck the north tower of the Trade Center. Seeing those awful scenes, I wonder how many of us reflexively mouthed the words "terrorist" and "Osama bin Laden."

By that fateful day—September 11—a little more than a year had passed since the Islamic Movement of Uzbekistan interrupted the lives of the players of this story. By summer's end, Juma Namangani's jihad had not returned to Kyrgyz soil, though no one believed the IMU had retired. Where were they? In February 2001 Namangani's hosts in the Tajik government, presumably under pressure from its Central Asian neighbors, once again persuaded him to leave Tajikistan peacefully. Adding spice to the mystery of who are the IMU's friends and who are its foes, Pakistani journalist Ahmed Rashid reported that Russian and Tajik military helicopters had airlifted Namangani with 250 of his followers from Tavildara in Tajikistan to a base in Afghanistan, but several hundred IMU men were said to remain in Tajikistan.

During my visit to Bishkek, journalists and officials expressed the feeling that Russia aids and abets the IMU. How else to explain the ease with which the IMU moves back and forth over the Afghan-Tajik border, through thousands of Russian and Tajik border guards and heavy armor? I learned a Russian saying in Bishkek: if you look at the sunrise often enough, you'll eventually see a conspiracy in it. Indeed, this sounded like conspiracy theory writ large. What was in it for the Russians? The answer, I was told, was that the irritant of Namangani—too small a force to topple Karimov, yet strong enough to create mayhem and fear—keeps the Uzbek regime toeing the Russian line and dependent on Russia's military. This gives Russia a powerful presence in the oil- and gas-rich regions of Central Asia. And then there is the opium—thousands of tons of it, stocked in warehouses in Afghanistan and moving north across the borders every day.

Reports surfaced in August 2001 that Namangani's men had been spotted fighting in Afghanistan on the side of the Taliban, against the armies of Ahmed Shah Massoud's Northern Alliance at a town set in a rocky wasteland called Koh-e-Siah Boz, near Taloqan. Reports also emerged in the Russian and Central Asian press claiming that Namangani was under the direct command of Osama bin Laden, acting as one of his top lieutenants, and that bin Laden was the de facto "defense minister" of Taliban forces. Later still, in November 2001 after the U.S. attack on Afghanistan, reports said Namangani had died from wounds after a bombing raid somewhere near Dashtiqala, near Taloqan, while Takhir Yuldashev was reported to have been among four hundred foreign fighters who had revolted after surrendering and fought to the death in an old fortress called Qalai-i-Jhangi, also near Mazar-i-Sharif. Perhaps they really were dead. Certainly, hundreds of IMU fighters had perished in the U.S.-led bombings. Though the Uzbek and Tajik presidents held press conferences to proclaim Namangani's death, the reports were fraught with conflicting information. Perhaps Namangani and Yuldashev were still alive, their deaths a fiction, and they had escaped to continue their jihad on another day.

THE CLIMBERS who were in the Karavshin in August 2000 have all moved forward with their lives, but the experience shadows them still. Kate Dooley, who slipped out steps ahead of the invaders because the late Captain Ruslan Samsakov ordered her out of the Karavshin ahead of schedule, sounded full of self-reproach in the aftermath of the experience. She wrote in an e-mail: "The whole thing makes me wonder about obnoxious and ignorant western climbers (I speak of myself as well as of the other groups there) stubbornly going into areas they have been warned away from and endangering their own and other peoples' lives." Dooley's group had known about the Japanese-hostage incident prior to leaving Australia, and travel agents in Bishkek had warned them of danger in the Karavshin. She went there anyway. It's in the nature of climbers to take calculated risks, whether it's to cross an avalanche-prone snow slope or to climb far from one's protection on a cliff, but terrorism is an objective hazard that no climber is prepared to meet. If there was a lesson to learn from the drama in Kyrgyzstan, it was as a cautionary tale to climbers and travelers in the hinterlands of the Third World to heed warnings, assume nothing, and be vigilant.

Natasha Kolysnik, the sole woman among the hostages in the Ak Su valley, talked about the personal resolutions her group made during an emotional, tear-filled vodka blowout in Batken after the army airlifted them to safety. She and her husband, "Vasya," had felt so near to death during their captivity that upon their release they immediately looked to the future. She was due to have a baby in September 2001. Igor Chaplinsky also talked of having another child, the third for him and his wife, and Mischa Volosovitch said he'd marry his girlfriend and start a family. Vasili Kolysnik even pledged to quit smoking.

Dickey, Caldwell, Rodden, and Smith, with their longer and more violent captivities and the media controversy surrounding their story, have had more demons to deal with. To those who do not know them closely, the four seem little different from the people they were prior to their journey to Kyrgyzstan. But there have been changes to their internal landscapes.

John Dickey feels the experience opened his eyes to the negative side of humanity, and he's noticed in himself "a greed to live life in greater saturation, and in greater intensity than ever before." At the end of 2001 he was still living in San Francisco with Rita Di Lorenzo, still odd-jobbing his way around photography and video production, still climbing in Yosemite and dreaming of expeditions to distant mountains. He accepts the motives driving the terrorists who struck the Karavshin—religion, politics, money, and ignorance—as inevitables in a harsh world, but he is less comprehending of the strangers who've dogged him with their speculations and accusations. In September 2001 the Man from Interfax returned with a scathing letter in *Climbing* magazine that scorned the climbers' honesty and put blood on their hands for the deaths of Kyrgyz soldiers. "While . . . the climbers are spending $1,000,000-plus in royalties from magazine, book and movie deals," the letter read, "they might well remember the little girl they left behind in Kyrgyzstan."

The writer was referring to Asel Raimbekov, whose father was the soldier gunned down at the bridge over the Ak Su on August 12. And no one had made a million dollars. The association left Dickey aghast. "We never wanted this experience or the attention it brought us. We were hostages. The situation was beyond our control. We had no idea this war was coming." But he adds, "I am not a victim of this experience. It simply 'is.' I'm living my life as I always have."

Of them all, Caldwell seems to have emerged the least damaged, due in part to the support of two loving families and to his own resilient, guileless personality. "I am still the same old Tommy Caldwell," he says. He has successfully distanced himself from the rebels who tormented him in Kyrgyzstan and from those who have doubted his word in America. He's even had the opportunity to look one of his accusers in the eye, at a crowded trade show of the recreation industry, and he felt no desire to rebuke her. Caldwell cured himself of Kyrgyzstan by throwing himself back into climbing. In the summer of 2001 he produced two notable feats: he put up the hardest free climb on the two-thousand-foot vertical granite wall of Long's Peak in Colorado, and he became the first person to free-climb the Muir Wall, a twenty-seven-hundred-foot route on El Capitan. Optimism as much as his physical strength kept him alive in Kyrgyzstan. He never doubted they would make it out of there.

When Caldwell climbed the Muir Wall his partner was Rodden. Returning to the airy verticality of El Capitan was a benchmark event for her. She'd been stricken with nightmares for months, and by a fear that around some corner she'd meet a vengeful terrorist. The act of climbing itself was even soured, as she associated it with her kidnapping. Only the immense patience of Caldwell, coaching her through a period of depression, allowed her to rediscover climbing.

Looking back on the person she was in Kyrgyzstan, Rodden sees a naïve young woman who took the world at face value. She has worked hard to put the experience into perspective. Though she wishes she could turn back the clock and erase the terrible things she saw, it seems that Rodden had some sort of epiphany out there too.

"The whole time during our captivity I was redefining my relationship with God, praying and asking for guidance." As they ran for their lives to Mazar that last night, she felt that she was joined by a protective presence. At Mazar, amid a hail of bullets in the night and with men forcing them facedown onto the dirt, jamming guns into their backs, she felt her terror replaced by a feeling of calm as she prepared to die. "There was nothing more I could do, the shot was going to come, and then that would be it. I felt a very weird thing at that point. I saw something like a light that I was going toward. I thought then about my family, and I asked God to let them know I was all right, and that I would be with them anyway, just not in the flesh."

She and Caldwell currently live in the Rocky Mountains of Colorado, and they have little doubt that they'll spend the rest of their lives together.

The one-year anniversary of the hostage ordeal saw Jason Smith and his friend Cedar Wright in the Canadian arctic, dodging ricocheting stones and climbing fast and light up the four-thousand-foot walls of Baffin Island. Since Kyrgyzstan he's lived in his van, working little so he can climb often. He talks as if he's still in survival mode: "When we were in the bivouacs with the rebels, I'd wake up for another night of marching around the mountains and say to myself, 'I'm alive.' I'd appreciate the moment, but I knew it might not stay that way. I still have that feeling whenever I wake up. Every day I feel I might get chopped. I'm much more aware of death." He also struggles with the disillusionment of shattered expectations. "We were *together*—then it was gone," he says of the suddenness with which the group drifted apart. To Smith they'd been a band of brothers, and a sister, and they'd reached some zenith of the human spirit. When the struggle was over, though, the brilliant thing that had kept them together and alive turned to dust and blew away. The separation was jarring. It's left him feeling hollow. He's found it difficult to see much of Caldwell and Rodden since they parted company in Bishkek, and vice versa. They brought out the best and the worst in one another; they gave one another everything they could. They used one another up.

The last time I heard from Smith before finishing this book was in the days following the terrorist attacks on the World Trade Center and the Pentagon. America was nervous, and Smith feared the worst. Furthermore, he was certain he had just seen Abdul/Sabir on television in an archival film clip of an entourage surrounding Osama bin Laden. "This is going to go big," Smith said of the coming conflict. "I know these guys. They don't give up." He'd just bought a plane ticket to the Buddhist nation of Thailand, which he figured was the safest place to weather the storm. He wasn't sure how long he planned to stay.

ON JUNE 22, 2001, a Kyrgyz military trial held behind closed doors in the southern capital of Osh sentenced Ravshan Sharipov and Ruslan Abdullin to death, with confiscation of all their property. Kyrgyzstan's moratorium on capital punishment would end in December 2001, yet the two rebels were still inhabiting the limbo of death row as this book went to press, in February 2002. In the meantime their Kyrgyz government–appointed lawyers have the right to appeal their sentences. Ironically, the FBI may factor in as a savior for Sharipov, as an agent from the Washington Field Office maintained in August 2001 that the sentencing in no way diminishes the agency's interest in prosecuting him. The FBI agent's comments came prior to the World Trade Center attack. Interest in extraditing Sharipov may have changed since then, and since the apparent destruction of the IMU.

The sentencing of Sharipov brought no joy to any of the former hostages, though none of them lost sleep over it. When John Dickey learned that the rebel might die he wrote me a note that expresses the ambiguity of all their feelings over the maelstrom in their lives that was Kyrgyzstan: "There are all these illusions we have in life about justice, fairness, and chance. We often do our best to ignore humanity's true face. I hope those guys get a good death."

About the Author

GREG CHILD is the author of *Thin Air: Encounters in the Himalayas; Climbing: The Complete Reference; Mixed Emotions: Mountaineering Writings of Greg Child; Postcards from the Ledge: Collected Mountaineering Writings of Greg Child;* and coauthor, with Lynn Hill, of *Climbing Free: My Life in the Vertical World.* A mountaineer who has summited K2 and Everest, Child lives near Moab, Utah.